# READING HARRY POTTER AGAIN

## AGAIN

### New Critical Essays

Edited by Giselle Liza Anatol

D0208538

**PRAEGER**
*An Imprint of ABC-CLIO, LLC*

A B C ⬤ C L I O

Santa Barbara, California • Denver, Colorado • Oxford, England

**Library of Congress Cataloging-in-Publication Data**

Reading Harry Potter again : new critical essays / edited by Giselle Liza Anatol.
   p.   cm.
  Includes bibliographical references and index.
  ISBN 978–0–313–36197–5 (hard copy : alk. paper) — ISBN 978-0-313-36198-2 (ebook)
   1. Rowling, J.K.—Criticism and interpretation.   2. Children—Books and reading—English-speaking countries.   3. Children's stories, English—History and criticism.
4. Fantasy fiction, English—History and criticism.   5. Rowling, J.K.—Characters—Harry Potter.   I. Anatol, Giselle Liza, 1970–
PR6068.O93Z843   2009
823'.914—dc22      2009005773

13    12    11    10    09    1    2    3    4    5

This book is also available on the World Wide Web as an eBook.
Visit www.abc-clio.com for details.

ABC-CLIO, LLC
130 Cremona Drive, P.O. Box 1911
Santa Barbara, California 93116-1911

This book is printed on acid-free paper ∞

Manufactured in the United States of America

# READING HARRY POTTER AGAIN

# Contents

# Acknowledgments

I offer profuse thanks to my editor, Suzanne Staszak-Silva, and to the contributors for their time and efforts; I'm especially grateful for those who had the patience to endure me as editor once again. I am indebted to the members of the Department of English at the University of Kansas, particularly Dorice Elliott for her generous support of the project, the participants of SAGE's Academics Anonymous, and Adam Long, without whom I never could have met my deadlines. Much appreciation goes to Tamara Falicov, Ann Rowland, and Kim Warren, the members of my Kansas City writing group, whose encouragement, enthusiasm, and intellectual rigor consistently helps me to focus my mind and energies. Dee Hurt deserves the greatest praise for assisting me with passages that were sure to ruin the surprises of the novels for her, and for always helping me to balance work and play. I thank Miles Hurt whose continued belief in magic inspires me to continue writing about it. And last, but certainly not least, I thank Mylisha Joi Hurt for continuing to ask the important questions that keep me on my toes, and showing me that great thinkers can come in all sizes.

# Introduction

When my first collection of scholarship on J.K. Rowling's Harry Potter series—*Reading Harry Potter: Critical Essays* (2003)—was published, many readers had been finished with book IV, *Harry Potter and the Goblet of Fire*, for months, and were eagerly anticipating the next installment in the seven-book sequence. *Harry Potter and the Order of the Phoenix* was released in summer 2003 to the usual eye-popping fanfare and earth-shattering sales; it was followed by *Harry Potter and the Half-Blood Prince* in 2005 and *Harry Potter and the Deathly Hallows* in 2007. As they finished the last page of *Hallows*, I suspect that many fans of Rowling's series reacted as I did: with a start of panic at the thought, "What am I supposed to do *now*?"

Many readers confessed to be suffering from withdrawal until summer 2008, when—on Harry's and Rowling's July 31 birthday—it was announced that *The Tales of Beedle the Bard* would be published on December 4. The title comes from *Harry Potter and the Deathly Hallows*, where Albus Dumbledore leaves Hermione Granger a copy of the collection of children's tales in his will. Rowling crafted seven duplicates of the handwritten illustrated work, giving six to friends and supporters; the seventh was auctioned at Sotheby's in London for a record-breaking £1,950,000 (US$4 million), to be donated to Children's High Level Group, the European children's charity cofounded by Rowling in 2005.[1] The successful buyer at the auction, Amazon.com, allowed readers to access the work through its website, and produced a collector's edition resembling the original; *Harry Potter* publishers Bloomsbury and Scholastic will release a cheaper edition of the tales, "translated from the original runes by Hermione Granger" and featuring an introduction and illustrations by Rowling.

Besides noting Hermione's participation in the project in a July 2008 statement, the Potter author claimed that the new text would include "notes by

Professor Albus Dumbledore, which appear by generous permission of the Hogwarts Headmasters' Archive."[2] Rowling effectively blurs the lines between author and character, creator and creation in this comment—much like she blurs the lines between the "real" and "fantasy" worlds throughout the Harry Potter series. Whereas in book I, Hogwarts, and the magical realm seem quite distinct from the normalcy-obsessed suburbia of Harry's upbringing in the Dursley household, by the time one reaches *Order of the Phoenix*, the dementors infiltrate Little Whinging, triggering "a breach in the great, invisible wall that divided the relentlessly nonmagical world of Privet Drive and the world beyond. Harry's two lives had somehow become fused."[3] In *Half-Blood Prince*, Voldemort himself enters nonmagical Britain, destroying the Brockdale Bridge and killing masses of nonmagical humans. And on the other side of the alleged divide, the secure boundaries of Hogwarts continue to deteriorate after Dumbledore's death. Ron states, "Everywhere's the same now," revealing the eradication of borders between safe and unsafe, private and public, inside and outside, even home (or home-like spaces) and away.[4]

On an individual level, Harry straddles many borders throughout the series. His age renders him a child for the majority of the narrative, whereas his skills, the problems he is required to solve, and his encounters with malignant forces suggest he is ready to be an adult. He occupies the position of both student and teacher as he combats Professor Umbridge's bureaucratic rules by secretly instructing the members of Dumbledore's Army in Defense Against the Dark Arts. Harry and Voldemort pierce each other's consciousness—the borders of self—on numerous occasions, perhaps most frighteningly when Voldemort possesses Harry at the end of *Phoenix*. And Harry enters the intriguing liminal space between life and death in the mystical King's Cross Station of book VII.

After the final battle in *Deathly Hallows* and the defeat of Voldemort's forces, Rowling suggests a complete erasure of social boundaries and hierarchies in that "nobody was sitting according to House anymore: All were jumbled together, teachers and pupils, ghosts and parents, centaurs and house-elves."[5] Even in front of the headmaster's study, the gargoyle does not require a password; it merely groans, "Feel free" when Harry asks if he, Ron, and Hermione can enter. Some might argue that the author encourages a radical reordering of not only the magical world, but the world in which readers live and are often constrained by hierarchical systems that privilege various groups on the basis of gender, race, ethnicity, socioeconomic class, sexual orientation, religion, occupation, title, or whatever it may be. Others might point out, however, that Rowling does not sustain this radical social vision. In the epilogue of the series, we see Harry's son Albus worrying about the sorting procedures as he is about to go off to Hogwarts for the first time. Clearly, a reinstatement of the practice of sorting the students into Houses signals the reestablishment of certain norms.

As I argued in *Reading Harry Potter*, despite the claims of well-known figures such as William Safire, Roger Sutton, and Jack Zipes, Rowling's series is critically significant and should be taken as seriously by adult critics as youthful fans. Children are not simply mesmerized by the plots and excitement of popular adventure tales; the future thinkers and leaders of societies worldwide are readily absorbing the social values and cultural mores imbedded within the literature they read. Even if, as Lana Whited argues, Rowling had not so successfully crumbled the stereotype that "works of great literary or artistic value do not enjoy commercial success," or, in other words, that "commercial success and literary value are mutually exclusive,"[6] the sheer popularity of the Harry Potter series merits a rigorous exploration of the texts. And thus, when, in the world of literary criticism and postcolonial studies Edward Said asks, "How does Orientalism"—or, I would add, *any* systematic way of thinking about the world—"transmit or reproduce itself from one epoch to another?"[7] critics in those fields often neglect the most obvious answer: through children's literature.

We find this concept brought to life in Rowling's *Deathly Hallows*. Hermione argues that "The Tale of the Three Brothers" contains no explicit reference to the objects known as the Deathly Hallows, to which true-believer Xenophilius Lovegood retorts, "[O]f course not.... That is a children's tale, told to amuse rather than to instruct."[8] As the contributors to this volume and many other scholars will attest, children's books—the Harry Potter novels among them—can certainly instruct and amuse at the same time. Children are inculcated with the moral, behavioral, and social codes of their time through a variety of "texts": their caregivers' lectures as well as urban legends shared on the playground; television programs as well as magazine advertisements; song lyrics and films; textbooks and comic books. In Rowling's novel, Ron astutely notes that children's stories such as that of the three brothers are one example "of those things you tell kids to teach them lessons.... 'Don't go looking for trouble, don't pick fights, don't go messing around with stuff that's best left alone!'"[9] The themes and "lessons" described in the current collection are often more subtle, but no less powerful in the messages they have the power to convey.

Metaphors for reading come up in the series yet again in the fifth book during Harry's Occlumency lessons. This skill is meant to protect the young protagonist against Voldemort's expertise at Legilimency—the ability to read the minds and emotions of others. Rowling's creation of the term Legilimency, with its root in the Latin word *legĕre*, which means "to read," heightens her reader's consciousness of the power involved in reading and penetrating a text. Professor Snape berates Harry: "The mind is not a book, to be opened at will and examined at leisure. Thoughts are not etched on the inside of skulls, to be perused by any invader. The mind is a complex and many-layered thing."[10] Texts, too, can be complicated, and the exchange provides an excellent model for anyone hoping to engage in an interpretation of the Potter series.

Although when I first began planning *Reading Harry Potter* there was very little analytical interrogation of Rowling's work, the past decade has seen a surge in literary criticism and cultural studies on the narratives: Lana Whited's *The Ivory Tower and Harry Potter*, Elizabeth Heilman's *Harry Potter's World* and

*Critical Perspectives on Harry Potter,* and Mercedes Lackey and Leah Wilson's *Mapping the World of Harry Potter,* to name just a few. The contributors of *Reading Harry Potter Again* and I are excited to enter into the existing critical conversation in several ways: not only by engaging with the writers of the mentioned texts, but also with each other, and with our writing Selves of five years past. Brycchan Carey, Lisa Damour, Ximena Gallardo C. and C. Jason Smith, Margaret Oakes, Rebecca Stephens, and I are delighted to have the opportunity to continue the strands we began in the earlier collection, re-addressing and revising arguments made there in light of the completion of Rowling's series. Tracy Bealer, Trish Donaher and James Okapal, Peg Duthie, Leslee Friedman, Lisa Hopkins, Michael Johnson, Chantel Lavoie, and Shama Rangwalla provide the new voices and new perspectives to some of the concepts introduced in the former volume and to some new topics as well.

Damour approaches the series with her expertise as a clinical child psychologist, and places the character of Harry Potter in a behavioral context. She demonstrates how, by depicting Harry as in the throes of emotional pain, Rowling creates a young protagonist who, far from acting abnormally irrational and melodramatic, is a realistic portrait of a normally developing teenager.

Stephens and Duthie both consider the radically different impact of the Potter narratives on various religious communities. In *Reading Harry Potter,* Stephens explored challenges to the Potter books as linked to anxieties about authority and hierarchy among conservative Christians; in *Reading Harry Potter Again,* she continues her examination of how the series has been interpreted as "anti-Church"—and this despite obvious spiritual signification in the novels, including Harry's search for the Deathly Hallows, a type of Holy Grail. Stephens tracks shifts in the sources of attempted censorship, arguing that a more conservative political climate in the United States has actually led to a *decreased* number of challenges. Duthie, on the other hand, probes how ministers from various congregations positively invoke Rowling's novels in their sermons to establish common cultural connections with their members.

Donaher, Okapal, and Hopkins investigate how the Potter series presents notions of destiny and free will. The existence of Professor Trelawney's prophecy regarding Voldemort's demise causes Donaher and Okapal to contemplate the validity of Harry Potter's heroic status: if Harry does not *choose* his actions, but merely *reacts* in accordance with some preordained plan, can he truly be considered a hero? Their chapter engages with the philosophical concepts of determinism, libertarianism, and compatibilism to investigate how Rowling's series presents notions of fate and choice. Hopkins, a literary scholar, compares Harry to canonical figures such as King Arthur and Prince Hal from Shakespeare's Henry plays—the former as a prime example of predestination; the latter, the emblem of independent thought and action whose choices enable personal growth.

Chantel Lavoie, a former contributor, shifts her topic from the sorting ritual and the traits associated with each of the Hogwarts dormitory Houses to a

consideration of lies and deceitfulness. Both of her chapters, however, inter-
rogate how Rowling subverts binaries and challenges traditional notions, such
as truth-telling as inherently "good" and lying as intrinsically immoral—an
important concept especially since the concept of "truth" becomes murky as
the series progresses. In book VI, is Harry lying when he soothes, "Yes . . . yes,
this'll make it stop" while tipping the poisoned potion into Dumbledore's mouth
in "The Cave" chapter? In book VII, Harry assumes that written texts contain
essential truths when, looking at a copy of Rita Skeeter's tell-all biography of
Dumbledore, he thinks: "Now he would know all the things that Dumbledore
had never thought it worth telling him."[11] He must learn, however, to account
for personal bias on the parts of both the reader and the writer; written documents must be interpreted, and not just taken as fact, whether they are tabloid
pieces, history textbooks, biographies, or autobiographies.

Correspondingly, when in *Half-Blood Prince*, Dumbledore informs Harry, "I
think you will find [my memory] both rich in detail and satisfyingly accurate,"[12]
the reader who recognizes the unreliability of remembrances must question the
veracity of this statement. Memories may be fixed in the mind of remembering
subject, but that does not mean they are necessarily *true*; they can be tempered
by the passage of time, one's current mood and circumstance, one's perspective
on the recalled event, and one's relationship with the recollected participants or
the person to whom the reminiscence is conveyed. Readers might recall that in
the sixth novel, Voldemort plants a false memory in Morfin Gaunt's mind after
using his wand to kill the Riddle family; Professor Slughorn's shame causes
him to modify his own memories of conversations with the schoolboy Tom
Riddle; Hokey's memories are distorted to cause her to recall putting poison
into her mistress's drink. Does this mean that Dumbledore—an eminently wise
man, and an old man—must be speaking tongue-in-cheek? Or has Rowling's
establishment of Dumbledore as a supremely heroic figure, along with his
ability to use Legilimency to pull the "real" memories from weak or altered
minds, plus the young reader's likely lack of perspective on the unreliability of
memory, reasserted a false binary of "true" versus "false" texts?

The next three chapters explicitly pursue the social issues of gender, race,
and class in the Potter books. Gallardo C. and Smith describe how upon reading
the second half of Rowling's series, with its apparent focus on Harry's connections to his father and emphasis on heteronormative paradigms, they at first
believed that their argument from *Reading Harry Potter*—that Harry is actually identified with the feminine more than conventional masculinity in the
novels—would be undermined. However a closer reading of the narratives led
them to conclude that Rowling's work actually unravels rigidly defined binaries
of "male" and "female," challenging common conceptions of what it means to
be gendered in contemporary society.

My chapter continues to push a reading of Rowling's narratives as harkening
back to much earlier children's books, especially stories published before the
fall of the British empire. Although the overt message of the Potter series is

antiracist, a conservative colonial ideology peeks forth in the author's allegorical renditions of racial "Others." Scholars like Karin Westman have asserted that "The multi-ethnic Hogwarts, with its students such as Cho Chang, Pavarti Patil, Lee Jordan . . . and top-notch black Quidditch player Angelina Johnson, hardly offers a rosy-hued return to a child-book Edwardian past."[13] I would counter, however, that these characters are hardly examples of social and cultural progress: they are portrayed in strongly assimilationist terms that render their cultural uniqueness all-but-invisible except for, in a couple of cases, their names. Further, Rowling's representations of the giants, centaurs, and goblins echo the tropes of the brutish (American) Indian, the Noble Savage, and the sneaky "Oriental" in ways that undermine the antiracist message of the series.

Rangwala uses a neo-Marxist approach to delve into issues of socioeconomic class in the novels. She asserts that Rowling's narratives work to produce and re-produce traditional middle-class values, including privileging the intelligentsia and critiquing the rampant consumption of a newer middle class. Oakes, also a former contributor, considers questions of inclusion and social exclusivity as well: she posits a reading of the books based on conventional definitions of alchemy. She identifies the Death Eaters' desires to see magic as an innate skill, with secret processes much like alchemy, and their fear of magic as a science, open to be learned and practiced by anyone, as related to their yearnings to preserve an elitist hierarchy of power in the wizarding world.

Carey's and Bealer's chapters fit together seamlessly; both address Rowling's encouragement of political participation in her young readers. Carey again takes up the question of the house-elves and their bondage; he argues that although Harry's struggle with Voldemort provides a productive site for the discussion of a democratic society's reactions to elitism, totalitarianism, and racism, Rowling's treatment of the house-elf issue becomes less and less radical as the series progresses. Nevertheless, he demonstrates how Rowling continues to tap into certain literary and historical tropes that suggest that she sees the elf/slavery problem as inseparable from larger political issues. Bealer focuses on a single Potter novel—*Order of the Phoenix*—to analyze the parallels between adult and student resistance movements against authoritarian regimes. Exploring how Harry's interactions with corrupted political institutions influence his existential conflict with the Dark Lord, Bealer proposes that the emotions of love and compassion are privileged as paramount to political strategy and agency.

The final two chapters take distinctly intertextual approaches to Rowling's work. Friedman reframes the processes of reading and writing, once seen as, respectively, passive and active, to examine how major female characters in the series access written texts and power. She compellingly asserts that various characters' success is predicated on their ability to read intertextually or between and among a variety of written materials. Johnson's chapter details the "magical" transfiguration of one text into another: Rowling's *Harry Potter and the Prisoner of Azkaban* into Alfonso Cuarón's film of the same name. Johnson surveys how several key themes get transformed in the process, as well as how the film fits into multiple cinematic traditions, from the classic Universal horror films of the 1930s to the French New Wave films of the late 1950s and early 1960s.

In *Harry Potter and the Deathly Hallows*, Dumbledore tells Harry, "That which Voldemort does not value, he takes no trouble to comprehend. Of house-elves and children's tales, of love, loyalty, and innocence, Voldemort knows and understands nothing."[14] Unfortunately, Voldemort is not the only one. And although this collection of essays cannot instill the values of uncompromising justice, love, loyalty, and kindness in our readers, we anticipate that our work will help readers of all types to value children's literature beyond its ability to entertain and come to a greater understanding of Rowling's work and the society in which we live.

## NOTES

1. Rowling's donations to charities are well documented: £500,000 to Britain's National Council for One Parent Families in 2000; the proceeds of *Fantastic Beasts and Where to Find Them* and *Quidditch through the Ages* to Comic Relief UK, for AIDS education and uniting war-torn families in the world's most impoverished nations, and so on.

2. Shannon Maughan, "Rowling's Rare Book to Hit Shelves in December." *Publishers Weekly*. July 31, 2008 <http://www.publishersweekly.com/article/CA6583159.html?nid=2788>.

3. J.K. Rowling, *Harry Potter and the Order of the Phoenix* (New York: Scholastic, 2003), 37.

4. J.K. Rowling, *Harry Potter and the Half-Blood Prince* (New York: Scholastic, 2005), 650.

5. J.K. Rowling, *Harry Potter and the Deathly Hallows* (New York: Scholastic, 2007), 745.

6. Lana A. Whited, "Introduction—Harry Potter: From Craze to Classic?" *The Ivory Tower and Harry Potter* (Columbia: University of Missouri Press, 2004), 7.

7. Edward W. Said, *Orientalism* (New York: Vintage, 1979), 15.

8. Rowling, *Hallows*, 409.

9. Rowling, *Hallows*, 414.

10. Rowling, *Phoenix*, 530.

11. Rowling, *Hallows*, 353.

12. Rowling, *Prince*, 263.

13. Karin E. Westman, "Specters of Thatcherism: Contemporary British Culture in J.K. Rowling's Harry Potter Series." *The Ivory Tower and Harry Potter*. Ed. Lana A. Whited (Columbia: University of Missouri Press, 2004): 305–28, 307.

14. Rowling, *Hallows*, 709.

# Harry the Teenager:
# Muggle Themes in a Magical Adolescence

*Lisa Damour*

The last three volumes of J.K. Rowling's Harry Potter series carry us into the heart of Harry's adolescence; Harry turns fifteen at the beginning of book V, *Harry Potter and the Order of the Phoenix,* and nears eighteen as the series comes to its close. In an earlier essay, I proposed that young readers are likely attracted to elements in Rowling's first four books that reflect the dynamic, unconscious elements of preadolescent psychological development.[1] Here, I argue that the last three books of the Potter saga not only spin a complex tale of the triumph of good over evil, but do so while exploring some central aspects of normal psychological development during adolescence proper. The story is a fantastic, magical tale with plenty to entertain adolescents and adults alike; it also offers a rich portrait of what nonmagical adolescence looks and feels like. Teenage readers likely find many reflections of their own experiences in Rowling's last three books. Adult readers who tune in to the more subtle aspects of Rowling's narrative stand to learn a lot about the complex relationships between teenagers and the adults who surround them.

Many elements in the last three books of the Harry Potter series hold an obvious appeal to the teenage reader. The arc of Ginny Weasley's tale—from having a giddy crush on Harry in *Harry Potter and the Chamber of Secrets* to becoming his girlfriend, then wife—surely delights any girl who ever pined for her big brother's best friend, or any older boy for that matter. This is no small club. In general, twelve- to thirteen-year-old girls are much more romantically inclined than their male age-mates and tend to channel their ambitions toward slightly older boys. Indeed, the "boy band" division of the music industry has profited massively from creating singing groups whose looks and lyrics are marketed straight at the romantically bereft young adolescent girl.

If Ginny's tale resonates with the girl who daydreams about emerging from adolescence as a witty dynamo who walks off with the most popular boy in the world, Neville Longbottom's story appeals to any boy who hopes to go from zero to hero. In the early Harry Potter books, Neville is a sad, bumbling nerd whose academic strengths are limited to herbology. He blooms in *Harry Potter and the Order of the Phoenix*, when he joins Dumbledore's Army. From there, he fights side by side with Harry in the Department of Mysteries, leads the resistance when Hogwarts is taken over by Death Eaters, and renders Voldemort mortal by decapitating his pet snake, Nagini. Our last look at Neville finds him "surrounded by a knot of fervent admirers."[2]

Rowling's creation and destruction of Dolores Umbridge is also understandably appealing to teenage readers. A highly sadistic character sporting a thin veneer of sickly sweetness, Umbridge represents a "type" with whom teen readers are undoubtedly familiar: the self-satisfied adult who freely abuses the power differential between grown-ups and children in order to serve her own needs. First appearing in *Harry Potter and the Order of the Phoenix*, Umbridge cruelly punishes Harry for insisting that Voldemort has returned, a fact vehemently denied by the Ministry of Magic for whom Umbridge works. In the end, Rowling more than evens the score with the punishments that befall Umbridge—she continually likens Umbridge to a toad,[3] has her beaten by centaurs whom she has publicly insulted, and ultimately has her tried and imprisoned for her cruelty to Muggle-borns.

The curriculum in Umbridge's first Defense Against the Dark Arts class must also confirm for teenage readers that Rowling "gets it." Despite massive evidence that Voldemort is alive, gaining followers, and on the march, Umbridge insists that the Hogwarts students do not need to be prepared or encouraged to actually *use* defensive spells:

"Now, it is the view of the Ministry that a theoretical knowledge will be more than sufficient to get you through your examination, which, after all, is what school is all about...

"And what good's theory going to be in the real world?" said Harry loudly, his fist in the air again.

Professor Umbridge looked up.

"This is school, Mr. Potter, not the real world," she added softly.

"So we're not supposed to be prepared for what's waiting out there?"

"There is nothing waiting out there, Mr. Potter."[4]

This scene must seem startlingly familiar to any adolescent who has ever attended an abstinence-only sex education class.[5] Even in classrooms that provide comprehensive sex education, teens consistently find that it's hard to get adults to talk realistically about what's "out there." This is not to say that the general adolescent attitude toward sexual activity matches the Hogwarts students' attitude toward fighting Death Eaters. Rather, it is to say that real teenagers and Rowling's teenagers share the misery of having to deal with adults who deny the reality, and risks, of that which lies plainly all around them.[6]

In addition to including plots with obvious appeal to teenagers the last three volumes in the Harry Potter series include subtle narrative threads that speak to some of the central challenges of adolescence. Harry's erratic emotionality, complex relationship with Dumbledore, and precipitous maturation at the end of the series display Rowling's deep and unusual appreciation for the less-than-obvious psychological strands of normal adolescent development.

Rowling understands that adolescence, by its nature, involves psychological distress. In the first four volumes of the Harry Potter series—Harry's eleventh to fourteenth years—Harry is a relatively mild-mannered boy, especially considering his extraordinary life circumstances. Harry's mood changes significantly in *Order of the Phoenix*. Featuring Harry as a fifteen-year-old, hardly a chapter of *Phoenix* goes by in which Harry fails to openly defy an authority figure, explode in rage at his friends, bicker with his Quidditch teammates, suffer from tormenting nightmares, make destructive choices, feel isolated and bereft, or seriously consider dropping out of school. Even when his outlook brightens somewhat in the following year, Harry's mood still ranges from kind and earnest to irascible and bellicose.

Through all the fireworks, Rowling never suggests that Harry is out of touch or unbalanced. In this, she sets herself apart from many contemporary adults who are increasingly unwilling to view adolescent distress as in some way developmentally essential. As part of a broader cultural war against negative emotions, even normal adolescent behavior has now become grounds for medical intervention; alarming statistics testify to the rising use of psychotropic medications to tame the emotions of children and teens. Antidepressant prescriptions for teenagers nearly doubled from 1997 to 2002, notwithstanding FDA black box warnings that some antidepressant drugs are associated with adolescent suicide.[7] Antipsychotic prescriptions for children and teens more than doubled in roughly the same period despite the fact that these powerful drugs are not well tested in children under the age of eighteen.[8] Prescriptions for Ritalin, a popular stimulant, increased almost threefold during the 1990s, and as many as 6 percent of American children are now treated with psychostimulant medications.[9]

To be sure, psychotropic medications *can* be a critical component in the effective treatment of some children and adolescents. Antidepressants and antipsychotics have the potential to be life saving when carefully prescribed to properly evaluated patients. The failure to consider psychostimulants when treating a child with bona fide attention-deficit/hyperactivity disorder is malpractice at best. Yet, the rapid rise of prescriptions for psychotropic medications for children and teenagers indicates a trend toward substituting diagnoses and medication for the thoughtful assessment of legitimate, and often developmentally normal, sources of psychological pain.[10]

In 1958, Anna Freud, Sigmund's daughter and an influential theorist in her own right, wrote the following:

I take it that it is normal for an adolescent to behave for a considerable length of time in an inconsistent and unpredictable manner; to fight his impulses and accept them; . . . to love his parents and to hate them; to revolt against them and be dependent on them; . . . to be more idealistic, artistic, generous, and unselfish than he will ever be again, but also the opposite: self-centered, egoistic, calculating. Such fluctuations and extreme opposites would be deemed highly abnormal at any other time of life. At this time they may signify no more than that an adult structure of personality takes a long time to emerge, that the individual in question does not cease to experiment and is in no hurry to close down on possibilities.[11]

Today, heavy-duty diagnoses, like bipolar disorder, and heavy-duty drugs, like lithium, are used more frequently to categorize and suppress "symptoms" that Anna Freud described, nearly fifty years ago, as the typical face of adolescent development. To her credit, Rowling gives us a Harry who matches Anna Freud's description (assuming, of course, that we substitute "parental figures" for "parents"). The reader and Rowling understand that Harry—in all his anger and despondence—makes sense. We do not question the basis of Harry's moodiness, but see it as the expectable outward sign of his painful past and conflicted present. For example, Harry's reunion with Ron and Hermione after a summer at the Dursleys' takes on a striking new tone in *Order of the Phoenix*. Rather than settling joyfully into his old friendships, Harry rails at his friends and accuses them of deliberately keeping him in the dark.[12] Even when Harry is at his most outrageous his struggle is depicted throughout as a meaningful, reasonable response to his circumstances and a catalyst for his personal growth. Rowling balances Harry's tantrum with a tender description of its source: "Every bitter and resentful thought that Harry had had in the past month was pouring out of him; his frustration with the lack of news, the hurt that they had all been together without him, his fury at being followed and not told about it: All the feelings he was half-ashamed of finally burst their boundaries."[13] Teenage readers are likely comforted by Rowling's clear recognition that it is not "crazy" for teenagers to have intense, conflicted, even bewildering emotions in response to the real and stressful challenges associated with growing up.

Rowling explores two other elements of adolescent development that are rarely acknowledged between parents and teenagers yet likely resonate with teenage readers: the influence of parents' *own* adolescent experiences on how they approach the task of parenting their teenage children and the sudden maturation that typically occurs when teens develop the ability to see their parents as having free standing psychologies that predate—and operate independently of—the parent–teen relationship.

Throughout book VII, *Harry Potter and the Deathly Hallows*, Harry struggles with a painful question: if Dumbledore knew that his own death was imminent, and knew that he was leaving Harry with the life-threatening task of vanquishing Voldemort, why didn't Dumbledore lead Harry to the Deathly Hallows, the three magical objects that make their owner immortal? Feeling hopelessly stuck, Harry becomes incensed: "'Look what he asked from me, Hermione! Risk your life, Harry! And again! And again! And don't expect me to explain everything, just trust me blindly, trust that I know what I'm doing, trust me even though I don't trust you! Never the whole truth! Never!'"[14] Harry's confusion about Dumbledore's silence deepens when it becomes clear that Dumbledore not only failed to *lead* Harry to the Hallows (as Harry originally assumed), but in fact failed to simply *give* Harry the Resurrection Stone and the Elder Wand, which were in his possession, and which, in combination with Harry's Invisibility Cloak, would have made the protagonist the owner of all three Hallows. When Harry meets Dumbledore in the limbo of King's Cross he asks:

"Why did you have to make it so difficult?"
   Dumbledore's smile was tremulous.
   [. . . . ] "I was afraid that your hot head might dominate your good heart. I was scared that, if presented outright with the facts and those tempting objects, you might seize the Hallows as I did, at the wrong time, for the wrong reasons. If you laid hands on them, I wanted you to possess them safely."[15]

Here, Dumbledore refers to the pivotal events of his own seventeenth year. Upon graduating as the finest student ever to attend Hogwarts, Dumbledore had no choice but to return home to care for his orphaned sister, Ariana. At King's Cross, Dumbledore explains to Harry that bitter resentment of his situation made him vulnerable to becoming "inflamed" by Grindelwald's belief that ownership of the Deathly Hallows would help them become the "glorious young leaders of the revolution" giving wizards power over the Muggle-born.[16] Dumbledore's association with Grindelwald sets into motion a chain of events that culminate with the accidental murder—perhaps by Dumbledore—of Ariana.

Ariana's death haunts Dumbledore for the rest of his life. While draining the goblet in the cave where Voldemort hid Merope's locket, Dumbledore revisits his sister's death: "'It's all my fault, all my fault,' he sobbed. 'Please make it stop, I know I did wrong, oh please make it stop and I'll never, never again'."[17] Dumbledore's shame about his adolescent mistake is so intense that he refuses to become Minister of Magic, fearing that he cannot be trusted with power, and he fails to give Harry information that might have eased Harry's mind, if not his mission.

In this thread, Rowling captures a prevalent dynamic between parents and their adolescent children: the parents' tendency to perceive their children through the scrim of their own adolescence. Two forces contribute to this common state of affairs. First, children typically become quite a bit more private when they enter adolescence. This often begins with the twelve- to thirteen-year-old closing her bedroom door to do the same, usually innocuous, things she used to do with the door open. It extends over time to sharing far more information with one's friends than one's parents and sometimes to living "in the home in the attitude of a boarder, usually a very inconsiderate one so far as the older and younger family members are concerned."[18] Teenagers create a blank space with their privacy, and parents inevitably fill in the blank with memories from their own adolescence. Parents who are fearful that their children will make irreparable mistakes during adolescence—as most are—find themselves filling in the blank with memories that are now quite frightening. Fathers recall how eager they and their friends were to make sexual progress with girls; mothers recall dicey scenarios involving unsupervised parties with drugs and drinking.[19] Add to this the reality that teenage behavior *is* often quite risky. Even if teens aren't telling their parents exactly what happened last Saturday night, parents can usually come up with enough information to fan the flame of selective memory.

Ideally, parents would draw on recollections of their own adolescence to empathize with their teenager's experiences and enforce fair but firm behavioral expectations. Yet, quite commonly, parents are ashamed of aspects of their adolescence and shame—one of the most slippery and toxic of all emotions—tends to get in the way of parenting in the same way that it interferes with Dumbledore's care of Harry. Rather than viewing the teenager for who he is, the parent treats the teenager as if he is on the verge of repeating the parent's own mistakes. Although the parent's anxiety comes from a loving place, it is experienced by real teens in the same way it is experienced by Harry: for reasons that aren't clear, the parent seems not to trust the child, especially in certain arenas. Unfortunately, this is generally an unconscious process. In other words, it is a rare parent who is fully aware that his distrust of his teenager derives from past events the parent feels bad about. Instead, the parent often feels justified in his suspicions and takes one of two tacks. Either he becomes entrenched in his refusal to get into the details of certain teenage topics, or he repeatedly warns the teenager of the risks associated with particular adolescent behaviors. Either way, the teenager feels hurt and bewildered.

For the most part, teens and their parents survive this misunderstanding. Otherwise good parenting can compensate for the presence of a few shameful memories, and sometimes, parents balance each other out. The father who can't stand to have his daughter go on a date is tamed by the mother who knows that the girl can take good care of herself; the mother who is fearful of letting her daughter attend a party is reassured by the dad who points out that "she's a careful kid." Ultimately, Harry makes sense of Dumbledore's strange omissions when he gets a full account of Dumbledore's painful early experiences and the pair ends the series on the warm terms they enjoyed in the early novels. This last point ties to a broader theme in the final three volumes: that Harry only truly "grows up" when he understands the early experiences and attendant psychologies of the critical adults in his world.

In the second half of the series, Harry and the reader learn the developmental histories of Albus Dumbledore and Severus Snape, the two adults with whom

Harry maintains the most intense—and intensely conflicted—relationships. We learn that Dumbledore's inscrutability derives, in no small part, from his painful and complex past as noted earlier. With regard to Snape, the first six volumes in the series lead the reader believe that Snape dislikes Harry because Harry—with his "boy who lived" status and daring hijinks—reminds Snape of James Potter, the popular boy who bullied Snape during their Hogwarts days. However, in *Deathly Hallows*, we learn that Snape loved Harry's mother Lily from the time they were children and that he lived out his days tortured by his own accidental role in her death. In the end, it becomes clear to Harry and the reader that Snape's poor treatment of Harry may have little or nothing to do with Harry's behavior (which, in actuality, is quite *unlike* James'[20]); Snape persecutes Harry because he is the spitting image of the man who ran off with the love of his life.

Armed with insight into Dumbledore and Snape's early lives, Harry suddenly, and completely, grows up. As Voldemort and Harry circle each other in their final meeting, Voldemort accuses Harry of being a "little boy"[21] with a "childish dream,"[22] but Harry makes it clear that he is no child. Harry tells Voldemort that he "won't be killing anyone else tonight"[23] and goes on to educate Voldemort about the truth behind Dumbledore's death, Snape's loyalty, and the ownership of the Elder Wand. In a final appeal, it's Harry who exhorts Voldemort to "Be a man."[24]

When Harry gains an objective understanding of the men who have "raised" him, he crosses the Rubicon that divides teenagers from true adults. Ideally, at some point in their late adolescence, teenagers come to appreciate that not every aspect of their parents' behavior should be taken personally.[25] Adolescents mature precipitously when their lifelong and developmentally normal egocentrism gives way to an ability to take an objective view of their parents' freestanding psychologies. For example, a daughter who was angered and hurt by her mother's persistent snooping might suddenly realize that her mother noses into everyone's business, and that she snoops not because she truly suspects she'll find anything, but because she's lonely. Even behavior that appears to be directed specifically at the child, such as Snape's clear dislike of Harry, can take on unsuspected dimensions. A son who feels humiliated by his father's persistent criticism from the sidelines of the sports field might come to appreciate that the father is struggling to make peace with his own aging. Rather than gracefully accepting middle age, the father may be wishing this his son's athletic prowess will make up for his own loss of potency. Suddenly, it becomes clear to the teenager that the problem is not his athletic ability but his father's narcissism.

It is hard to overstate the developmental shift that occurs when teenagers begin to view their parents objectively. Instead of thinking that the parent's behavior accurately mirrors some aspect of the teenager—untrustworthiness, athletic incompetence—teens can see that the parent's behavior often derives from sources that may have little or nothing to do with them. Rather than feeling hurt by the adult and thrust into an effort to disprove, or at least try to make sense of, the parent's view, the teenager becomes merely annoyed by his or her parent's quirks and empathetic to their vulnerabilities. At that point, a world of possibility opens up. Less reactive to life at home, the teenager is now more fully prepared to face life at large. Relieved of some of the effort of living up to, or at least negotiating with their parents' expectations, young adults begin to grapple with what they want for themselves. No longer trying to make sense of Dumbledore and Snape, Harry directs his full force at Voldemort, telling him "It's just you and me."[26]

As coming-of-age tales go, Harry Potter's is hard to beat. Harry not only saves the world but also does so while acting in developmentally appropriate ways from ages eleven to seventeen. In the epilogue to the final volume, Rowling underlines Harry's full-blown maturation; seven volumes of Harry's pure distaste for Snape are capped by the adult Harry's plausible reference to Snape as the "probably the bravest man I ever knew."[27] In Rowling's stories the easily observable elements of childhood and adolescence are undergirded by a pitch-perfect depiction of the more subtle aspects of normal development. For teenage readers, Rowling creates adolescent characters who feel reassuringly real, even as they navigate an utterly fantastical world. For adults, Rowling provides an insightful guide to the thorny aspects of the parent–teen relationship while laying out some of the essential catalysts of adolescent maturation.

## NOTES

1. Lisa Damour, "Harry Potter and the Magical Looking Glass: Reading the Secret Life of the Preadolescent," in *Reading Harry Potter: Critical Essays*, ed. Giselle Liza Anatol (Westport, CT: Praeger, 2003), 15–24.

2. J.K. Rowling, *Harry Potter and the Deathly Hallows* (New York: Scholastic Press, 2007), 745.

3. J.K. Rowling, *Harry Potter and the Order of the Phoenix* (New York: Scholastic Press, 2003), 146.

4. Ibid., 244

5. At present in the United States, any state that uses federal funding to support the teaching of sex education must emphasize abstinence until marriage as the ideal option for teenagers and may only discuss contraception in the context of failure rates. Heather D. Boonstra, "The Case for a New Approach to Sex Education Mounts: Will Policymakers Heed the Message?" *Guttmacher Policy Review* 10, 2 (2007): 2–7. http://www.guttmacher.org/pubs/gpr/10/2/gpr100202.html (accessed 30 June 2008).

6. One can easily extend this scenario to the many ways in which adults make themselves somewhat ridiculous to teenagers. The same adults who fail to raise an eyebrow at "Harold and Kumar" movies (about two potheads) will become surprisingly cagey and moralizing when asked about real-life marijuana use. Teens who listen to rapper Lil' Wayne's sexually explicit lyrics—as many teens do—would be hard pressed to find an adult who will speak frankly with them about the physical acts Lil' Wayne describes.

7. B. Vitiello, S. Zuvekas, and G. S. Norquist, "National Estimates of Antidepressant Medication Use among U.S. Children, 1997–2002," *Journal of the American Academy of Child and Adolescent Psychiatry* 45, 3 (2006): 271–79.

8. N. Patel, et al., "Trends in the Use of Typical and Atypical Antipsychotics in Children and Adolescents," *Journal of the American Academy of Child and Adolescent Psychiatry* 44, 6 (2005): 548–56.

9. J.M. Rey and G. Sawyer, "Are Psychostimulant Drugs Being Used Appropriately to Treat Child and Adolescent Disorders?" *The British Journal of Psychiatry: The Journal of Mental Science* 182 (2003): 284–86.

10. The strangeness of this situation is hardly lost on the teenagers themselves. On more than a few occasions, a teenaged patient of mine has arrived at our appointment in a fury: "You're not going to *believe* this! My friend's parents are divorcing and haven't been on speaking terms for months. When my friend told her pediatrician that she was crying all the time and had trouble sleeping, do you know what happened? The pediatrician put MY FRIEND on antidepressants!"

11. Anna Freud, "Adolescence," *The Psychoanalytic Study of the Child* 13 (1958): 255–78. 275.

12. Rowling, *Phoenix*, 65–66.

13. Ibid., 65–66.

14. Rowling, *Hallows*, 362.

15. Ibid., 720.

16. Ibid., 716.

17. J.K. Rowling, *Harry Potter and the Half-Blood Prince* (New York: Scholastic Press, 2005), 572.

18. Freud, "Adolescence," 269.

19. In all likelihood, parent's memories of adolescence are weighted toward the risky moments. People tend not to dwell on their good decisions; tamely hanging out with friends may not make much of a mark on memory.

20. As the series unfolds, the reader learns that James Potter, although charming and talented, was also quite a bully as a teenager. For example, in *Phoenix* Harry sneaks into a memory that Snape meant to hide in a Pensive for the duration of their Occlumency lesson. In the memory, Harry watches as his father and Sirius torment Snape for their own entertainment. The scene ends with Snape suspended in midair, and James Potter asking his classmates "Who wants to see me take off Snivelly's pants?" Never does Harry's behavior even approximate the kind of cruelty in which James and Sirius Black engaged. Rowling, *Phoenix*, 649.

21. Rowling, *Hallows*, 741.

22. Ibid., 740.

23. Ibid., 738.

24. Ibid., 741.

25. Indeed, Phineas Nigellus—the former Hogwarts headmaster—chastises Harry for his egocentricity. Traveling between his portraits at Hogwarts and Grimmauld Place in *Phoenix*, Nigellus transmits a terse message from Dumbledore telling Harry to stay with his friends at the Order's headquarters. Harry bristles at the instruction, fearing that has become a dangerous weapon under Voldemort's mental control.

"So that's it, is it?" [Harry] said loudly. "*Stay there?* . . . Just stay put while the grown-ups sort it out, Harry! We won't bother telling you anything, though, because your tiny little brain might not be able to cope with it!"

"You know," said Phineas Nigellus, even more loudly than Harry, "this is precisely why I *loathed* being a teacher! Young people are so infernally convinced that they are absolutely right about everything. Has it not occurred to you, my poor puffed-up popinjay, that there might be an excellent reason why the headmaster of Hogwarts is not confiding every tiny detail of his plans to you?"

Nigellus' derisive tone aside, his point is a good one. Harry, like most teenagers, sometimes lacks perspective on the behavior of others. Rather than considering possibilities which do not place him at the center, Harry sees Dumbledore's brevity as a personal insult, rather than as the strategic move that it is. Rowling, *Phoenix*, 649.

26. Rowling, *Hallows*, 737.

27. Ibid., 758.

# I

# Religion and Morality

# 2

# The Lightning Bolt Scar as a Lightning Rod: J.K. Rowling's Harry Potter Series and the Rhetoric of the Extreme Right

*Rebecca L. Stephens*

Witches and witchcraft have long served as a sort of social lightning rod, symbols onto which members of a society project their fears about their culture, especially in those times and places that witchcraft itself was a real and present danger. We can see this clearly in the *Malleus Maleficarum* (*The Hammer of Witches*), the 1486 manual by Heinrich Kramer and James Sprenger used to prosecute witches during the Inquisition. We can see the Church's fear of women's power and sexuality in the section titles, such as "Concerning Witches who copulate with Devils. Why is it that Women are chiefly addicted to Evil Superstitions?" and the attempt to shore up the masculinization of medicine in "The Witches who Midwives in Various Ways Kill the Child Conceived in the Womb and Procure an Abortion; or if they do not this, Offer New-born Children to Devils."[1] We can also see this in the Salem witch trials, where the accused were often those who were outsiders to the society, like Tituba, the Barbadian woman accused of spell casting and divination. In Arthur Miller's retelling of the Salem witch trials in *The Crucible* (1953), witchcraft becomes a metaphor through which to speak about the fears that generated the Red Scare and Communist witch hunts of the 1950s. Maryse Condé's novel *I, Tituba, Black Witch of Salem* (1986) also recounts the Salem story to highlight the cultural monovision of the Puritan culture and the continuing American fear of the racial and sexual "Other." Jodi Picoult's recent retelling of *The Crucible* in turn uses witchcraft as means by which a sexually abused teenage girl seeks to gain power over one of our own contemporary culture's worst nightmares—the pedophile—neatly transferring witchcraft to a less fearsome thing than the "real" threat of an alleged sexual predator.[2] In each case, witchcraft serves as a lightning rod, absorbing a culture's fears of what seems most terrifying at a given moment.

As a series that has generated controversy from the beginning of its mammoth popularity for its portrayal of witchcraft, the Harry Potter books work in much the same way—as a symbol of the contemporary social anxieties of various groups, particularly within American culture. In *Reading Harry Potter*, I explored fears surrounding challenges to authority and hierarchy. These underlying fears are still applicable, but the landscape of protest has changed in some surprising ways since that chapter was published. Based on continuing media coverage, especially of recent court cases involving the books, I anticipated that my research would find that the challenges to the Harry Potter series would have continued the established pattern—that the challenges would stem from established conservative Christian groups, like Concerned Women for America and Focus on the Family, that had previously objected to the books and supported parents who initiated challenges to the books in schools throughout the United States. With more careful reading, however, what instead became apparent was that the attempts to censor Harry had actually decreased and that these attempts had for the most part shifted to different sources. In fact, some of the very groups that had previously censured the series, most prominently Focus on the Family, were now encouraging followers to read the books. At the same time as these groups—most of whom are readily recognizable to most Americans as the virtual "face" of organized conservative Christianity in this country—became more accepting, a swelling number of less publicly visible groups even further on the political right had taken up the censorship banner. Many of these groups, which seem to exist in isolated pockets around the United States, but communicate in a big way through the Internet, voiced condemnation of Harry Potter in increasingly histrionic and beleaguered tones.

What had happened in the intervening years to account for the reduction in challenge events and the shift in the source of would-be censors? One prominent factor is that the country itself has shifted generally to the right in recent years. The Bush Administration's support of faith-based initiatives, the appointment of more conservative judges to the U.S. Supreme Court, and the growing number of states adopting amendments to their constitution banning gay marriage are just a few of the public policies that have created a political and cultural climate that is more reflective of conservative Christian values and have, therefore, given conservative Christian groups a greater sense of political capital. The climate, however, seems not to have swung far enough to the right to those at the extreme end of the conservative spectrum. True to theories about identity creation that suggest that the most effective way for groups to solidify a cohesive collective identity is by establishing how "us" differs from "them," these far-far-right-wing groups have sought to differentiate themselves from the now-more-mainstream Christian right by focusing on how the groups have actually failed to live up to "true Christian values" in the culture wars. Thus, as a continuing cultural phenomenon Harry and his witchcraft have become the a lightning rod that deflects and reflects the insider and outsider status of these two types of Christian groups and their power (or lack of) within this cultural moment.

The Harry Potter series has been involved in several legal cases since *Reading Harry Potter* was published. The first time Harry went to court was in July 2002, when a student and her parents sued the Cedarville, Arkansas, school board that had placed the books on restricted access in the district's school libraries after a parent complained that the series "might promote disobedience and disrespect for authority"[3] and that it depicted witchcraft. But, ultimately, a U.S. District Court judge ordered the school to return the books to its library shelves, stating that the restriction violated the First Amendment rights of the students.[4] A more recent court decision pertaining to school challenges of Harry Potter came in May 2007, when Georgia Superior Court Judge Connie Bachelor upheld a 2006 decision by the state board of education to retain the series in the school system's library media centers.[5] This case also started with a complaint from a parent, Laura Mallory, who alleged that the books are "not educationally suitable and have been shown to be harmful to some kids." She also argued that the Harry Potter series promoted the Wiccan religion and that assigning the books was tantamount to school sanctioning this religion over Christianity. Before going to trial, the hearing before the Gwinnett School Board pitted Mallory and six others objecting to the books against a crowd of almost ninety who turned out in support of the books, including a number of high school students who wore shirts protesting the detrimental effects of censorship on education.[6] Most recently, the American Civil Liberties Union filed suit in May 2008 on behalf of a public library assistant, Deborah Smith, near St. Louis, Missouri, when Smith refused to work her normal shift during the celebration of the release of *Harry Potter and the Deathly Hallows*. A Southern Baptist, Smith felt that the series "popularize[d] witchcraft and the practice of the occult."[7]

Other challenges to the books were not so sedate. The books were publicly burned by Rev. George Bender in rural Pennsylvania in 2001 and burnings were repeated by fundamentalist church groups in other states from 2001 to 2003.[8] And since my last survey of the censorship events, bannings continue to spread to other countries. In 2002, school officials in the United Arab Emirates removed the Harry Potter series from schools along with other books that they deemed had "written or illustrated material that contradicts Islamic and Arab values."[9] Other countries where the books have been removed from schools include Australia, Britain, Finland, and Sweden.

As the court cases and other challenges illustrate, the most common objection to the Harry Potter books continues to be the books' representation of witchcraft, cited repeatedly as a doorway to occult practices and as a tempting lure to Christian children to practices that many conservative Christians persist in linking to Wicca. In *Counts v. Cedarville School District*, for example, the defendant board members argued that the presentation of witchcraft amounted to the books' promoting a particular religion, by implication, the Wiccan religion, and one member stated that if the Harry Potter series advocated Christianity, "'he would not object to them'."[10] An added twist on these witchcraft objections, however, is a more widespread idea that the witchcraft is specifically anti-Christian, even though through the entire series, the books mention no religion of any kind. In fact, this absence was noted in a much-quoted article *Time* magazine article by Lev Grossman, "[i]f you want to know who dies in Harry Potter, the answer is easy: God. Harry Potter lives in a world free of any religion or spirituality of any kind. He lives surrounded by ghosts but has no one to pray to, even if he were so inclined, which he isn't."[11] This rhetoric is especially obvious on the more extreme conservative Christian views voiced on radical websites. On the "Straight Talk on Harry Potter" page, for instance, William J. Schnoebelen, who claims to have "spent sixteen years as a teacher of witchcraft, spiritism and ceremonial magick . . . [and] seven years in the Church of Satan,"[12] along with years as a Freemason and a Mormon and whose website includes links explaining the evils of these organizations, makes the following complaints about the series:

The morals presented in the Potter books are anti-God and anti-Christian. More importantly, the lifestyle of magick is presented as fun. Few kids would find magick so appealing if they knew they had to grapple with a hideous demon to acquire it; and even then have a good chance of being slaughtered before the end of the ritual. Not only that, the books are definitely drawing kids towards witchcraft. "Who wouldn't choose a wizard's life?" asked TIME magazine. Even authentic, real Wiccans are "charmed" by the Potter series, according to the Associated Press. Anything that witches find good and charming certainly ought to be viewed with suspicion by serious Christians. More important than that—these books enflame what C. S. Lewis called a "spiritual lust" for occult knowledge and power. They tickle the desire to become "little gods" and fill the child's head with violence, blood sacrifice and a world view which is decidedly anti-Christian.[13]

Likewise, on the Fill the Void Ministries website, which shares the extreme discourse style and spiritual warfare preoccupations with Schnoebelen and others of his ilk, Kathy Smith asserts on the "Who Is Harry Potter"[14] page that "Christian ideals are totally ignored throughout these books, but they have an anti-Christian theme to them. . . . Everything a Christian is, the Harry Potter books are not. Everything God is, the Harry Potter books are not."[15] Another website from Let Us Reason Ministries warns that the Harry Potter series "influences our children to be open to pagan spirituality, this is not just imagination. What we are watching is an all out assault on biblical values and a Christian worldview."[16]

Others on the extreme Christian right have made virtual cyber-cottage industries out of deploring Harry Potter and sensationalizing the fears about witchcraft and the occult. On its "Is 'Harry Potter' Harmless" page, the site ChristianAnswer.net pushes a documentary, *Harry Potter: Witchcraft Repackaged*, which it says:

studies elements of Rowling's imagery and writings, including the use of the "Potter" name in Pagan religion, shapechanging, meditation, human sacrifice, feminine power,

Wicca (the religion of witchcraft), the tools, spells and curses used in witchcraft, Christian youth and their involvement, communicating with the spirit world, reincarnation, situational ethics in witchcraft, the lightning bolt as a power symbol, broomsticks and witches' hats as phallic symbols, dabbling in divination and sorcery, recruitment, teaching children dark arts, *Scholastic Inc.'s* involvement, and more.[17]

One can't help but notice how the fears catalogued in the description echo those enumerated in the *Malleus*, particularly in referencing feminine power as one of the dangers of the Harry Potter books. Steve Wohlberg, a Christian Right radio host, peddles *The Hour of the Witch*, a documentary that promises to help viewers "discover hidden dangers within Harry Potter" and to "protect your family from deadly supernatural forces." Wohlberg's words are characteristic of the fear-laden language that permeates those actually selling Potter opposition. Painting their audience as at the mercy of unseen but constantly menacing spiritual threats, these sales pitches rely on the hope that inspiring their viewers to feel frightened, vulnerable, and beleaguered by the ambushes waiting in the wider culture will force them to grasp at a single source of their spiritual angst that can be (conveniently) solved by purchasing the video or book. The most frequently cited web detractors in articles examining the censorship of the Harry Potter series are Berit and Andy Kjos whose Kjos Ministries site contains twenty lengthy pages with titles ranging from "Harry Potter and the Postmodern Church" to "The Deadly Magic of Potter Movies—Not Just Fantasy!" All are devoted to criticizing what they view as the myriad anti-Christian qualities of the books.[18]

One of the other key elements of the Harry Potter as anti-Christian allegations turns on the assumption that the depiction of Muggles, especially of Harry's relatives the Dursleys, is Rowling's critique of everyone who is opposed to witchcraft. Linda Harvey's essay "Harry Potter and Anti-Christian Bigotry" on *WorldNetDaily* provides a vivid example of this reasoning. She describes Rowling's unlovely characterization of Vernon Dursley and his fear that others will discover Harry's powers as "classic bigotry" and concludes that because of this depiction:

The message that screams from these pages for children to absorb is that these despicable people who object to "magic" are worthy of the worst scorn. And that's mostly what they receive throughout the Potter books. Our children quickly figure out that Muggles equate to traditional conservatives. And who are the most fervently "anti-magic" in real-world America? Christians. If kids don't get this right off, the mainstream media's frequent, negative caricatures of Christians will connect the dots for them. Might this be one more clue to explain the rise in virulent anti-Christian sentiment in recent years? In the Potter books, it's OK to hold such people in thorough contempt and sometimes openly mock them.[19]

Harvey is just one of the many commentators who read Muggles as an indictment of religious people. This misinterpretation results, in part, because they misunderstand the Muggles in the series as uniformly opposed to magic, rather than simply not able to practice it. The Let Us Reason Ministries site, for example, describes Rowling's depiction of Muggles as threatening, particularly to young children's understanding of what it means to be Christian: "The muggles, who are ordinary people (the adults) ungifted with the powers of a wizard are the blind, pictured as cruel, mean, narrow and self-indulgent. The wizards and other creatures are the good guys who have wisdom and help Harry. The adults are depicted as strict, controlling, unloving and against the kids. . . . The author does a good job of reassuring the child how safe they are among the children who have the powers."[20] The problem with this statement, of course, is that although the Dursleys' treatment of Harry is indeed almost uniformly cruel, Muggles are not monolithically evil, nor are magical people or creatures universally good. Hermione's relationship with her Muggle parents is clearly warm and open, as we see in *Deathly Hallows*, when she is forced to rename her parents and to modify their memories of having a daughter in order to protect them from persecution under the Voldemort-controlled Ministry of Magic. Erasing her parents' recollection is vital because she has told them a lot about Harry and Ron over their years at Hogwarts and she clearly mourns the loss of even temporary connection to her family. Additionally, most of the continued tension throughout the series turns on whether Snape actually warrants Dumbledore's trust—an answer that we ultimately learn is far from a simple yes or no. Rowling's characters are consistently much more complex than just magic folks, good/Muggles, bad.

An additional source of criticism comes from a relatively new group engaged in the outcry against Harry Potter: ultraconservative Catholics. Although the Vatican produced a document in 2003 that expressed opposition to New Age practices in general, the composers of the document found Harry Potter unobjectionable. Teresa Osorio Goncalves, an official with the Pontifical Council for Interreligious Dialogue, which authored the statement, described the Catholic reaction to Harry Potter as "more balanced, looking at the impact on children," and Rev. Peter Fleetwood said at the same time that the books aren't serving as a "banner for anti-Christian ideology," concluding that he saw "absolutely no problem with Harry Potter."[21] Recently, however, Harry Potter has come under attack from the Catholic writer Michael D. O'Brien, whose writings focus on what he perceives as an apocalyptic decline of religious values in contemporary culture. O'Brien weighs in on the Dursleys as a symbol of anti-Christian sentiment, saying that in the books, "Conservative people are bad, anti-magic dogmatists are really bad and deserve whatever punishment they get (hence the delicious retributions against the Dursleys)."[22]

Another problem with an "anti-Christian" argument based on a reading of the Dursleys and Muggles becomes abundantly clear now that the series is concluded. In *Deathly Hallows*, the long-term objection by Harry Potter and his group, especially Hermione, to Muggle subjugation comes to the forefront as a key element of the battle against evil. Voldemort and his Death Eaters

are the group that tortures, imprisons, and slaughters Muggles, seeking repeatedly to place magical over nonmagical beings. Harry Potter's side fights
the mistreatment of Muggles throughout the book in tandem with their fight
against Voldemort. One of the first of the many actions they take to stop
Voldemort's goal of achieving a hierarchy elevating wizards over Muggles and
other creatures in *Deathly Hallows* occurs when Harry, Ron, and Hermione
break into the Ministry of Magic to try to find the Horcrux necklace held by
the odious Dolores Umbridge. Initially, they are horrified by the newly erected
statue reflecting a Ministry now in the grip of Voldemort's power: "a gigantic
statue of black stone" that shows "a witch and wizard sitting on ornately carved
thrones," which actually turn out, on closer inspection, to be "mounds of carved
humans: hundreds and hundreds of naked bodies, men, women and children,
all with rather stupid, ugly faces, twisted and pressed together to support the
weight of the handsomely robed wizards." The statue is captioned "MAGIC IS
MIGHT."[23] The fight that later ensues over the Horcrux actually allows Harry
and his friends to save the Muggles awaiting interrogation from imprisonment
and death. The three make sure the Muggle-borns escape the Ministry before
they leave and urge those freed to take their families into hiding to avoid further
persecution by the Ministry.[24]

Significantly, Harry's most profound, though only temporary, disillusion-
ment with Dumbledore comes after reading Rita Skeeter's description of the
headmaster's former relationship with Grindelwald. Harry's comment—"here
we are, risking our lives to fight the Dark Arts, and there he [Dumbledore]
was, in a huddle with his new best friend [Grindelwald], plotting their rise to
power over the Muggles"[25]—illustrates how deeply the books support an egalitarian philosophy. Repeatedly, Harry's actions demonstrate the importance of
treating everyone, regardless of magical status, the same. Harry digs a grave
for Dobby the house-elf with his own hands, which encourages the goblin
Griphook to aid the trio in breaking into Gringotts to claim Helga Hufflepuff's
cup, now another Horcrux to be destroyed. Giving the house-elf Kreacher a
treasured wizard family heirloom means that later Kreacher leads the charge of
the house-elves in the climactic battle to defend Hogwarts. Finally, despite arguments like O'Brien's that allege that the Dursleys are "deliciously" punished
and humiliated, in fact the most reprehensible of the Dursleys—Dudley—is
instead allowed redemption in the final book. As the Dursleys leave their house
and Harry for the last time, Dudley acknowledges that Harry previously saved
his life (which Harry describes as almost "I love you" coming from Dudley)
and the two shake hands as their final amicable interaction.[26]

In addition to the textual arguments that can be made to refute the treatment
of Muggles as anti-Christian many more self-identified Christian writers in
recent years have reacted to these claims with illustrations of how the books
are not only not anti-Christian, but are actually solidly Christian in their values. Emily Griesinger, a self-identified Christian academic, argues that "despite
potential problems associated with witchcraft, Rowling's magic, like the magic

of Tolkien and especially the 'deeper magic' of Lewis, is best understood as a narrative device that articulates hope."[27] In *God, the Devil, and Harry Potter*, John Killinger "comes to the aid of 'the boy who lived,' arguing that he is an 'often unwitting Christ figure' whose story draws on Christian themes and teaches useful lessons."[28] The Vanguard Church, a Southern Baptist congregation in New York City uses skits developed from the Harry Potter stories "as a springboard to teach spiritual truths . . . we're using them almost like a bridge," said a co-founder of the church.[29] Dan McVeigh answers his own question, "Is Harry Potter Christian?" with a qualified "yes": some "passages hardly make the books apologetic: but they remind the reader of Christian assumptions and, perhaps leave her [Rowling] open to Christian possibilities."[30] In fact, Peggy Lin Duthie's article in this volume is devoted to exploring the many ways that religious leaders have incorporated "the Potterverse" into conveying their spiritual messages. All of these trends clearly illustrate that *Harry Potter* has become more acceptable to Christian groups in general.

One would have expected that the publication of *Deathly Hallows* with its emphasis on the soul through its storyline about Voldemort's Horcruxes and its presentation of a type of afterlife where Harry meets and speaks with the dead Dumbledore would have set off a storm of controversy. Contrary to these expectations, however, many of the groups who previously discouraged Christians from reading the works have actually taken more moderate approach to the books. Lindy Keller (formerly Beam) of the group Focus on the Family initially expressed strong reservation about the series for the lack of moral authority, saying that "Rowling does not write from the basis of Judeo-Christian ethics." That page has been since taken down from the Focus on the Family website,[31] and her current reviews of the Potter narratives have become distinctly more Harry-friendly: each review starts with a section on the positives of the book or movie. In fact, in a review of *Deathly Hallows*, Keller says that "In Rowling's world, characters embrace many of the same values Christians in the real world espouse. But as Harry, Ron and Hermione struggle to choose between right and wrong, and sort out grey areas, it is the human heart that decides, rather than any divine authority or maxim. Still, *Deathly Hallows* has a feel for spirituality that comes across as very believable at times. It is even sprinkled with Scripture."[32]

Additionally, many books and articles have come out since the first volume of *Reading Harry Potter* by authors who identify themselves as conservative Christians who actually advocate for the series—some even recommending the novels as teaching tools for Christian values. The editor of Apologetics Index states that "parents should not overreact to the Potter series. Rather, they should be well informed so that they can provide their kids with balanced information. Make sure they know they difference between fantasy and reality. Christian parents may want to encourage their kids to discover the possible allegories in the Potter stories."[33] Likewise, an editor at *Christianity Today*, Ted Olsen, writes,

I can attest that there are a number of Christians out there who adamantly feel that the books endorse evil—or are evil themselves. They have tried hard to get *Christianity Today* to change its view on J.K. Rowling's works, but without success.... Whether similar efforts have convinced Colson, Dobson, and some others to take a slightly stronger stance against Harry Potter is unknown.... Regardless, their heart doesn't seem in it. I still don't think there's a groundswell of opposition to the Potter books. But what opposition does exist, it seems clear, is originating in the pews rather than the pulpits.[34]

The challenge numbers seem to agree with Olsen's conclusion that the groundswell of opposition to the books is generally waning among even the conservative Christian groups that formerly opposed the Harry Potter series. Surprisingly, even the announcement of Dumbledore's homosexuality, which one might have assumed would ignite a new round of challenges, has been quiet after the initial flap. What many called J.K. Rowling's "outing" of Albus Dumbledore—her October 2007 remark to a group of Potter fans at Carnegie Hall that Dumbledore was gay—created a furor in the mainstream media and in cyberspace. Reponses ranged from "Dumbledore's gay (yawn)"[35] to laudatory comments to vehement condemnation; speculation over Rowling's motives in making this statement also ran rampant. Some accused her of pandering for additional profits, whereas others praised her effort to promote tolerance. Many others predicted that the news would prompt a storm of controversy from the Christian right and it looked like that tempest would erupt immediately after the announcement when ever-comment-ready Berit Kjos was interviewed in the *Toronto Star* saying that "'My first response was "Thank you, Lord," because this helps us show others that these books should not be used in the churches to illustrate Christianity. Because Dumbledore has been revealed as a homosexual, it helped me communicate my message,' she said."[36] Casey Seiler of the *Times Union* in Albany, New York, posited that "Dumbledore could provide a cash windfall for conservative bastions such as the Media Research Council and Pepperdine University, where laptops were no doubt steaming last week to promote grant reports with titles like "Good Witch/Bad Witch: The Homosexual Agenda in Fantasyland."[37] The anticipated firestorm of objections, however, never got off the ground. By June 2008, searches on the subject yielded almost no references beyond those reacting to Rowling's initial comment in late 2007.

This nonreaction is even more surprising given a recent trend in overall book challenges. While the Harry Potter books were number one on the American Library Association's (ALA) Hit List of most challenged books from 1999 to 2002, J.K. Rowling dropped off the ALA's list of most challenged authors after 2003, when her books ranked second on the list, and the Harry Potter series does not appear at all in the organization's list of Most Challenged Books for 2006. The most challenged title for 2006 was *And Tango Makes Three* (2005), written by Justin Richardson and Peter Parnell, which was targeted "for homosexuality, anti-family, and unsuited to age group." These reasons were reflective of a trend throughout the 2006 list; just one book on it—*Scary Stories* (1981) by Alvin Schwartz—was challenged on the grounds of occult/Satanic content, whereas four of the top ten works were objected to based on the presentation of homosexuality.[38] This is yet another shift from that which Amanda Cockrell noted in "Harry Potter and the Witch Hunters" when she argued that one reason for censorship attempts on Rowling's books was a change "in the focus of censorship efforts from sex to the occult."[39] Cockrell is referencing the shift from the 1980s challenges to Judy Blume's work to a focus in the late 1990s on challenging fantasy novels, but the ALA data bears out that a temporary shift did seem to occur but that the pendulum has now swung back to objections based on sexual content: the number of challenges for "occult/Satanism" increased by sixty-nine cases between 1999 and 2000, but by 2007, eight of the ten on the ALA list were again there because of sexual explicitness.

Maybe Dumbledore's sexual orientation provided little ongoing basis for censorship justification because of the extratextual form of its announcement and the fact that there are no overt references that make it clear in the books' events. It's as easy, perhaps even easier, to read Dumbledore as asexual—which many argue is the proper depiction of any adult in children's literature—as it is to perceive him as gay. But perhaps the relative silence on the subject has more to do with the same factors of shifting social context that have influenced the decline in challenges overall. The text itself is firmly established in culture, even in mainstream Christian culture. The series is also now complete, so its full dimensions have been revealed (although, of course, other completed works remain perennials on challenge lists, many series stay on because new books are produced, such as the "Alice" series by Phyllis Reynolds Naylor). Another factor may be the relatively short time frame that it takes for a young adult book to achieve status as part of the young adult literary canon. Because of the immediacy of most young adult fiction and the rate at which its readers grow past its readership age, a "generation" for a young adult novel can be as little as ten years. Finally, it may also be that at the end, the books come down decisively on the side of good. Voldemort is utterly and finally vanquished through Harry's selflessness in a stunning battle where the forces of good rout the Death Eaters for the last time. And nineteen years later, Harry's scar has never pained him again.[40] Moreover, in the Epilogue, Harry and his friends have grown up to be paragons of the nuclear family values so dear to conservative hearts. Harry, Ron, and Hermione are all married with children of their own who are continuing the family tradition of leaving for school from platform 9 and 3/4s.

More indirect causes of the decreasing number of challenges may be related to the context surrounding the groups who previously protested the books. In recent years, the preoccupations of the Christian right and the political realities for these groups have shifted, as has their impact on politics and public policy.

Under the Bush Administration and the power of so-called "wedge issues," such as gay marriage, the United States has perceptibly shifted to the right in many ways. Alongside President Bush's re-election in 2004, eleven bans on gay marriage were passed in states around the nation; access to abortion has been restricted; faith-based initiatives have received strong support from the White House. Similar changes can be seen in Catholicism. As the church hierarchy steadily becomes more conservative with the selection of the staunchly traditional Pope Benedict, many liberals have left the church, leaving the lay population more conservative in general. Although Pope Benedict has not been as hard-line as many feared when he was first named, he has reaffirmed that the church will not change its position on issues like women in the priesthood, priestly celibacy, birth control, or other points where many liberal Catholics differ from the official church's position. Additionally, Pope Benedict has sought to bring back into the fold some groups previously shunned as overly reactionary. For instance, the recent Vatican removal of restrictions on the Latin Mass is seen by many as an effort to reconcile with followers of Archbishop Marcel Lefebvre who was excommunicated after his opposition to the Vatican II council's introduction of mass in the vernacular.[41]

The result of these mainstream moves toward the right seems to be for groups at the more extreme end of the conservative Christian spectrum to seek ways to differentiate themselves. They strive to separate themselves from the now less radical positions in order to maintain their group identity and sense of place in the social order. In other words, as mainstream groups become more sure of their political power and gain confidence that they can effect cultural changes, their attempts to censor Harry Potter actually decrease since it becomes less important to distance themselves from the mainstream—because it is now their milieu as well. But as the Harry Potter books become more accepted by mainstream conservative Christian groups, those at the even farther right of the conservative Christian spectrum become more vociferous and radical in their protests against the book. Why has this happened?

Two points are particularly helpful in examining the meaning of this rhetorical strategy around the censorship of Harry Potter. The first comes from Jayne Seminare Docherty's book *Learning Lessons from Waco*, which explores the violent standoff in Texas at the Branch Davidian Compound in 1993 in terms of colliding worldviews. Docherty analyzes the ways that conflict over metaphors and conflicting ways of perceiving the world contribute to disputes: tension arises about a shared metaphor: "over which metaphor is appropriate for a particular situation [or...] disagreements over whether or not a metaphor is literal or merely figurative speech."[42] Harry Potter can be seen as just such a metaphor. In "The Potterverse and the Pulpits," Duthie tells of a Methodist pastor's perturbation that a small group of Potter antagonists are seen as representing all Christians. On the other side, many ultraright Christians seem to perceive accepting Harry Potter as synonymous with buying into a dangerously secular culture and repudiating a duty to perceive the world through a "true" Christian lens. The more moderate groups see Harry Potter's witchcraft as metaphorical and that view opens the books up to interpretation for spiritual truths, whereas the more extreme end sees the series' witchcraft as literal and, therefore, inappropriate for Christian readers. Because Harry has become such a cultural phenomenon, embraced by even many conservative Christian groups, his acceptance or rejection has become a means by which these ultraright groups can distance themselves from the larger culture. The use of witchcraft and its supposed anti-Christian meaning seems to fit precisely with the disagreement over the literal or figurative nature of Harry as a metaphor for conflicting worldviews, even within seemingly similar religious groups.

A second theoretical concept can further help us to untangle the significance of the decline in current challenges by more mainstream conservative Christian groups and the intensifying rhetoric of the more extreme Christian fundamentalists. Titus Hjelm's article "Between Satan and Harry Potter" explores the ways that Wiccans in Finland have sought to legitimate their religion in Finland in "response to the media discourse which, from the Wiccans' point of view plays down the religious aspect, either by connecting Wicca with Satanism or ridiculing it with allusions to 'Harry Potter religion'."[43] Drawing upon James R. Lewis's book *Legitimating New Religions*, Hjelm identifies Finnish Wiccans' strategies of distinguishing themselves from popular representations of witchcraft as evil or trivial through "knowledge of the intellectual aspects of their faith," "putting doctrine into practice," and establishing a sense of community through shared ritual.[44] Fascinatingly, however, the very practices used to legitimate a new religion like Wicca can also be seen as strategies employed by certain religious ultraconservatives when they write about Harry Potter as a metaphor for their worldview. The extreme right discourse demonstrates the strategy of intellectual knowledge, or as Lewis phrases it, offering evidence of superior insight or wisdom:[45] the sites' insistence that they see spiritual dangers in the Harry Potter books that other Christians do not. Jon Watkins's web page "Harry Potter: A New Twist to Witchcraft" on the site *Exposing Satanism and the New World Order* is a graphic illustration of this strategy:

And what is sickening, Christians, or so-called Christians, are part of the fan club. I knew nothing of Harry Potter until mail started coming in asking if it was ok for teachers in Christian schools to be reading children books about mythology and witchcraft!!!! Did you read that correctly? In Christian schools!!!! Are we now so far gone that the church can't tell what Witchcraft is?[46]

Thus, acceptance of Harry Potter has been established as an element which marks the "them" to the extreme right's "us." As Watkins's words exemplify, support for the books among other Christians actually becomes a betrayal of Christian identity; conversely, rejecting the books then becomes the mark of a "true" Christian.

As discussed in my first essay, establishing a communal identity is attempted by establishing a sense of a shared ritual and knowledge base. In many of these oppositional groups—whether conservative Christians, orthodox Catholics, or Wicca—we can see a profound opposition to a larger culture that does not differentiate enough in their minds between their beliefs and those of the mainstream. The Let Us Reason site is equally clear in its rejection of identifying with other Christians across denominational boundaries: "The tact [sic] of the enemy of God has been and still is to introduce other religions as equally valid and a uniting with them to destroy the truth in Christianity."[47] The Jeremiah Project site, whose commentary on Harry Potter and Halloween purportedly caused one reader to burn all of her Halloween decorations, sees other Christians as needing to be warned about the spiritual hazards of ecumenism: "The glittering terminology of ecumenism is seen, on close examination, to be as hollow as a soap bubble and just as slippery and hard to hold onto. Where is the 'common ground' between belief and unbelief? A believer cannot ignore the 'major theological differences' between him and an unbeliever. Instead, he should be cutting through those differences with the Sword of the Word to win the unbeliever to the Lordship of Jesus Christ."[48]

As Lewis notes, groups are driven to use these strategies when outside and more powerful groups seek to delegitimize them in some way. Because politically organized conservative Christian groups like the Christian Coalition and Focus on the Family have grown in recent years and become allied with more mainstream sources of power, more extreme groups might feel besieged, not only by the secular culture, but also by the larger, more politically powerful conservative Christian groups—witness the mentality of constant assault expressed by the persistent references to spiritual warfare expressed in their rhetoric. Driven by this mindset, they must focus on what sets them apart, and Harry Potter serves as is an ideal marker because of the books' popularity—the series' widespread acceptance makes it a very clear line of demarcation.

Examining the rhetoric of the extreme far-right groups, however, is not to point fingers or to apply labels (like the *Washington Post* reporter who named Laura Mallory "Idiot of the Year 2006" in his blog[49]); it is instead an attempt to understand the sources of opposition to Harry Potter. Analyzing the language and context of challenges can help us to understand how powerful and complex the dynamics that cause censorship can be. Harry Potter is a case which, because of its position as a publishing and reading phenomenon, makes us aware of the delicacy of the balance of the multiple ingredients that make up the social stew of book challenges. It illustrates how forcefully popularity plays a role in prompting objections. In "Harry and Hierarchy," I noted popularity as a stimulus for challenges and described the surprising lack of opposition to Phillip Pullman's *His Dark Materials* trilogy. However, when the film industry brought Pullman's series into the public eye, a spate of protests promptly followed the release of the movie version of *The Golden Compass*. In my own small-town newspaper, a series of letters to the editor exhorted readers to boycott the movie, echoing almost word for word the language of the Catholic League's censure of the film.[50] These letters also parallel another point that *Harry Potter* helps us to explore: how the impact of group identification and perception of a group's position within a social milieu can spur people to challenge actions.

In practical terms, for those concerned with book challenges in general and opposition to Harry Potter in particular, thinking about political climate and monitoring the sites and rhetoric of these groups might help teachers, scholars, and librarians anticipate where their next challenge might come from. Identifying the sources and ideology behind objections might aid us in negotiating with a parent whose worldview prompts her or him to voice concern. In "Questioning Witchcraft and Wizardry as Obscenity: Harry Potter's Potion for Regulation," Lee Ann Diffendal notes that "magic pragmatically posits harm to society and is quite capable of producing socially toxic anxiety. That is, if individuals could predict the future, alter reality, transform nature, and use magic to harm others, an increasing distrust among individuals might develop, causing the social contract to falter."[51] She writes ironically, but raises a crucial point: even without the reality of actual witchcraft, examining the censorship attempts surrounding Harry Potter can show us the deep divisions within our society, even among groups that to outsiders might look homogeneous. Looking at the Harry Potter series as a lightning rod that informs certain group identities perhaps raises more questions about future challenges than it answers. If the political pendulum swings back to the left in this country, will it set off a new outbreak of challenges? Or has Harry Potter become so firmly a part of our culture that it has lost its charge to electrify would-be censors? Even if we can't answer these questions now, looking at the rhetoric and identity construction of the groups using Harry Potter as a metaphor can perhaps help us to sort out conflicting worldviews and achieve more effective social negotiations with those whose worldviews are profoundly different than our own. As Jayne Docherty notes, "we all bring our Gods to the table." Maybe Harry Potter can help us illuminate some of those differences, whichever God (or Goddess) sits by our sides.

**NOTES**

1. Heinrich Kramer and James Sprenger, *The Malleus Maleficarum*, Trans. Rev. Montague Summers (New York: Dover Publications). Rpt. 1971.

2. Jodi Picoult, *Salem Falls* (New York and London: Washington Square Press, 2001).

3. Todd A. DeMitchell and John J. Carney, "Harry Potter and the Public School Library," *Phi Delta Kappan* 87 (October 2005): 159–65, 163. http://www.ebschost.com/ (accessed June 9, 2008).

4. Nicholas J. Karolides, Margaret Bald, and Dawn B. Sova, *120 Banned Books* (New York: Checkmark Books, 2005), 241.

5. *American Libraries*, "Harry Potter Foe Loses Challenge," August 21, 2007. http://www.ebschost.com/ (accessed June 2008).

6. Laura Diamond, "Hearing draws Potter Foes, Fans" *The Atlanta Journal-Constitution* April 21, 2006: J1. http://www.proquest.com/proquest (accessed June 9, 2008).

7. Quoted in Betsy Taylor, "'Potter Event Led to Rights Violations,' ACLU Says," *St. Louis Post-Dispatch*, B7, May 28, 2008. http://www.proquest.com/proquest (accessed June 9, 2008).

8. Blaise Cronin, "The Dean's List," *Library Journal* February 15, 2003, 48. http://www.ebschost.com/ (accessed June 9, 2008).

9. Quoted in Karolides, Bald, and Sova, *120 Banned Books*, 243.

10. Quoted in DeMitchell and Carney, "Harry Potter and the Public School Library," 164.

11. Lev Grossman, "The Doubting Harry," *Time*, July 23, 2007, 15. http://www.ebschost.com (accessed June 9, 2008).

12. William J. Schnoebelen, "Bill Schnoebelen Biography," *With One Accord*, http://www.withoneaccord.org/store/Biography.html (accessed June 9, 2008).

13. Schnoebelen, "Straight Talk on Harry Potter," *With One Accord Ministries*, http://www.withoneaccord.org/store/potter.html (accessed June 9, 2008).

14. The "Who is Harry Potter" page is also rhetorically interesting in that it plays eerie music when opened and is illustrated with a skull and crossbones. The graphics suggest, indeed, that the books are not only anti-Christian, but are actually dangerous to Christians given the common use of the skull and crossbones image to denote poisonous substances.

15. Kathy A. Smith, "Who is Harry Potter?" *Fill the Void Ministries*, http://www.fillthevoid.org/children/HarryPotter2.html (accessed June 9, 2008).

16. *Let Us Reason Ministries*, "Harry Potter: A Sorcerers Tale,'" http://www.letusreason.org/current16.htm (accessed June 9, 2008).

17. Eden Communications, "Is 'Harry Potter' Harmless," *ChristianAnswers.Net*, http://christiananswers.net/q-eden/harrypotter.html (accessed June 11, 2008).

18. Berit and Andy Kjos, "Harry Potter Articles," *Kjos Ministries*, http://www.crossroad.to/articles2/007/harry-links.htm (accessed June 9, 2008).

19. Linda Harvey, "Harry Potter and Anti-Christian Bigotry," *WorldNetDaily*, http://www.worldnetdaily.com/news/article.asp?ARTICLE_ID=56715 (accessed June 9, 2008).

20. *Let Us Reason Ministries*, "Harry Potter: A Sorcerers Tale.'"

21. *America*, "Vatican Questions New Age, Supports Harry Potter," February 17, 2003, 4–5. http://hwwilsonweb.com (accessed June 1, 2008).

22. Michael O'Brien, "Harry Potter and the 'Death of God," *LifeSiteNews.com*, http://www.lifesitenews.com/ldn/2007/aug/07082003.html (accessed June 9, 2008). O'Brien also condemns the books for their heretical approach, which he argues serves secular humanism at the expense of Christianity:

> Throughout the series there is overwhelming evidence that a Gnostic worldview is being slowly but surely presented. In fact, it is a new form of that ancient archipelago of heresies, a neo-gnosticism that borrows remnants of Judeo-Christian symbols and mixes them with cultic concepts of life and afterlife. For example, toward the end of the final volume, Harry's headmaster and mentor, Dumbledore, meets with Harry in a nebulous otherworldly zone, after Dumbledore's death and Harry's pseudo-death, before the latter's mysterious "resurrection." Yet even these and other metaphysical references are merely used to serve the author's real goal, which is the exaltation of the humanist ideal.

One of the bases for O'Brien's abhorrence of the series is a letter from Pope Benedict—when he was still Cardinal Ratzinger—that warned of the "subtle seductions" toward witchcraft in the Harry Potter series. The official Vatican position on the books has not altered since Ratzinger became Pope, however. In January 2008, the Vatican newspaper, *L'Osservatore Romano*, published two articles, one in favor of and one against Harry Potter, under "The Double Face of Harry Potter."

23. J.K. Rowling, *Harry Potter and the Deathly Hallows* (London: Bloomsbury, 2007), 198–99.

24. Ibid., 217.

25. Ibid., 294.

26. Ibid., 39–40.

27. Emily Griesinger, "Harry Potter and the 'Deeper Magic': Narrating Hope in Children's Literature," *Christianity and Literature* 51, 3 (2002): 455–80.

28. *Publishers Weekly*, "Pwforecasts," Nov. 11, 2002, 58.

29. Quoted in Mindy Sink, "The Split Verdict on Harry Potter," *The New York Times*, March 8, 2003, B6. http://www.proquest.com/proquest (accessed June 5, 2008).

30. Dan McVeigh, "Is Harry Potter Christian?" *Renascence* 54, 3 (2002): 197–214.

31. Lindy Beam, "What Shall We Do With Harry?" *Plugged In (Focus on the Family)*, http://www.family.org/pplace/pi/genl/A0008833.html (accessed May 5, 2001).

32. Lindy Keller, review of *Harry Potter and the Deathly Hallows Plugged In On-line*, http://www.pluggedinonline.com/articles/a0003326.cfm (accessed June 9, 2008).

33. *Apologetics Index*, "The Harry Potter Debate," http://www.apologeticsindex.org/p03.html (accessed June 9, 2008).

34. Ted Olsen, "(A Bit Less) Positive About Potter," *Christianity Today Magazine Online* July 26, 2007. http://www.christianitytoday.com/ct/2007/julyweb-only/130–43.0.html?start=2 (accessed June 9, 2008).

35. Leonard Pitts, "So Dumbledore is Gay: (Yawn), It's All in the Details," *Sunday Gazette-Mail* (Charleston, WV), Oct. 28, 2007, 3C. http://www.proquest.com/proquest (accessed June 9, 2008).

36. Raju Mudhar, "More than Robes in Wizard's Closet," *Toronto Star* Oct. 23, 2007. http://www.proquest.com/proquest (accessed November 7, 2007).

37. Casey Seiler, "Opinion: Tolerance Thrives in Fantasyland." *Times Union* Oct. 28, 2007. http://www.proquest.com/proquest (accessed November 7, 2007).

38. American Library Association, "Challenged and Banned Books," http://www.ala.org/ala/oif/bannedbooksweek/challengedbanned/challengedbanned.cfm.

39. Amanda Cockrell, "Harry Potter and the Witch Hunters," *The Journal of American Culture* 29.1 (2006): 24–30, 24. http://www.ebschost.com/ (accessed June 9, 2008).

40. Rowling, *Hallows*, 607.

41. National Public Radio, "Pope Revives Latin Mass in Concession To Tradition," *Weekend Edition Sunday*, July 8, 2007. http://www.npr.org/templates/story/story.php?storyId=11813687 (accessed June 11, 2008).

42. Jayne Seminare Docherty. *Learning Lessons From Waco* (Syracuse, NY: Syracuse University Press, 2001), 75.

43. Titus Hjelm, "Between Satan and Harry Potter: Legitimating Wicca in Finland," *Journal of Contemporary Religion* 21, 1 (2006): 33–48. http://www.ebschost.com (accessed June 10, 2008).

44. Hjelm, "Between Satan and Harry Potter," 43.

45. James R. Lewis, *Legitimating New Religions* (New Brunswick, NJ: Rutgers University Press, 2003), 13.

46. Jon Watkins, "Harry Potter: A New Twist on Witchcraft," *Exposing Satanism and the New World Order*, http://www.exposingsatanism.org/harrypotter.htm (accessed June 11, 2008).

47. *Let Us Reason Ministries*, "Ecumenism," http://www.letusreason.org/Ecumen17.htm (accessed June 9, 2008).

48. Vic Bilson, "The Modern Ecumenical Movement," *The Jeremiah Project*, http://www.jeremiahproject.com/prophecy/ecumen01.html (accessed June 9, 2008).

49. Emil Steiner, "OFF/Beat: Idiot of the Year Awards," WashingtonPost.com, http://blog.washingtonpost.com/offbeat/2006/12/idiot_of_the_year_awards_1.html (accessed June 10, 2008).

50. The position of the Catholic League on *The Golden Compass* is described at http://www.catholicleague.org/release.php?id=1342 and in a booklet published by the League, *The Golden Compass: Agenda Unmasked*. The letters to the editor referenced appeared in the *Stevens Point Journal*'s Opinion page on December 14 and 15, 2007 under the titles "Movie is Atheism for Kids," and "Parents Should be Cautious About the Golden Compass."

51. Lee Ann Diffendal, "Questioning Witchcraft and Wizardry as Obscenity: Harry Potter's Potion for Regulation," *Topic: The Washington & Jefferson College Review* 54 (2004): 55–62.

# 3

# The Potterverse and the Pulpits:
# Beyond Apologia and Bannings

*Peggy Lin Duthie*

In *Reading Harry Potter*, Giselle Liza Anatol asserts that "it cannot be stated enough times that works for children and young adults have incredible influence. This body of literature is a powerful tool for inculcating social roles and behaviors, moral guides, desires, and fears."[1] She also observes that adults intent on regarding the Harry Potter books solely as entertainment may resist considering how the series is "subject to the ideological structures that motivate all actions and underpin the workings of our daily world."[2] Both of these statements can be applied to the works of organized religions: worship services and religious education classes can be powerful tools for promoting spiritual reflection and moral conduct, but adults intent on viewing religious practice as an escape or refuge from the everyday world may reject any attempts to question or analyze the traditions that have shaped their beliefs and habits. As Rebecca Stephens suggests in "Harry and Hierarchy," the would-be censors of the Harry Potter series see themselves as countercultural in their priorities, upholding what they believe to be traditional values in an era of moral decay,[3] but the vehemence of book-burning clerics has reinforced a stereotype of devout Christians as out-of-step extremists, much to the dismay of their more moderate colleagues. Dave Barnhart, a Methodist pastor, recounted a meal with some college students where "the subject came up about Harry Potter and I said, 'Oh yeah, I'm really looking forward to the next book'—and one of them said, 'You're a minister, and you've read Harry Potter!?'" Barnhart reported feeling deeply disturbed by the student's reaction because it showed him how "a small vocal minority of Christians" are seen as speaking "for everybody"—and also because it indicated that his dinner companions had originally felt they had to conceal their enjoyment of the books from him, which in turn implied that they regarded Christianity as irrelevant to certain aspects of their lives.[4]

In response to the series' opponents, a number of Christian writers have penned faith-based defenses—*apologia*—of J.K. Rowling's work. In their zeal to present Rowling's work as inspired and influenced by Christian messages and values, some of these writers have been judged guilty of wishful interpretation, but they have also earned praise for their efforts to deepen their audiences' understanding of both literary and theological matters.[5] The interest in Rowling's use of religious phrases and images can also be seen in academic presentations such as a course on Christian theology and Harry Potter taught at Yale[6] and conference panels such as "Mere Fantasy Meets Mere Christianity,"[7] "Church, Woods, or Open Field: Religion in the Wizarding World,"[8] and "The Education of Harry Potter," the last a sold-out event featuring an ordained Anglican priest (Francis Bridger), an ordained Eastern Orthodox lector (John Granger), and a tenured professor of philosophy (David Baggett).[9]

Although the antagonism directed at the series has been significant enough to deter many Christian booksellers from including it in their inventories,[10] an editor for *Christianity Today* argues that the media's portrayal of widespread evangelical denunciations of Harry Potter is "as fictional as the Potter books themselves."[11] He acknowledges that the books have their enemies (some who unsuccessfully pressured *Christianity Today* to repudiate the books), but he also suggests that those enemies aren't as active in their opposition as they used to be—a trend explored by Rebecca Stephens in her chapter in this volume. Connie Neal, who describes herself as "the first Christian to publicly take a stand against attacking the Harry Potter books,"[12] concurs: "I only get calls screaming at me that I'm leading people to the devil maybe once every three months now instead of once a week."[13] Simon Barrow surmises that journalists have been sometimes led astray by the desire for a good fuss, citing reporters overly eager to claim that "the C[hurch] of E[ngland] was somehow asking people in the pew to read Harry's adventures instead of Bible stories" when it was "rather manifestly doing nothing of the sort."[14]

Rowling herself identifies as a member of the Church of Scotland, and according to a 2008 profile, she has said that the New Testament verse quoted in the final book—"The last enemy that shall be destroyed is death"—is the theme of the entire series. At the same time, she also maintains, "I did not set out to convert anyone to Christianity. I wasn't trying to do what C.S. Lewis did. It is perfectly possible to live a very moral life without a belief in God, and I think it's perfectly possible to live a life peppered with ill-doing and believe in God." In the same interview, Rowling states that the opposition to her stories has been balanced by the times they "have been lauded and taken into pulpit, and most interesting and satisfying for me, it's been by several different faiths."[15]

In the rest of this chapter, I explore some of the ways the Potterverse has been invoked by religious leaders in order to introduce or enhance their messages. By "the Potterverse," I mean not only the texts of the books themselves, but also the films, the criticism, the hype, the fandom, and other components of the books' cultural presence—in short, both the fictional universe of the books and the real-life universe of human individuals interacting with the stories, their prominence in contemporary culture, or both. I do not attempt to generalize about specific denominational attitudes toward the Potterverse or the theological soundness of their representatives' claims; rather, my goal is to demonstrate the diversity of spiritual approaches to—and appropriations of—a secular phenomenon.

The production, preservation, and study of religious texts is subject to a number of variables that may not be readily apparent to individuals who are not themselves involved in the creation, implementation, or distribution of sermons, educational curricula, or collateral materials such as newsletters, bulletins, and website content.[16] Many of these texts are unavailable to the general public: be they online and/or in print, the development and upkeep of organized, comprehensive archives require fiscal and volunteer resources that many organizations cannot command or spare. Moreover, some churches and synagogues deliberately restrict access to their publications in order to protect the privacy of their members or to discourage electronic spammers and trolls.[17]

The availability of contemporary homiletic literature is further complicated by the very nature of the genre: some preachers do not script their sermons, preferring to extemporize from outlines or improvise on the spot. Some speakers tweak their exhortations as they are delivering them—sometimes to accommodate logistical constraints (such as a worship service running longer than anticipated due to the length of its other elements), and sometimes to incorporate a more effective phrasing or pithier anecdote that has come to mind—and others deliver multiple versions of a fully drafted homily, refining each iteration in response to audience reactions. The text versions of most sermons are seldom word-for-word transcripts of the preachers' actual speeches, but rather snapshots of their authors' intentions.[18]

Furthermore, some ministers are wary of releasing their words outside of the original environment for which they were intended, fearing misquotation or mischaracterization of their messages by uninformed or unfriendly outsiders.[19] During the 2008 presidential primary season, several commentators cautioned against assessing the Reverend Jeremiah Wright's remarks without taking into account the congregational and cultural dynamics of Wright's ministry, echoing Wright's insistence that "black worship is different from European and European-American worship."[20] One observer noted, "As a preacher myself I know that I've said a few things over the years that, if pulled from their context, would sound far different than they had when I preached them. I've even preached some things that if they were heard in their totality would be controversial."[21] Another asserted, "Good ministers say dramatic things, stir things up, and push people hard to look at what they believe and how they act. That's their job. To hold their congregants accountable for every word they say in a sermon is absurd, and shows the people who attack them for such that they don't understand religion very well."[22] All these considerations and variables problematize the use of sermons as evidence of literary or sociological trends.

On the other hand, the technological advancements of the past decade have significantly expanded the scope of spiritual outreach. Internet access has become so commonplace that many houses of worship *do* choose to publicize their activities online, and tools such as blogging software and MP3 recorders have enabled scores of religious professionals to connect to readers and listeners they would not have encountered through predigital means of communication. The rise in affordable, distribution-efficient options for self- and small-press publication has likewise provided outlets for potential ministry that would have been considered beyond the scale of many budgets but a generation ago. I have confined my analyses in the rest of this chapter largely to sermons and programming produced under the aegis or endorsement of official religious organizations, but it bears noting that there exists an abundance of devotional texts and theologically framed commentary outside of formal ministry and religious education with neutral or positive references to the Potterverse. These include Logospilgrim's "ministry of compassion" in the garb of Severus Snape;[23] off-the-cuff commentary on the personal blogs of religious professionals;[24] editorials by parents praising Rowling's storytelling choices;[25] and heated comment-thread debates among fans of the Potterverse, its detractors, and third-party participants astounded (and sometimes appalled) at the depth of feeling fueling both sides.[26] It is also worth noting that many individuals employ aliases when participating in online forums or fandom conventions as a measure of self-protection. Some do so to safeguard their personal data against theft or misuse, and others disguise themselves in order to prevent their extracurricular activities from harming their professional careers, be it in terms of reputation or effectiveness (e.g., not being taken seriously by colleagues or clients due to mainstream stereotypes of science-fiction-and-fantasy fans). Ministers and seminarians who have adopted this strategy thus comprise another under-visible presence in the history of religion and literature's cross-pollinations.

With such factors in mind, it would be foolish to draw sweeping conclusions about the Potterverse's overall effects on religious practice; that said, the documentation that *is* available reveals a variety of expository and exegetical strategies that may surprise readers unaccustomed to evaluating sermons as vehicles of literary influence. These approaches have included highlighting parallels between Harry Potter characters and biblical or contemporary heroes, discussing how elements of the novels and movies echo lessons found in the Bible, critiquing objections to the Potterverse from faith-based perspectives, and issuing calls to social action that incorporate Rowling's depictions of good versus evil.[27]

The extent to which a minister can fit references to the Potterverse into a homily depends in part on the type of service he or she is expected to lead. The format and flavor of services can vary widely not only across a denomination but within a single congregation as well, both among churches large enough to staff multiple clergy and those too small to employ a minister full time or

at all (relying on guest speakers or lay leaders on a regular basis). The human and financial resources available to a congregation affect the placement of
children during sessions of worship, with some congregations conducting fully
intergenerational services as a result of economic necessity rather than choice.
When children remain with their parents for the duration of a service—be it
because child care or Sunday school programming happens to be unavailable,
or because the service has been specifically configured for all ages—their presence can affect how the preacher tailors his or her text, especially given the
controversy over whether good parents should allow their children access to
the Potterverse at all.[28]

When preachers choose to illustrate their sermons with allusions to works
of popular fiction, they must consider to what extent the members of their
audiences will be acquainted with those works. In the case of *Harry Potter*, the
series has been wildly, unquestionably popular in terms of book sales and movie
screenings, but assessing the general public's familiarity with the actual story
is more complex than it may initially seem. On the one hand, the basic plot
has become well known enough to inspire products such as "Republicans for
Voldemort" and "Democrats for Wormtail" bumper stickers,[29] as well as references to its characters in conventional cultural and political commentary.[30] On
the other hand, there are many adults who will not read the books despite their
popularity, for reasons ranging from lack of interest in fantasy fiction to active
dislike of Rowling's writing style.[31] There will continue to be generations of
children who will be restricted from direct access to textual versions of the series
until their parents and teachers deem them old enough to handle the books'
darker scenes, which in turn limits the extent to which the series' plot twists
can be openly discussed by its existing fans and critics without impacting future
readers' potential enjoyment of the story's suspenseful elements. The extended
gaps of time between the release dates of different formats also has affected
discussion of the series' arc and conclusion: a number of budget-conscious consumers have deferred reading each volume until its more affordable paperback
edition became available to them, and another segment of Rowling's audience
has followed only the motion picture renderings of her story. For the final book
in the series, *Harry Potter and the Deathly Hallows*, there were two years
between the scheduled publication dates of the hardcover and U.S. paperback
editions (July 2007 and July 2009, respectively) with an additional two years
before the final film is expected to premiere (May 2011).[32]

These factors make the use of references to the Potterverse both tempting
and challenging for preachers seeking to expand the reach of their messages.
Tempting, because drawing connections between beloved fictional characters
and real-life issues can be a means of engaging readers who already identify with the characters. Challenging, because preachers simultaneously risk
alienating listeners who are either indifferent or even hostile to the series and
its popularity. In attempt to strike an appropriate balance among the different types of potential audience members, preachers must also assess to what

degree they feel obliged to avoid revealing key plot developments. The challenge of creating a meaningful yet spoiler-free message is a motif that appears in a number of sermons. One Unitarian Universalist minister prefaced his sermon with, "I want to try to discuss the Harry Potter series. Since I suspect that many of us, but not all of us, have read one or more of these books. I will do my best to try to talk about these books in as concrete a manner as I can *without* giving 'too much' away in terms of how any of the stories actually come out."[33] A Lutheran lectionary preacher outlines the difficulty in more detail:

I'm going to go out on a limb this morning and say that this fifth book in the series helps us to understand our very difficult reading from St. Paul this morning. What is all Paul's talk about boasting, not in colorful visions of heaven, but of boasting in the power of weakness? As our family has digested this Harry Potter book in its first two weeks, I'm struck by how its themes very much resonate with our Second Reading.

This is going to be a bit tricky. I need to tell some of the story without giving too many important details for those who haven't had time yet to finish all 870 pages. But I need to also tell enough so that folks who haven't read any of these books, or seen the movies, might glean enough of the story to understand how it might help with hearing what St. Paul is talking about with power in weakness.[34]

These considerations are echoed by a pastor who advises his listeners who *haven't* completed the series to clap their hands over their ears whenever he heads into spoiler territory.[35] Other preachers opt to go ahead and incorporate major plot revelations into their texts, particularly as time elapses between the publication date of *Deathly Hallows* and the scheduling of new sermons. In August 2007, one such minister warned, "Lest there should be any disappointment later, I should offer a spoiler alert and make it explicitly clear that if you don't want to hear any details about these books—including the most recent one—then I'll encourage you to leave and spend some time, perhaps, with our children in their religious education class this morning."[36] One witnesses here the tension worship leaders must perpetually navigate between invitation and inclusiveness: when a speaker elects to treat a text as one familiar to the majority of those present—be it *Harry Potter*, the Bible, or responsive readings favored by the congregation in question—it unavoidably creates a separation between those who are indeed acquainted with the text in question (or who at least feel they ought to be) and those who are not. This is not in itself necessarily a bad thing: being "in the know" about specific customs and rituals is one of the ways in which individuals develop a sense of belonging to a larger community. At many churches, this knowledge of liturgical practices and sacred texts is often transmitted to visitors and newcomers via classes, prayer books, handouts, and other learning aids, or taught through regular, guided opportunities to participate in services. However, these strategies of cultivating a collective religious literacy are not designed to address blanks in a worshipper's familiarity with secular icons and touchstones. Ministers who choose to integrate popular culture references into their homilies are acting on the hope—often a reasonable one—that such allusions will help improve the odds of their words being remembered beyond the moment of delivery because they are essentially suggesting to their listeners points of association likely to be more immediate and contemporary than, say, the commentary of faceless prophets and distant sages. At the same time, preachers who employ this gambit may discover it backfiring on them if their perceptions strike members of their audience as dated, labored, irrelevant, or patronizing. In revealing what one views as basic knowledge within one's community—even for details as arguably trivial and tangential as *Saturday Night Live* punch lines and the endings of classic motion pictures—one displays one's assumptions about what one considers "the norm" in terms of access to and attitudes toward the sources in question. For instance, in the case of the minister directing spoiler-averse congregants to an alternate religious observance cited above, the expectation inherent in that church's organization of its morning was that most of its adult members would have obtained and read *Deathly Hallows* within a month of its hardcover debut, which in turn indicates a level of financial and educational resources common to the majority of those expected to be in attendance. An option being provided for individuals not meeting the anticipated norm speaks to the series' current, unusual status as a demi-classic—its popularity such a given that a speaker can reasonably assume widespread audience familiarity with the story, but not yet at the level of undisputed classics such as *Star Wars* or *Gone with the Wind*, where the stories' developments and denouements have become so well known that spoiler warnings are no longer *de rigueur* for mentions of Darth Vader's relationship to Luke Skywalker or Rhett Butler's with Scarlett O'Hara. As such, its incorporation into a worship setting carries with it a range of potential ramifications in relation to issues of communal identity—the Potterverse can enhance a preacher's attempts to connect with his or her audience, but it can also prompt or deepen feelings of alienation among individuals unenthusiastic about Rowling's work.

The potential structure of a sermon can also be affected by the time allocated for its delivery. Among some congregations, homilies lasting over an hour are commonplace, whereas others expect speakers to conduct their expositions within fifteen minutes or less. There are also calendar-based considerations: many congregations adhere to a denomination-wide schedule of scriptural readings (often referred to as a *lectionary* among Christians and as a *parashah* or "Torah portion" among Jews);[37] the prescribed texts for a given week consequently shape the direction of the message to be developed for that Sabbath. This is not necessarily a constraint, as many preachers are adept at spinning thematic connections between assigned verses and secular milestones, such as the release dates of Harry Potter books and films. For example, on the Sunday before the release of *Harry Potter and the Half-Blood Prince*, Baptist minister Tom Cullen asked his listeners whether they were "wild about Harry" as a prelude to urging them to become "wild about God":

On Friday night there will be millions of people around the world who will line up outside their local bookstores in order to get a copy of this next installment in Harry Potter's life. These people are wild about Harry.

If you are wild about Harry you can buy Wild about Harry tote bags, buttons, you can buy Wild about Harry t-shirts, And of course the Wild about Harry coffee mug. Even your dog can be Wild about Harry!

So in this world there are all sorts of things you can be wild about.

*Do you get a sense of what it means to be wild about God? It means to be so in love with him that He is the focus of your life.* [emphasis in the original][38]

Cullen proceeded to describe Psalm 150—that week's text—as a call to become "wild about God," referring again to the intensity of Harry Potter fans when he characterizes God's love for His people. Cullen's usage of the Harry Potter phenomenon as a point of a comparison between secular and sacred manifestations of devotion is a feat of both zeal and tact: Cullen fervently exhorted his listeners to give themselves wholeheartedly to God, but he refrained from direct condemnation of those who had focused their adoration elsewhere. By describing what his listeners stood to gain from placing God at the center of their lives without resorting to negative critiques of secular priorities, Cullen kept his message palatable to existing Harry Potter fans that might have been present: if Cullen *had* chosen to disparage the affection exhibited by fans of the Potteverse, he might well have placed a segment of his audience on the defensive, which in turn would have undermined his efforts at persuading them to redirect their ardor towards God.

Another Baptist minister, Ernest R. Flores, used the publication of *Deathly Hallows* as a lead-in to his discussion of scripture. After describing his own family's participation in book release festivities the night before, Flores spoke approvingly of how the book's title reflects a series-wide preoccupation with death, and praised its author's willingness to dwell on the subject, stating that "if J.K. Rowling can in an entertaining way help my children deal with these issues, I'm all for it."[39] This declaration set the stage for his claim of how Christians transform the tragedy of death into a triumph of comfort and hope: "Nobody takes tragedy and turns it into triumph like Jesus. And that's what we have here in our text from John 13:31 all the way into the 14th chapter."[40]

One Presbyterian chaplain, prompted by Colossians 2:6–15, likened the concerns of contemporary parents to St. Paul's battle against heresy. In her view, the efforts of twenty-first–century parents to shield their children from harmful entertainment and "dark, dangerous and death-dealing" messages spring from the same fierce commitment to love that propelled St. Paul to sound urgent warnings against non-Christian philosophies "packed with empty deceit." The Harry Potter phenomenon was utilized in this sermon on two levels: the books were initially cited as an example of an entertainment that has been judged both as unacceptably pagan and as "wholesome family entertainment."

The preacher later evaluated the books' depiction of love's power in the light of Paul's charge to other Christians to live lives deeply rooted in faith, speaking of Lily Potter's sacrifice of her life to save her son's as a supreme demonstration of love's triumph over evil. The sermon concluded with an assertion that the *Harry Potter* books and the Epistle to the Colossians display a common mission:

Harry's task is, in many ways, the same as the task Paul gives to the Colossians, and it's our task too: to be rooted and built up in the love that gave itself for us. To remember that love, and carry on in the light of it. To resist philosophies (whether human-manufactured or wizard-manufactured) which allow anything else to take that love's place in our hearts. Love: a force so powerful it marks us forever. Not every book gives us this message. Thank God for the ones that do.[41]

Rowling's work was also utilized as a teaching aid in a Yom Kippur sermon by Reconstructionist rabbi Alex Lazarus-Klein, who employed the Potterverse at length to make sense of "the very surreal Torah reading from Parashat Acharei Mot in Leviticus describing the ritual of the scapegoats." He asserted that in explaining Harry's story, "I will also explain our own." In Lazarus-Klein's view, Harry's life is divided among competing states of existence and incompatible desires (magical vs. Muggle; heroic vs. normal; the visions in Mirror of Erised vs. the realities of the present), and the hero's ultimate challenge is to realize and retain his authentic self through it all. The story of the goats is similarly a message to Jews to tend to their core identities—to steer clear of being torn apart by the claims of different realms.[42]

Among the preachers who choose to expound on the moral lessons of the Potterverse, several approaches yield particularly provocative results. When ministers who are themselves fans of Rowling's work critique fundamentalist objections to the Potterverse, their attitudes toward their colleagues' fears reveal several schools of thought regarding how observant believers should interact with both works of imagination and with the wider world in general. For many Potter-friendly clergy, the series supports their assertions that the grace of God is visible in unexpected locations for those willing to see. One Baptist pastor urged concerned parents and grandparents to engage in creative and critical measures to keep the books in proper perspective, including the identification of "redemptive analogies and spiritual metaphors in the literature and films you consume. They are everywhere, often in what seem the most unlikely places."[43] A Presbyterian pastor compared her initial resistance to Al-Anon meetings with that of adults who believe children's literature has nothing to teach them: speaking of a colleague's well-publicized Potter-themed preachings, she said,

I shudder to think of the spiritual tools I would have missed out on, if I had continued to avoid Al-Anon. Hopefully John Zingaro's congregation knows they would be the poorer for not having learned how to see God's insights in the mundane and ordinary adventures of modern life, even as revealed in children's literature.[44]

Regarding a Harry Potter service conducted at her church, a Unitarian Universalist director of religious education wrote, "I personally am drawn to the idea that we all (adults and children alike) are spiritual beings in the midst of a human experience, so that everything we do, everything we encounter, can be seen from a spiritual perspective.... One's spiritual life neither begins nor ends at the door to the sanctuary; every moment is one in which to become spiritually aware."[45]

In some respects, the injunction to cultivate spiritual awareness in everyday settings can be seen as part of a Christianity that encourages engagement with the secular world rather than retreat from it. This approach to living a life of faith is echoed in Dave Barnhart's passionate argument that Harry's encounter with the Mirror of Erised sheds light on how Christians can choose to interact with the world:

It's a powerful scene in the book—but I also think it's a metaphor for us and how we live our lives and how we read books and how we look at the world, because oftentimes our vision is shaped by what we desire the most—what's in our hearts. And for people who desire Jesus Christ, when we look at the world, or when we read Harry Potter, or when we look into the face of someone who's homeless, we see Jesus Christ. If you desire Jesus, it's amazing how often He shows His face to you. It's like the world is a great big mirror which shows you your heart's desire.[46]

This sensibility—that of discerning grace in all the things one encounters in this world—is *not* displayed by or embodied in any of Rowling's protagonists. Their actions are driven neither by universalist visions of fairness nor of all wizards (let alone all humans) being creatures of equal standing;[47] after all, Rowling's narrative was created not to serve as a model of applied theology but to captivate its readers with a tale of good triumphant over evil. Even so, the series' historical sweep, symbolism-rich setting, and diverse cast add up to a combination conducive to multiple personal interpretations that go beyond the author's discernable intent (and, in some cases, subverting it on purpose); the series' status in contemporary culture can make it an attractive launching pad for circulating one's own opinions on issues such as love, anger, and justice, even when said opinions are neither directly inspired nor in actual alignment with those expressed by Rowling.[48] In their explorations of what readers respond to in the books, a number of preachers focus on how the flaws of Rowling's heroes allow ordinary humans to identify with them—as well as how Harry, Dumbledore, and other protagonists ultimately triumph in spite of their mistakes and foibles, which reflects a recurring theme in the Bible itself. Rabbi Allison Vann compares Harry to Moses, asserting that "both are flawed leaders, totally human even in their super-human tasks. Harry is a lousy communicator and terrible at asking for help. Moses loses his temper and asks God, some could say, for too much. I believe we are attracted to Harry, as to Moses, for they could be any of us. As imperfect beings taking on tremendous, often overwhelming tasks, they prove to us that each of us has within ourselves the power to change the world."[49] Unitarian Universalist minister Elizabeth Greene also observes that Harry "is no angel of perfection. He never acts like some kind of saint, always feeling kind and forgiving toward everybody. He has hateful feelings just like the rest of us." As a result, "this scrawny, sometimes-hateful, often-insecure, regular kid (from a terribly deprived background!) makes choices that come from a great heart, and he gives us hope that we can do it, too."[50]

Another theme that regularly appears in faith-based defenses of the Potterverse is the tenacity of theism, as demonstrated by Christianity's history of flourishing in environments far more inhospitable and heathen-dominated than that of the Information Age. One could even argue that this offers another arc of identification for Christians reading the series, since the books can be read as a history of Harry and his allies (Dumbledore's Army and Order of the Phoenix) persisting in their quest to vanquish Voldemort despite persecution by Ministry figures and other grave obstacles. Some of the sharpest dissections of fundamentalist anti-Harry antics have come from devout Christian commentators assessing their co-religionists' behavior as itself a variation of "magical thinking," where the wielding of prayers like magic spells (e.g., "if I say $x$, God will grant me $y$") speaks more of superstition than genuine faith.[51] Others have noted that the exaggerations of religious extremists "probably turn more people away from Christianity than Harry Potter ever will!"[52] and that "attacking the Harry Potter phenomenon, and burning the books, and instilling fear into people who have not read the books or watched the film only increases promotion and makes more people inquisitive."[53]

The Potterverse has aided ministers wishing to speak to their congregations about topics such as identity, friendship, heroism, holidays, love, courage, imagination, myth, and storytelling, and the choices to be pondered in relation to these matters. Beyond the pulpit, there have been countless classes, workshops, camps, Vacation Bible Schools, fundraisers, and fellowship events organized around Harry Potter scenarios and themes. In short, the Potterverse is substantially present in the practice of contemporary mainstream religious practice, not as a target of latter-day Pharisees but as an inspirational resource. For scholars fascinated by the ways literature can be appropriated, circulated, and transformed in the name of goals external to the original text, there is an abundance of Potter-related content and concerns to analyze, ranging from the ways religious professionals elect to characterize the Hogwarts Houses (especially Slytherin) to their generalizations about genre fiction. The willingness of many preachers to incorporate elements from the Potterverse within their own narratives of morality suggests readings of fantasy fiction that are more diverse and sophisticated than those propagated by Christianity's noisier factions.

## NOTES

1. Giselle Liza Anatol, "Introduction," in *Reading Harry Potter: Critical Essays*, ed. Giselle Liza Anatol (Westport, CT: Praeger, 2003), xv.

2. Ibid.

3. Rebecca Stephens, "Harry and Hierarchy: Book Banning as a Reaction to the Subversion of Authority," in *Reading Harry Potter*, ed. Giselle Liza Anatol (Westport, CT: Praeger, 2003), 61–62.

4. Dave Barnhart, "Defense Against the Dark Arts." Preached at Trinity United Methodist Church (Homewood, AL), 12 August 2007. http://www.trinitybirmingham .com/worship/sermon_audio/archives. The websites cited in this chapter were accessed during June 2008.

5. For an example of this type of commendation, see Dave Kopel, "Deconstructing Rowling," *National Review Online* (9 June 2003). http://www.nationalreview.com/ kopel/kopel062003.asp. Connie Neal provides links to similar reactions at http://www .connieneal.com/special-harry-potter-section.htm.

6. Patrick Lee, "Pottermania lives on in college classrooms." *CNNU* (25 March 2008). http://www.cnn.com/2008/SHOWBIZ/books/03/25/cnnu.potter/index.html.

7. The panel consisted of seven teachers from California Baptist University—Erika J. Travis, Nicole DeLaRosa, Amanda Copen, Jennifer A. Newton, DawnEllen Jacobs (the university's assistant provost), David E. Isaacs, and Jennifer Tronti—who described their offering thus: "As fans of fantasy, we have fallen under Harry Potter's spell; as teachers at a Southern Baptist institution, we have found interesting connections between our faith communities and the writings of J.K. Rowling. Harry has been much maligned by some of our fellow believers, but we have found a great deal in Harry Potter's world that connects with our beliefs. Join us for a two-part panel that both compares Rowling's world with that of the Inklings (a.k.a. the Oxford Christians) and explores connections between her works and other fantasy texts." Presented at *Lumos, a symposium* (Las Vegas: HP Education Fanon, 29 July 2006).

8. *Lumos* (28 July 2006). The well-attended panel was moderated by Lisa Evans, a graduate of Hartford Seminary. Its members included Rita Wilbur, a graduate of Chicago Theological Seminary and the pastor of two churches in Texas; Morgan Howard, who had obtained her master's degree in English from Bob Jones University (a conservative Christian institution); and Karen Dougherty, a twenty-year member of a druid fellowship.

9. *Lumos* (29 July 2006). The conference also included solo presentations by the three men, as well as by Amy O. Miller (a Jewish cantor) and "Professor Servus Logospilgrim" (the pseudonym of an influential Eastern Orthodox blogger). Granger, Miller, and Logospilgrim have all appeared at multiple Harry Potter conferences, some of which include the granting of Continuing Education Units to teachers, librarians, and other scholastic professionals.

10. "Christian bookstore sells Harry Potter: Most religious shops avoid the popular novels." *msnbc.com* (1 February 2005).

11. Ted Olsen, "(A Bit Less) Positive About Potter: How Focus on the Family, Prison Fellowship, and others have—and haven't—changed their views about the books over the years." *Christianity Today* (July 2007). http://www.christianitytoday.com.

12. Connie Neal, "A Christian Defense of Albus Dumbledore" (21 October 2007). Published on the *Dallas Morning News* religion blog on 1 May 2008. http://religionblog. dallasnews.com.

13. Matt Kennedy, "Christian themes in Potter books make good evangelism tools, some say." Associated Baptist Press (31 July 2007). http://www.abpnews.com/www/2682.article.print.

14. Simon Barrow, "Reading Harry Potter too religiously," *Ekklesia* (30 July 2007). http://www.ekklesia.co.uk/node/5504.

15. Nancy Gibbs, "J.K. Rowling" (part of a series on the runners-up for 2007 Person of the Year). *Time* 130, no. 27 (31 December 2007). http://www.time.com/time/specials/2007/personoftheyear.

16. Disclosure: I am a lay preacher, and two of my own sermons have incorporated extended references to the Potterverse: "The Inherent Worth and Dignity of Every Person" (extemporized, 13 August 2006) and "Unicorns, Hippogriffs, and Bisexuals" (scripted, 22 July 2007; archived at http://www.nashpanache.com). My background has also included managing events for an Episcopalian cathedral and serving on the worship, administration, and associate minister advisory committees of First Unitarian Universalist Nashville.

17. Central Presbyterian Church (Baltimore) offers a thoughtful and thorough "Website Ministry FAQ" that addresses many opportunities and challenges applicable to offline as well as online communications. http://www.centralpc.org/admin/webminfaq.htm.

18. One senior pastor wrote the following disclaimer for his church's website: "All sermons in our archives were preached live in our Sanctuary and were written for the ear and not the eye. This is why some of the grammar, punctuation, and word patterns may appear unusual. All of our pastors passed 7th grade English . . . even though it might not look like it" (http://www.centralpc.org/sermons/sermons.htm). Likewise, Thomas Schmidt issues a similar plea, noting that the online texts of his sermons "do not include notes on inflection and tone and do not carry forward reading and music the original audience may have experienced and may have given meaning to something barely referenced in the sermon. Thus, subtle attempts of humor made evident to the audience by tone and inflection may easily be misconstrued as insulting or derogatory to the reader. Please keep this in mind and read with an open mind and inquiring spirit" (http://www.thoughtsandstories.com/id23.html).

19. My thanks to Gail Seavey, senior minister of First Unitarian Universalist Nashville, for this insight.

20. Don Gonyea, "Wright Decries 'Out of Context' Criticisms of Sermon," *All Things Considered*, 28 April 2008. http://www.npr.org.

21. Erik Walter Wikstrom, "Rev. Wright in a Different Light." *A Minister's Musings* (8 April 2008). http://a-ministers-musings.blogspot.com.

22. Mike Lux, "Ministers and Their Sermons." *Huffington Post* (28 April 2008). http://www.huffingtonpost.com.

23. Logospilgrim, *Just a Thistle* (self-published: lulu.com, 2005), 18.

24. For instance, James Ishmael Ford (whose profile warns that his statements "probably do not, and certainly should not be assumed to represent the views of any organization to which I belong") greeted one of Rowling's controversial post-canonical revelation with a succinct "Dumbledore is gay. Ain't it loverly?" ("Breaking News," *Monkey Mind* [21 October 2007]. http://monkeymindonline.blogspot.com). Another blogger joked, "Now . . . *accio* sermon!" at the end of a post where she admitted she was procrastinating on its writing ("Wotcher Harry! or, Accio Friday Five!" *Magdalene's Musings* (13 July 2007). http://magdalenesmusings.blogspot.com).

25. For an example, see Caryn Rivadeneira, "Bringing Harry Potter to Church," *Gifted for Leadership: A Community of Christian Women* (23 July 2007). http://blog. christianitytoday.com/giftedforleadership.

26. Ibid.

27. For examples, see Amy Zucker Morgenstern's "Democracy, Fascism, and Magic" (preached at Unitarian Universalist Church of Palo Alto [CA], 4 November 2007; http://www.uucpa.org/sermons_07/sermon071104.html) and Donnie Miller's "Of Muggles, Mudbloods and Pureblooded Wizards" (preached at Trinity Family Church of the Nazarene [Gardner, KS], 20 November 2005; http://www.trinityfamilyonline.com/about-us/sermons).

28. For instance, Jerome D. Cooper addresses both parents and children in a sermon given the Sunday before Christmas: "As a parent, be discerning, know what your children are reading and follow your conscience. Don't be led to do something by pressure one way or the other, but also don't judge those who might make a different decision. If you are a child: obey your parents." In "Harry Potter and Jesus." Preached at Central Presbyterian Church of Baltimore, 23 December 2001. http://www.centralpc.org/sermons/2001/s011223.htm.

29. The "Republicans for Voldemort" slogan first appeared in "Goats," a webcomic by Jonathan Rosenberg, on 8 August 2003 (http://www.goats.com/archive/030808.html). "Democrats for Wormtail" appears to have been established as an online on-demand store sometime during 2007 (http://www.cafepress.com/wormcrats).

30. For example, when Tilda Swinton wore a sack-like frock to the Academy Awards, Eric Wilson trashed her decision with the words, "Bless her Dobby the House Elf-loving heart" ("The Red [Can't Go Wrong] and the Black [Sober Is So 2008]." *New York Times* [25 February 2008]). During the 2008 presidential campaign, Arizona congresswoman Heather Wilson compared Democratic leaders' treatment of Hillary Clinton to how "young Harry Potter and his male friends initially reacted to Hermione Granger" ("Hermione Clinton." *New York Times* [8 June 2008]); in a similar vein, political columnist Maureen Dowd suggested that anti-Clinton voters saw her as a "Lady Voldemort" ("Surrender Already, Dorothy." *New York Times* [30 March 2008]).

31. See, for instance, "This Seems Like a Fine Time for a Startling Admission," where Hugo-winning author John Scalzi's statement that he hadn't read any of the Harry Potter books prompted over two hundred comments from his readers on whether the series was in fact worth reading and their own reasons for enjoying or avoiding it. *Whatever* (20 July 2007). http://www.scalzi.com/whatever/2007/07/20/this_seems_like_a_fine_time_fo.html

32. SLJ Staff, "Paperback Edition of 'Deathly Hallows' Slated for July 2009." *School Library Journal* (29 September 2008). http://www.schoollibraryjournal.com/article/CA6599861.html; Geoff Boucher, "Final 'Harry Potter' book will be split into two movies." *Los Angeles Times* (13 March 2008). http://www.latimes.com/entertainment/news.

33. William Sasso, "The Theology of Harry Potter." Preached at Carbondale (IL) Unitarian Fellowship, 18 July 2004. http://www.cuuf.net/minister/sermons/Harry%20Potter%20Theology.html.

34. Paul J. Nuechterlein, "Harry Potter and Power in Weakness." Preached at Our Savior's Lutheran (Racine, WI), 6 July 2003. http://girardianlectionary.net/year_b/proper_9b_2003_ser.htm.

35. Barnhart.

36. Paige Getty, "What I've Learned From Harry Potter." Preached at Unitarian Universalist Congregation of Columbia (MD), 19 August 2007 (http://www.uucolumbia .net/files/sermon20070819_HarryPotter.pdf). In another example, a October 2007 program announcement at the Unitarian Universalist Church of Palo Alto (CA) was annotated with the following advisory: "Fair warning: This service will not give away the ultimate plot twists, but you might want to start reading now so that subsequent services on a Potter theme don't spoil it for you" (http://www.uucpa.org/sermons/ sermons_index_07.html). The Unitarian Universalist Fellowship of Fayetteville (AR) similarly cautioned prospective visitors that a sermon on "Harry Potter and the Flaming Chalice of Transformation" might include spoilers for book VII ("A Summer of Sundays." *The Beacon*, June 2008. http://www.fayettevilleunitarian.org/beacon/2008June .pdf).

37. Vanderbilt Divinity Library offers an excellent introduction to lectionaries in its FAQ for the Revised Common Lectionary, including links to print resources and other popular lectionaries. http://divinity.library.vanderbilt.edu/lectionary.

38. Tom Cullen, "Wild About God." Preached at Markham (Ontario) Baptist Church, 10 July 2005. http://www.markhambaptist.com/sermons/05sermons/ 0507sermons/050710.html.

39. Ernest R. Flores, "The Hallowing of Death." Preached at Second Baptist Church of Germantown (PA), 22 July 2007. http://secondbaptistgermantown.org/written/ sermon-2007-07-22.htm.

40. Ibid.

41. Magdalene6127 (pseud.), "The Gospel According to Harry Potter: A Sermon on Colossians 2:6–15." *Magdalene's Musings*, 29 July 2007. http://magdalenesmusings .blogspot.com.

42. Alex Lazarus-Klein, "Harry Potter and the Mystery of the Scape Goat." Preached at Temple B'nai Abraham (Bordentown, NJ) on 22 September 2007 (Yom Kippur). http://www.bnai-abraham.org/docs/rabbi/5768_YK_Day_Sermon.pdf.

43. Rod Benson, "Reading Harry Potter With Christian Eyes." Preached at Blakehurst Baptist Church (Sydney, Australia), 6 January 2002. http://jmm.aaa.net.au/ articles/1178.htm.

44. Eileen Parfrey, "Signs of the Times: Gifts." Preached at Springwater Presbyterian Church (Estacada, OR), 6 January 2002. http://www.springwater-pres.org/ sermon01–06-02.html. Zingaro, now pastor of First Presbyterian Church of Newton, NJ, self-published several editions of an anthology titled *The Harry Potter Sermons* beginning in 2001.

45. Kerrie Lirosi, "Religious Enrichment News." First Congregational Parish (Kingston, MA) newsletter (April 2003). http://kingstonuu.org/news-april.html.

46. Barnhart.

47. For a provocative, highly critical examination of Rowling's theology, see Daniel Hemmens, "Harry Potter and the Doctrine of the Calvinists." *FerretBrain*, 17 August 2007. http://www.ferretbrain.com/articles/article-161.html.

48. For instance, the "Nineteen Years Later" ending to the series displeased many longtime fans of the series, with some regarding it as a specimen of substandard storytelling and others who felt it cemented a highly conventional, heteronormative worldview that they had hoped the series would transcend. A collective desire to explore some of the themes Rowling hadn't satisfactorily addressed helped fuel the development of

hundreds of "Epilogue, What Epilogue?" (EWE) fanfics in the months following the publication of *Deathly Hallows*.

49. Allison Bergman Vann, "Why I Love Harry Potter." Preached at Temple Beth-El (San Antonio, TX), 3 August 2007. http://www.beth-elsa.org/abv080307.htm.

50. Elizabeth L. Greene, "Harry Potter, The Sequel: Doing the Right Thing." Preached at Boise (ID) Unitarian Universalist Fellowship, 4 November 2001. http://boiseuu.org/sermons/11401harrypotter.pdf.

51. Cf. Barnhart, "Who's Afraid of You-Know-Who?" (preached at Trinity United Methodist, 19 August 2007); Bill and Sherry Rankin, "Bringing Harry Potter to Church" (workshop at *The Upside Down Kingdom: Living the Sermon on the Mount* (65th Annual Bible Lectures at Pepperdine University, Malibu, CA), 1–2 May 2008); and John E. Manzo, "The Allure of That Which Is Bogus" (preached at St. Marks United Church of Christ [New Albany, IN], 12 August 2007; http://www.stmarksucc.org/081207.pdf).

52. Marlin Lavanhar, "Hell, Holidays, and Harry Potter." Preached at All Souls Unitarian Church (Tulsa, OK), 16 December 2001. http://cc25980.hostcentric.com/sermons.asp.

53. Benson.

# 4

# Causation, Prophetic Visions, and the Free Will Question in Harry Potter

*Patricia Donaher and James M. Okapal*

To describe Harry Potter as a hero involves a moral assessment of his character because heroism necessitates choosing good over evil. Heroism, in fact, requires that Harry has the *freedom* to choose right action over wrong, but how are we to make sense of Harry's heroism given Sibyll Trelawney's prophecy in *Order of the Phoenix*? The prophecy accurately, if obliquely, describes events that occur after the prophecy is made: Harry is born in July to parents who fought Voldemort three times; Voldemort tried to kill Harry, giving the protagonist his famous scar; Harry does in fact kill Voldemort in *Deathly Hallows*. The prophecy and the way the events unfold suggest that the Harry Potter universe is designed in such a way that Harry does not choose his actions, but that his actions are mere effects of some preordained cosmic plan. Unless there is some way of interpreting the narratives such that Harry can make choices, he may not really be a hero.

Both fans and scholars have discussed these doubts about the possibility of freedom of choice in the Harry Potter series.[1] One article of note is Gregory Bassham's "The Prophecy-Driven Life: Fate and Freedom at Hogwarts" in the 2004 *Harry Potter and Philosophy: If Aristotle Ran Hogwarts*.[2] Bassham argues for a libertarian interpretation in which freedom of choice operates despite the deterministic elements in Sibyll Trelawney's hero prophecy. Our contention in this chapter is that Bassham does not argue effectively for the presence of free will in the Harry Potter universe, nor does he adequately address the role of prophecy in the series. Our interpretation of the books allows for limited freedom within the larger deterministic framework through the creation of "new first causes," that is, events that do not have antecedent actions as their impetus. In other words, a resolution is possible for the apparent existence of both free will and determinism in the Harry Potter universe. This interpretation keeps Harry's heroism from being undermined by the deterministic forces at work in the novels. Furthermore, in examining closely the prophecy, ambiguity and intentionality emerge as important factors in keeping Harry's actions from being fated, thus opening up the possibility for the kinds of choices and self-determination that Albus Dumbledore consistently argues for in the series, but that initially do not appear possible to Harry or the reader.

The terms *determinism*, *libertarianism*, and *compatibilism* describe the primary positions in debates about free will; therefore, definitions of these terms are necessary to following our argument. *Determinism* is a view in which current events (including actions) are caused by antecedent events such that the antecedent events are sufficient to determine only one future. This view precludes the possibility of choice for the characters by assuming that freedom and causality are incompatible and by arguing that we act in accordance with causal laws. One opposing view, the view defended by Bassham, is *libertarianism*. Libertarianism holds that current events (including actions) are *not* caused by antecedent events. Libertarianism agrees with determinism that freedom and causality are incompatible but argues that our actions are not constrained by causal laws. The final view we discuss is called *compatibilism*. Compatibilism is the view that current events (including *some* actions) are caused by antecedent events, but the antecedent events are not sufficient to determine only one possible future. This view disagrees with the assumption made by the determinist and the libertarian that freedom and causality are incompatible.


## DETERMINISM

Although Bassham dismisses the idea that Rowling's plot is completely deterministic, a strong case can be made for a deterministic interpretation of the Harry Potter universe. The ability to rewind time, for example, and yet not change events, as when Harry and Hermione go back to save Buckbeak and Sirius in *Prisoner of Azkaban*, is one such case. Events are repeated exactly as they occurred the first time around—something most clearly demonstrated by the reader's realization that the "unmistakable swish and thud of an axe" during the execution scene did not signal Buckbeak's death, but the executioner's anger over losing his prize and by Harry's realization that it was not his father's Patronus that saved him, but his own.[3] Viewing the events in *Prisoner of Azkaban* as if Harry and Hermione were merely repeating actions already completed suggests that no other outcome is possible. Harry was destined to save Sirius; Buckbeak was destined to be freed.

Rewinding time is just one piece of evidence for a deterministic interpretation of the novels. In the novels, nothing appears to be left to chance: Harry is "sorted" into a specific house apparently based on his heritage and on personal preferences that were cultivated en route to Hogwarts.[4] Furthermore, Harry's assertions that he was lucky or that he had help in his encounters with

Voldemort do not align with facts indicating that antecedent events help Harry deter, and eventually kill, Voldemort. In the *Sorcerer's Stone*, Harry's touch, made deadly to Voldemort by his mother's love, cripples the embryonic Voldemort so that he cannot return to life at that point.[5] In *Goblet of Fire*, the relationship between the core of Harry's wand and Voldemort's causes a cascade reaction that allows Harry time to reassess his situation.[6] In every encounter with Voldemort, the Dark Lord's own arrogance and lust for vengeance cause him to make errors in judgment with regard to Harry, including the errors he makes in choosing a wand with which to defeat Harry in *Deathly Hallows*.[7] Thus, whether these events are produced by prior circumstance or intrinsic character traits, it appears that freedom of choice is not wholly functional within Rowling's universe.

Consider, for example, how Harry's upbringing, the circumstances of his birth, and the difficulties of his childhood living with the Dursleys compare strikingly with Voldemort's birth and childhood in the orphanage. Voldemort, placed in an orphanage with relatively sympathetic caregivers, may in fact have had an even more advantageous upbringing.[8] Yet only one of the two orphaned boys turns evil. It could be that genetics predetermines one's future self in Harry Potter, more so than the environment. Voldemort, as the heir of Slytherin, could merely embody the particularly mean psychological traits of his ancestors, like selfishness and sadism,[9] whereas Harry could merely embody a different set of psychological traits from his father, like a propensity for rule-breaking and rash action,[10] and from his mother, like a kind heart and sensitivity to others' feelings.[11]

Perhaps the clearest example that Harry lacks free will is that he is regularly called the "Chosen One," not because he appears to make choices to be a hero but because Trelawney and the rest of the wizarding world assume his status is predetermined. Well before Harry hears his Divination professor's prophecy in *Order of the Phoenix*, his character becomes associated with the concept of destiny, with its implied sense of fate and determinism. For example, although Dumbledore is hesitant to explain to young Harry his special status in the *Sorcerer's Stone*, others are not so reticent, like wand salesman Mr. Ollivander, who asserts that Harry will do "great things."[12] Scrimegeour summarizes the sentiments of the wizarding world in *Half-Blood Prince*: "The idea that there is somebody out there who might be able, who might be *destined*, to destroy He-Who-Must-Not-Be-Named—well, naturally it gives people a lift."[13]

Despite his proclamations about "choice," even Dumbledore appears to assume there is causation at work in the universe, or he would not have guided Harry as he did in both the *Order of the Phoenix* and the *Half-Blood Prince*.[14] At the end of book V, when Harry finally hears Professor Trelawney's entire prophecy, the headmaster's proclamation that "there is no doubt that it *is* you" suggests the importance of causal chains in the Harry Potter universe.[15] Once Voldemort makes his choice of Harry over Neville, then subsequent events unfold as a result of the previous event: in attempting to kill Harry, Voldemort instead bestows upon the boy the trademark lightning bolt scar, confers upon him certain advantageous powers that he can ultimately use against Voldemort, enhances the power of unselfish love that Harry's mother died to bequeath him and that Voldemort can never fully understand or respect, and propels Harry forward to their final, deadly confrontation. A harshly deterministic interpretation of Sibyll's prophecy is even accepted by Harry, who recasts the confusing proclamation that "either must die at the hand of the other for neither can live while the other survives" simply as "one of us has got to kill the other."[16]

However, interpreting the series along determinist lines raises an important issue with regard to Harry's ability to act heroically: if we interpret the Harry Potter universe as merely causal, then it is not possible to consider Harry a hero because he is not responsible for his actions. Instead, all of his actions, begun by Voldemort's reaction to the prophecy, and continuing through Lily's, Dumbledore's, and Snape's responses to Voldemort, appear to be merely effects. If this is correct, then freedom of action, free will, and, subsequently, responsibility and heroism are precluded. In short, if Harry lacked the ability to make choices, then his actions are mere stimulus reactions and cannot be used as evidence for his heroic character.

## LIBERTARIANISM

Although there is evidence to support a deterministic interpretation of the series, Rowling herself does not appear to endorse determinism. Instead, throughout the series, the narrator and characters stress the role of "choice," and therefore, free will, in shaping an individual's path, suggesting that Rowling's universe supports a libertarian point of view. As already mentioned, one of the earliest and most important scenes in the series is when Harry is sorted into Gryffindor. Bassham also uses this scene to argue that there is choice in the Harry Potter universe by reminding us that Harry had input into the Hat's decision making.[17] Harry, himself, in the epilogue to *Deathly Hallows*, believes in the power of free choice as well when he tells his own son, Albus Severus, that the Sorting Hat will place Albus in Gryffindor if that is what Albus chooses.[18] However, it would be a mistake to suppose that if there is one example of free choice, then the universe lacks causation. For example, in the case of the Sorting Hat, it is not clear whether Harry's or Albus' wish or desire is not also a link in the causal chain of the Sorting Hat's decision-making process, thereby becoming one of several causal influences on the Sorting Hat. It is even possible that these desires are the effects of previous events. When we consider that only a true Gryffindor could pull Godric's sword from the Hat, and that both Neville and Harry are able to do so, it may be that Harry's wish to be in Gryffindor is only a mirror of his own true, predetermined Gryffindor nature.[19]

However, this is not the only textual evidence in favor of a libertarian interpretation. Crucial scenes in *Deathly Hallows* point to the existence of free will in the novels. First, in chapter 34, "The Forest Again," Harry chooses to march into Voldemort's midst, knowing that he will die at Voldemort's hands. The chapter opens with Harry believing that he is predetermined to die, that "his life span had always been determined by how long it took to eliminate all the Horcruxes" and that he had a "true destiny."[20] Suddenly, however, the chapter shifts into being about making independent, antecedent-free choices. Harry sees Neville and asks him to destroy Nagini. The narrator describes this request as an "idea . . . *out of nowhere,* born out of a desire to make absolutely sure" that Nagini is eradicated. [italics added][21] In the next chapter, "King's Cross," the exchange with Dumbledore's apparition after Voldemort apparently kills Harry also indicates that choice is an integral part of the storyline. Dumbledore tells Harry, "We are in King's Cross you say? I think that if *you decided* not to go back, you would be able to . . . let's say . . . board a train." [italics added][22] He goes on to add, "I think . . . that if *you choose* to return, there is a chance that [Voldemort] may be finished for good. I cannot promise it." [italics added][23] The metaphorical significance of a hub, coupled with the direct suggestion of choosing, clearly indicates the presence of free will in the Rowling universe. Furthermore, Dumbledore's claim that he does not know whether Harry's returning will finally destroy Voldemort suggests that the outcome is uncertain. This uncertainty in turn suggests that a single, specific outcome is not entirely determined by antecedent events.

In examining the possibility of free decision making in the Harry Potter universe, it is also important to reconsider the interpretation of the prophecy. Bassham reconciles free will and foreknowledge by identifying the inherent ambiguity that can result from certain if–then statements and by pointing out that *"logical must"* is not the same as *"causal must"* since foreknowledge does not necessarily cause someone's actions.[24] He asserts that "foreknowledge imposes only a 'necessity of the consequent,' rather than a causal necessity" which "does not in any way affect the freedom or responsibility of those involved."[25] Such a position rightly disconnects foreknowledge from causation, which Dumbledore also does in *Half-Blood Prince* when he reminds Harry that "what the prophecy says is only significant because Voldemort made it so";[26] however, neither Bassham nor Dumbledore successfully reconcile the libertarian and deterministic elements in Harry Potter's world. Rather, prediction of the future, like in the reading of the tea leaves,[27] is only a mechanism by which the future is known; it does not deal specifically with the question of whether causation is operative.

Perhaps some of the most important evidence for freedom of choice in the books is the way Voldemort's actions are described once he hears the prophecy. In *Order of the Phoenix,* Dumbledore emphasizes that Voldemort had a choice as to which child he would personally attack: the half-blooded Harry or the pure-blooded Neville.[28] In *Half-Blood Prince,* while Harry, Hermione, and Neville are on the Hogwarts' Express, Harry thinks about how his and Neville's places could so easily have been reversed. The texts emphasize that Voldemort, for unspecified reasons, chose to believe that Harry was the one named in the prophecy. Harry also wonders if, had Voldemort chosen differently, there would have been no "Chosen One."[29] Finally, in *Half-Blood Prince*, Dumbledore notes that the prophecy itself is not sufficient to determine the course of events. In order for the prophecy to have efficacy, Voldemort had to make a choice and thereby put in place the first piece of a puzzle whereby the prophecy might come to describe future events.[30] Furthermore, Dumbledore states the prophecy does not compel Harry to act; Harry chooses to believe that Voldemort should be stopped.[31] Thus, the prophecy no longer describes future events that *must* happen, but is a special kind of guess about one of many possible futures. This possible future understanding is reinforced when Dumbledore points out that not every prophecy kept by the Ministry of Magic has been fulfilled.[32] Therefore, prophecies describe what might come to be, given certain conditions, but are not descriptions of predetermined events. This evidence moves us toward a libertarian interpretation in which Harry can be a hero. He has the freedom to make heroic choices, and Voldemort has the ability to make malicious, self-serving ones.

So, there is evidence that there is free will in the Harry Potter universe. If determinism and libertarianism were the only possible interpretations, this would be sufficient to defend a libertarian interpretation. However, there are all manner of problems with the evidence we have cited above. We have already mentioned, when discussing the scenes about the Sorting Hat, that some choice does not push all causality out of consideration. Furthermore, since logical and causal necessity are distinct, we cannot use the presence or absence of one type of necessity to argue for or against the presence of the other. Next, Dumbledore's lack of knowledge at King's Cross could merely indicate limits on his knowledge and not be evidence for a libertarian interpretation. Finally, even if Voldemort made a choice to kill Harry, it seems to have been an antecedent cause to many effects, such as Harry's scar, some of Harry's powers, and an influence on the actions of Harry and many others. In short, free will may be just as operational as causality, but the libertarian interpretation requires that all causality be disregarded because freedom and causality are not compatible.

## COMPATIBILISM

How do we make sense of a world in which causation is operating and yet one can choose to act with freedom? The answer is to recognize that we do not have to accept that causation and free will are mutually exclusive in the way that the libertarian and hard determinist jointly assume. Instead, we can interpret the Harry Potter universe along compatibilist lines, which will allow for both the predetermined fact that Voldemort will be defeated and for the free choice on the part of Harry (and, as we shall see, Neville) to act heroically.

The key is to establish that the novels allow for the influence of new first causes in which antecedent events are not the impetus for current conditions. Common sense would seem to understand choices as events that *do not necessarily have antecedent causes*. The compatibilist endorses this commonsense view. The problem for the compatibilist is to explain how new causes are possible. One way we can establish the possibility of new causes in Harry Potter is through what we will term the *ambiguity view*. According to this view, language can be ambiguous in ways that require choices, understood as new causes. A second way we can establish new causes in the novels is through what we will term the *intentionality view*, which is based on the concept that moral responsibility requires that we form mental states that in turn cause actions. Accepting either view is sufficient to make both freedom of action and causation coexist in the novels, allowing Harry to be heroic.

## Ambiguity View

One of the difficulties of determining whether the Harry Potter universe is deterministic or governed by free will are the inherent ambiguities of Trelawney's two prophecies.[33] Bassham's work, as noted previously, touches on a certain ambiguity in the hero prophecy; however, his argument centers on what he sees as the lack of causality in if–then statements and as we've shown, does not reconcile the libertarian and determinist viewpoints. A deeper analysis of the ambiguities in both prophecies can reveal ways to reconcile the incompatibility.

In language study, one common form of ambiguity is structural. *Structural ambiguity* focuses on the multiple interpretations possible for a longer phrase or sentence. For example, think about the old gag line, "The matron fed her dog biscuits." Do we read the sentence as the matron feeding her dog a snack called a biscuit, or do we read the sentence as the matron feeding some unnamed woman some dog's biscuits? Trelawney's hero prophecy uses structural ambiguity when it states that "either must die at the hand of the other for neither can live while the other survives." What is ambiguous about this expression is that statements of the form "either ——— or ———" can have at least two interpretations. The first interpretation can be "either ——— or ———, but *not* both"; the second interpretation can be "either ——— or ———, and possibly both." Both Harry and Dumbledore, as we noted earlier, interpret the prophecy in *Order of Phoenix* as "one of us has got to kill the other,"[34] utilizing the first interpretation for an either–or expression; however, as we find out at the end of *Deathly Hallows*, we should understand the prophecy to mean "Either Harry or Voldemort will die at the hands of the other, and possibly both." In fact, both of them appear to die, but only Voldemort does so in a permanent way, whereas Harry, Christ-like, rises from the dead to ensure the complete material death of Voldemort.[35] Thus, the use of structural ambiguity in Trelawney's hero prophecy requires choices by Harry to resolve the structural ambiguities, and these choices are examples of new causes in the Harry Potter universe.

Similarly, Trelawney's prophecies also display what we might term *referential ambiguity*, a kind of ambiguity that results when it is unclear who or what is the focus of a statement. This type of ambiguity often bedevils teachers grading student compositions. In a sentence like, "I went to the mall with my mom and grandmother, and *she* bought me a new sweater," it is not clear who the "she" refers to: the mother or grandmother. Like other ambiguities, a referentially ambiguous expression can have two or more possible interpretations and, more importantly, it seems to require that a choice takes place to resolve the ambiguity. Looking at the servant prophecy, we see that Trelawney's use of the word "servant" four times instead of a particular name involves this form of referential ambiguity, making it appear at first to refer to Sirius Black, but by the end of the novel we come to realize the reference is to Peter Pettigrew.[36] The hero prophecy utilizes more substantial referential ambiguities that open up a trio of choices as to who will defeat Voldemort: Harry, Neville, or, amazingly, Snape. The first statement in prophecy, "The one with the power to vanquish the Dark Lord approaches," could have referred to Harry or Neville as Dumbledore argues in the *Order of the Phoenix*.[37] Alternatively, it could refer to Snape, who *interrupts* the prophecy as it is delivered and who goes on to be a key figure in Voldemort's downfall.[38] Additionally, the phrase, "the power" becomes referentially ambiguous. To what does it refer: Snape's love for Lily and his skill at Occlumency, Harry's power to love, or Neville's unexpected, extraordinary courage? The second statement in the prophecy, "Born to those who have thrice defied him, born as the seventh month dies" could refer to either Harry and Neville, or possibly both Harry and Neville if we read the prophecy not as three repetitive statements, but three independent clauses, the first referring to Snape, the second to Harry (or Neville), and the third to Neville (or Harry).[39]

At first, these referential ambiguities appear merely to be complex plot devices to keep the reader guessing. The unnamed servant, whether Sirius, Peter, or some other wizard meeting the provided description, is moving down a specified path. Similarly, the one with the power, whether Harry or Neville or even Snape, is moving down yet another specified path. To eliminate the ambiguity in each prophecy, we must secure the referents, even if a particular phrase has multiple referents. This closure, however, must take place in a particular way, namely, by a character making a choice. In the case of Snape, the powers of love and occlumency provide him with the ability to choose which side of the great conflict he will defend.[40] In choosing a side, Snape's action secures one referent of the first sentence of the hero prophecy by making it clear that he is at least one of the people mentioned. Then, consider what Dumbledore says of Voldemort after Voldemort heard part of the hero prophecy: Voldemort had a choice as to who he would kill, Harry or Neville, and thus mark as his archrival.[41] Voldemort's choice did at least two things. First, it clarified that Harry was in fact one of the referents of the first sentence of the hero prophecy; second, it causally contributed to Harry's future to a large extent. Voldemort's choice marked Neville as well because Neville's character, seen often in opposition to Harry's, is also shaped by the fact that his parents were tortured with the Cruciatus Curse to the point of insanity.[42] Furthermore, although we have established that Voldemort's choice is an antecedent cause for the development of certain powers in Harry, like his ability to speak Parseltongue, we have not yet established well-grounded antecedents for the choice itself. Dumbledore's assumption, when he reveals the full prophecy to Harry in *Order of the Phoenix*, is that for psychological reasons, Voldemort chose the individual most like him, a "half-blood," but not even Dumbledore has enough information to make a definitive statement about Voldemort's choice.[43] The best way secure the referents and assign cause is to have it be the case that there is both causality and free choice in the Harry Potter universe.

Note, however, that Voldemort's choice was not sufficient to close off Neville from having a key role in Voldemort's destruction. Even in the final scenes of *Deathly Hallows* the referential ambiguity of the prophecy continues to leave open possibilities. In the end, Neville kills Nagini, the last of Voldemort's Horcruxes, while Harry kills the remnants of Voldemort, the physical person.[44] Who ultimately ends Voldemort's reign? Did not both boys, "born to those who have thrice defied him, born as the seventh month dies," kill Voldemort?[45] And, it seems, that both Neville and Harry had to contribute new causes for this to happen. First, Neville has to agree to make the attempt to destroy Voldemort even though Neville, up until the last book, appears to lack the confidence and skill needed to complete this task.[46] Second, Harry has to ask Neville to destroy Nagini and then he has to make a choice at King's Cross to return to his physical body after accepting his own death so willingly, thus setting him on a new path toward the successful destruction of Voldemort's physical body.[47]

The use of prophecy in Harry Potter with its attendant ambiguities, therefore, seems to suggest that under the surface of its well-ordered deterministic universe, there are factors, events, and motives that cannot be accounted for as mere effects. In particular, the structural and referential ambiguities of the prophecies create the possibility of choice and are what allow Harry and Neville to act heroically and bring both plot closure and logical closure in which a referent is assigned to the variable which created the original ambiguity in the prophecy.

### Intentionality View

There is an alternative way to argue for the compatibilist interpretation, which we call the *intentionality view*. This defense of compatibilism relies on the creation of mental states known as intentions. Intentions, whatever else they are, function as the causes of actions. These mental states are similar to beliefs and desires in that once formed they have definite content. A belief represents a state of affairs that currently exists; a desire represents a state of affairs that might come into being. An intention, however, is the motivation to move from the current state of affairs into some unrealized state. If one forms an intention, the motivational aspect of the intention can cause someone to act. Thus, intentions can be new causes when they are properly formed. Intentions are important in moral evaluation because they can be the locus of responsibility.[48] In developing this defense of compatibilism, we will show that Harry is capable of forming intentions independent of antecedent events.

To assign responsibility in a completely deterministic world is difficult because by virtue of having no choice in our actions, there is the implication that we don't think about our actions, rationalize them, juxtapose them with others' actions, and so on. The phrase "no choice" even implies that all of our actions are done *without intent* and thus are done without responsibility. The importance of intention as a new cause is highlighted in *Half-Blood Prince* when Harry revisits the question of destiny with Dumbledore. This critical scene continues to refine both Harry's and our understanding of how the results of Voldemort's choices, not the prophecy, created causal chains in Harry's life. A prophecy, then, in the Harry Potter universe is not necessarily a prediction for future events, but an explanation of the causal chains that will occur should certain actions be taken in the first place. If a prophecy is not heard, the events may or may not unfold as foretold because prophecy itself can be a motivator for the actions it seeks to explain. As Dumbledore reiterates to Harry, even Harry's actions can be viewed independently of the prophecy. Dumbledore argues that "the prophecy does not mean you *have* to do anything! But the prophecy caused Lord Voldemort to *mark you as his equal.* . . . In other words, you are free to choose your way, quite free to turn your back on the prophecy!"[49] Still, Harry must fight Voldemort to the death, but now he understands the subtle difference in the "must" as "the difference between being dragged into the arena to face a battle to the death and walking into the arena with your head held high."[50] Moreover, if Harry had never heard the prophecy, his own honorable attributes, including what Dumbledore deems the "power of a soul that is untarnished and whole,"[51] would still guide Harry's decision making and lead him into battle with Voldemort. This "power of the soul" provides the internal formation for an intention to act, and the prophecy, again, is a convenient mechanism for *explaining* some of what occurs in the novels, but does not *determine* those events since it is the intentions formed by characters like Harry which become new causes.

This compatibilist interpretation of the series is supported by Aristotle's Virtue Theory, which offers an explanation of how free will and responsibility can occur in a largely deterministic universe. Virtue Theory is a moral theory that focuses on character traits that help a person to flourish. These character traits are described in terms of intentionality, and intentionality is sufficient to generate moral responsibility. First, Aristotle points out that deliberation is such that "no one deliberates about what cannot be otherwise or about what cannot be achieved by his action."[52] This is because "we deliberate about what is up to us, i.e., about the actions we can do."[53] In other words, the concept of deliberative thought implies freedom because if we are predetermined, we would have nothing to deliberate about; deliberation only occurs in the absence of determination. Second, actions that are taken as a result of deliberation are voluntary, and "what is voluntary seems to be what has its origin in the agent himself."[54] To say that some action has "origin in the agent himself" is to say that an action is the result of an internal mental state, which is an intention. This intentional state expresses free will. Intentional action is voluntary action and actions "receive praise or blame when they are voluntary."[55] Thus, intentionality both defines an avenue for free choice and provides a basis for the assignment of responsibility.

In his article, Bassham makes an argument that appears to undercut this compatibilist interpretation by ignoring intentionality and declaring that the "definition [of compatibilism] *doesn't* work for many cases in which a person does what he desires but lacks any effective control over what he desires."[56] However, there is a distinction between a desire and the control of the desire. It is the control, what we might call the "choice" of which desire to follow, which is a person's intention, and an intention is a cause internal to one's consciousness. Framing his argument with a description of the Imperius Curse, Bassham claims that desires alone color our evaluation of the actions to which they are connected. He assumes that the Imperius Curse controls actions by changing desires, which he lumps under the phrase "by changing a person's will."[57] This is an issue for the compatibilist because Bassham makes the additional assumption that "free will is simply the ability to do as one desires."[58] There are at least two problems with this argument. First, it assumes that the Imperius Curse controls actions by changing desires; however, the Curse might simply change actions, *not* desires. In fact, this is exactly how it appears to act against Harry in *Goblet of Fire* in his graveyard confrontation with Voldemort.[59] If the Imperius Curse can control actions without changing desires, then there is no problem for the compatibilist since there is action not in accordance with desire. Alternatively, the curse might change desires, as Bassham indicates, but that is not sufficient to show that a person chooses to act in accordance with the Curse. If the Imperius Curse controls desires without changing intentions, then actions cannot be considered freely chosen. This lack of control helps us combat the second assumption of defining free will as "the ability to do as one desires." Free will can be defined as action which is not influenced by external factors. An action properly so called is one that has as its motivation mental states internal to the agent that eventually performs those actions. Since the Imperius Curse is an external factor, it alters a subject's psychological makeup by substituting a consciousness-external cause for an internally produced cause. Free will can be exercised if and only if there are no consciousness-external influences. Given this definition of free will, we can see that the characters in Harry Potter at least occasionally form intentions without external influence, thereby securing freedom and responsibility.

Throughout the series, textual evidence exists for intention formation free of external influence. Harry *has the intention* to do the right thing and he acts upon those intentions freely. The machinations of Dumbledore, his friendships with Hermione and Ron, and the unhappy circumstances of his life teach Harry about perspective, empathy, and morality, necessary traits for a heroic aspect. The key, however, is that only by forming an intention with a motivational aspect are these traits efficacious. Harry must, independent of his external influences, choose between different courses of action, and when he chooses, he generally forms an *intention for good or right action*. Harry's experiences lead him to deliberate and make intentional choices; these intentions become part of the causal chain, which subsequently effect action. Although there may not be a lot of choice in the Harry Potter universe, when choice is possible, its importance is manifest. For example, when Harry chooses to allow Cedric to tie with him in the maze at the end of *Goblet of Fire*, his decision to share victory with Cedric comes out of both his deeply ingrained sense of fair play and a spur of the moment decision that winning the challenge is not that important.[60] Such decisions are new causes, free of external stimuli, and are the basis of moral responsibility and heroism.

The test of whether Harry acts intentionally for the good and can be seen as a hero involves additional analysis of the events in *Deathly Hallows*. At any point in the series prior to this novel, Harry can choose to give up his quest to defeat Voldemort. The likely outcome of such a choice is certain death.[61] However, by not choosing to give up and by surviving his previous encounters with Voldemort, Harry must make yet another choice in *Deathly Hallows*: whether to defy Voldemort one last time. Harry's actions in this novel are best understood as emanating from internally formed intentions. To see that Harry forms new intentions in *Deathly Hallows*, we must recognize the choices he makes. First, he *chooses* an attitude of acceptance toward the events in his life. In doing so, he also *chooses* to accept the responsibility to end the cycle of violence begun by Voldemort, and he *chooses* not to seek Hermione or Ron's help after seeing Snape's memories unfold.[62] Harry then *chooses* to accept his fate as described by Dumbledore in Snape's memory; he *chooses* the path by which he will be the instrument of Voldemort's destruction *more* willingly than unwillingly, and like his decision to ask for Neville's help, "his understanding was coming so fast it seemed to have bypassed thought."[63] Harry then makes more choices: he asks Neville to carry on the quest if he fails; he uses the Snitch's contents to confer with his departed loved ones about the nature of death; and he conceals the Resurrection Stone by dropping it on the forest floor.[64] Finally, Harry *chooses* not to fight when he faces Voldemort in the forest in what he assumes will be his final encounter.[65] Each action suggests an active consciousness in which Harry forms intentions and acts upon them.

Moreover, in the dreamland of King's Crossing, Harry's discussion with Dumbledore reiterates the active power of the mind—the active power of consciousness—in framing and shaping our decisions and actions.[66] If Trelawney's hero prophecy really entailed a hard determinism, then Harry would not have had the freedom to make these choices in his final encounter with Voldemort. In making these decisions, Harry demonstrates limited free will and an acceptance of responsibility worthy of praise or blame. And because we as readers praise his actions, he becomes to our minds a hero.

## CONCLUSION

Freedom, responsibility, and the evaluation of a person's character are issues that face us in both real life and in literature. Our actions sometimes feel as if they are freely chosen, and sometimes as if they are compelled; a literary character's actions, such as Harry's, can have the same qualities. This dualism creates tension since we seem to lose responsibility if our actions are not freely chosen and we cease to be the objects of praise or blame. Like in our own world, there is evidence in the novels that both causation and free will are at work in the wizarding world. Such evidence seems to leave the reader with competing, mutually exclusive interpretations of the story unless we accept a compatibilist interpretation in which free will and causality coexist. According to this schema, the prophecy's ambiguities necessitate choices for plot closure, and Dumbledore's and Harry's discussions amplify the free will that flows from an ability to form intentions without antecedent causes. Finally, only a compatibilist interpretation explains how Harry can be heroic, despite the strong deterministic elements at work.

## NOTES

1. See, for example, Veronica L. Schanoes, "Cruel Heroes and Treacherous Texts: Educating the Reader in Moral Complexity and Critical Reading in J.K. Rowling's Harry Potter Books," and Chantel Lavoie, "Safe as Houses: Sorting and School Houses at Hogwarts," in *Reading Harry Potter: Critical Essays*, ed. Giselle Liza Anatol (Westport, CT: Praeger, 2003); Edmund M. Kenn, *The Wisdom of Harry Potter: What Our Favorite Hero Teaches Us about Moral Choices* (New York: Prometheus Books, 2008); and David Baggett and Shawn E. Klein, eds., *Harry Potter and Philosophy: If Aristotle Ran Hogwarts* (Chicago: Open Court, 2004), which includes the article whose assumptions about the nature of prophecy, fate, morality, and choice we examine here in detail.

2. Gregory Bassham, "The Prophecy-Driven Life: Fate and Freedom at Hogwarts" in *Harry Potter and Philosophy: If Aristotle Ran Hogwarts*, ed. David Baggett and Shawn E. Klein (Chicago: Open Court, 2004), 213–26. Note that Bassham's article is entitled "The Prophecy-Driven Life: Foreknowledge and Freedom at Hogwarts" in the book's table of contents.

3. J.K. Rowling, *Harry Potter and the Prisoner of Azkaban* (New York: Scholastic Press, 1999), 331 and 402, 397–417, and 411. Limited perspective suggests Buckbeak's demise through the recording of what Harry and Hermione heard upon leaving Hagrid's cottage; however, Buckbeak's supposed death is described in the same words as his salvation upon the rewinding of time: "There was a swishing noise, and the thud of an axe." The description of what is heard does not necessitate Buckbeak's death in the first telling. Given the amplified perspective of Harry's experience with his Patronus, where the event does not change in any detail, Rowling appears to deal consistently with time-travel chronology. See also Michael Silberstein, "Space, Time, and Magic" in *Harry Potter and Philosophy: If Aristotle Ran Hogwarts*, ed. David Baggett and Shawn E. Klein (Chicago: Open Court, 2004), 186–99, for an explanation based on a tenseless view of time.

4. J.K. Rowling, *Harry Potter and the Sorcerer's Stone* (New York: Scholastic Press, 1997), 79, 121.

5. Ibid., 294–95.

6. J.K. Rowling, *Harry Potter and the Goblet of Fire* (New York: Scholastic Press, 2000), 665–69.

7. J.K. Rowling, *Harry Potter and the Deathly Hallows* (New York: Scholastic Press, 2000), 656–57, 702–05, and 742–44.

8. J.K. Rowling, *Harry Potter and the Half-Blood Prince* (New York: Scholastic Press, 2005), 264–75.

9. See, for example, Chapter 10, "The House of Gaunt" in Rowling, *Prince*, 194–216, when Harry enters the Pensieve and encounters Voldemort's cowering mother, antisocial uncle, and violently prejudiced grandfather via Ministry agent Bob Ogden's memories.

10. For examples, see Rowling, *Azkaban*, 424–25, and J.K. Rowling, *Harry Potter and the Order of the Phoenix* (New York: Scholastic Press, 2003), 645–49.

11. Rowling, *Phoenix*, 649.

12. Rowling, *Stone*, 299 and 85, and Rowling, *Hallows*, 733.

13. Rowling, *Prince*, 345.

14. Dumbledore's assumptions in *Prince* are discussed in the next two sections.

15. Rowling, *Phoenix*, 842.

16. Ibid., 844.

17. Bassham, 225–26.

18. Rowling, *Hallows*, 758.

19. Rowling, *Chamber*, 319 and 333.

20. Rowling, *Hallows*, 692 and 693.

21. Ibid., 695.

22. Ibid., 722.

23. Ibid., 722.

24. Bassham, 224.

25. Ibid., 225.

26. Rowling, *Prince*, 509.

27. See, for example, Chapter 6, "Talons and Tea Leaves," in Rowling, *Azkaban*, 107 and 109, where tea leaf reading produces "omens," not actual predictions.

28. Rowling, *Phoenix*, 842.

29. Rowling, *Prince*, 139–40.

30. Ibid., 509.

31. Ibid., 511–12. This point is developed further in the section on compatibilism.

32. Ibid., 510.

33. Ambiguity should not be confused with vagueness. An ambiguous word or sentence has multiple meanings, whereas vague expressions are those that allow for fuzziness in interpretation. Consider as an example of vagueness the question, "When does someone become bald?" Clearly, a person who has lost all of his hair is bald, but it can be hard to determine when one's receding hairline disappears enough to be considered bald. The prophecies are not vague in this sense, i.e., there is no problem with a borderline case of someone being Harry or not being Harry; instead, the issue becomes one of how to interpret correctly the who and the what of the prophecies since untangling the ambiguities points to the coexistence of determinism and freedom in Harry Potter.

34. Rowling, *Phoenix*, 844.

35. Rowling, *Hallows*, 723–24.

36. Rowling, *Azkaban*, 324 and 371.

37. Rowling, *Phoenix*, 842.

38. Rowling, *Azkaban*, 545 and 549.

39. Rowling, *Phoenix*, 841. In addition to structural ambiguity, the prophecies use lexical ambiguity, which focuses on the multiple meanings inherent in a single word or phrase treated as a single idea, like the word "glasses," which could mean something used to improve your vision or something from which you drink. Sibyll's first prophecy in *The Prisoner of Azkaban* includes two lexical ambiguities, first it describes some unnamed follower of Voldemort as "chained" for the past twelve years (which appears to refer at first to Sirius's prison term in Azkaban, but ultimately becomes a reference to Peter's self-imposed chains as Ron's pet Rat, Scabbers) and second it declares that this follower will "break free" (which appears to refer back to Sirius's prison break, but again becomes a reference to Peter and his escape from Ron). Rowling, *Azkaban*, 324.

40. Rowling, *Hallows*, 678, 687, 4, and 655.

41. Rowling, *Phoenix*, 842.

42. Rowling, *Goblet*, 602–3.

43. Rowling, *Phoenix*, 842.

44. Rowling, *Hallows*, 733.

45. Rowling, *Phoenix*, 841.

46. A careful re-reading of the texts in which we examine Neville's heroism would show that although we and Harry are rather surprised by the disheveled, but commanding Neville that comes out of Aberforth's mirror, Neville's potential for heroism and bravery is subtly highlighted from the beginning of the series when Neville tries to stop Harry, Ron, and Hermione from leaving the Gryffindor common room in *Stone*, and later when Neville is struck down by the Cruciatus Curse (the same curse that caused his parent's insanity) while valiantly dueling by Harry's side in *Phoenix*. Rowling, *Hallows*, 570–72; *Stone*, 272–73; *Phoenix*, 800–802.

47. Rowling, *Hallows*, 722.

48. See, for example, Alfred R. Mele's article on "Intention" for additional information about the concept as we discuss it, in *Encyclopedia of Philosophy*, 2nd ed., Donald M. Borchert, ed. (Detroit: Macmillan Reference USA, 2006), vol. 4: 700–704. *Gale Virtual Reference Library*, http://go.galegroup.com (accessed 10 June 2008).

49. Rowling, *Prince*, 512.

50. Ibid., 512.

51. Ibid., 511.

52. Aristotle, *Nicomachean Ethics*, Trans. Terence Irwin (Indianapolis: Hackett Publishing Company, 1985), Book VI, Chapter 5, lines 1140a33–34.

53. Ibid., Book III, Chapter 3, lines 1112a32–33.

54. Ibid., Book III, Chapter 2, lines 111a22–23.

55. Ibid., Book III, Chapter 1, lines 1109b30–31.

56. Bassham, *The Prophecy-Driven Life*, 217.

57. Ibid., 217.

58. Ibid., 216.

59. Rowling, *Goblet*, 661–62.

60. Ibid., 635.

61. Rowling, *Prince*, 512.

62. Rowling, *Hallows*, 693.

63. Ibid., 698.

64. Ibid., 695, 698, and 703.

65. Ibid., 704.

66. Ibid., 722.

# 5

# Harry Potter and Narratives of Destiny

*Lisa Hopkins*

When the sword emerges from the water in *Harry Potter and the Deathly Hallows*, it offers clear confirmation of the importance of Arthurian motifs in the sequence. The silver doe that leads Ron and Harry to the sword[1] recalls the mystic white hart that in Arthurian legend appears to herald the start of a quest:[2] at first the sword in the pool looks to Harry like a cross,[3] this rare glance at Christian iconography reinforcing the sense of sanctity associated with the grail and with other Arthurian quests. In this chapter, I argue that the Arthur narrative is an important paradigm for the Harry Potter books, but also, like other narratives that are evoked during the series, a paradigm that is there ultimately to be deviated from since the story of Arthur is one of an appointment with destiny, whereas the story of Harry is one of choices and decisions—the very distinction that Dumbledore tries so hard to explain to Harry, and that ultimately makes Harry's own position not only tolerable but survivable.

The connection between the Harry Potter books and the Arthurian legend has already been hinted at in previous books. First, there are the obvious similarities between Merlin and Dumbledore (who is indeed a member of the Order of Merlin). Both are much older and wiser mentor figures who guide the young hero toward fulfilling his potential; both can perform formidable magic; and Dumbledore, like Merlin, is involved in arranging the young hero's fosterage. Moreover, like King Arthur, who when mortally wounded was taken away in a boat by the Lady of the Lake, Dumbledore too is borne toward death in a boat, across a lake in which a human hand eerily appears, and is buried by a lake, as Arthur is said to sleep in the island of Avalon until the time comes for him to return. The sense of a parallel is further underlined by Ron's conviction that, despite all the evidence to the contrary, Dumbledore might somehow have returned, as Arthur, the "once and future king," was prophesied to do. Dumbledore also echoes the structural role of King Arthur himself in the Arthurian narratives because both stand back from the action and allow the heroic deeds to be done by others, whether Harry or the Knights of the Round Table.

There are also other echoes of the Arthur story in Dumbledore's given names. Albus recalls Albion, an early name for England, and one explicitly linked with the Arthur story in Shakespeare's *King Lear*, where the Fool couples "the realm of Albion" with the prophecies of Merlin.[4] Percival was the name of one of Arthur's knights, who failed in his quest to find the Holy Grail, just as Dumbledore thinks that he himself failed in his quest to reunite the Hallows because he was unworthy.[5] A Brian of the Isles is mentioned in the first part of *Le Morte d'Arthur*,[6] and Wulfric evokes two separate figures, both with pertinent associations. First, there is Wulfric of Haselbury (known as St. Wulfric although he was never in fact canonized), and that Rowling may have had this Wulfric in mind is suggested by the fact that he spent part of his early life at Deverill, and Rowling gives the name Barnabas Deverill to a former possessor of the Elder Wand. Second, Wulfric was the name of the brother to whom St. Dunstan, Abbot of Glastonbury, entrusted the worldly affairs of the monastery while he himself concentrated on spiritual matters.[7] Glastonbury is, according to legend, a prime candidate for King Arthur's Avalon, not least after a cross was allegedly disinterred there in the twelfth century bearing the words "Hic jacet sepultus inclitus rex Arturius in insula Avalonia" ("here lies buried the famous king Arthur in the isle of Avalon").

It is suggestive, however, that not only the names of good characters recall names from the Arthurian legendarium. For example, Slytherin student Blaise Zabini invokes Blaise, the legendary teacher of Merlin, and some Harry Potter fans have linked the name of Voldemort's uncle Morfin Gaunt to that of the Arthurian knight Sir Morfan.[8] According to William of Malmesbury, the first chapel in the Isle of Avalon was built by monks who had traveled from the court of King Lucius,[9] which is the given name of Draco Malfoy's father. It is also worth noting that bad people as well as good have been drawn to the Arthur story: Hitler, who clearly lies behind Rowling's creation of Grindelwald, avidly sought the Holy Grail like Arthur and believed himself to wield the Spear of Destiny; he was also a passionate devotee of Wagner, whose operas included the Grail-themed *Parsifal* and the equally Arthurian *Tristan und Isolde*. It is perhaps partly an awareness of such associations that accounts for the fact that at the same time as Rowling evokes the Arthur story, she also destabilizes it as a model for her own narrative, allowing other, competing narratives to be recalled.

The name of Draco itself may also allude both to Arthur and another, related concern: the power of the stars to dictate human fate. There exists an old theory that the sudden rise of Arthur, son of Uther Pendragon, had something to do with the movement in the sky of the constellations of Arcturus and Draco.[10]

Moreover, in *Dragonheart*, dir. Rob Cohen (1996), a film of which Rowling might well have been aware since Jason Isaacs, who plays Lucius Malfoy in the Potter films, and David Thewlis, who plays Lupin, are both in it, there is a dragon called Draco, who ultimately ascends to the stars. The film also features a quest for Avalon and a symbiotic relationship between dragon and man similar to that between Harry and Voldemort.

Astronomy is certainly important in Rowling's books, and this, too, bears on the same issues of identity and destiny as in the Arthur story since it raises the question of whether human actions are the result of chance or choice. The Astronomy Tower—the site of Harry's, Ron's, and Hermione's lessons in the subject—is also notable in that it is on top of this tower that Dumbledore is killed. Moreover, many characters—particularly those associated or having family connections with Slytherin—are named after heavenly bodies. Voldemort's mother, Merope, shares her name with one of the Pleiades. Both Sirius and Regulus Black are named after particularly bright stars (*Regulus* being, in fact, the name of a newsletter for amateur astronomers).[11] Their uncle Alphard also shares a name with a star, while their cousin Andromeda bears the name of a constellation and Bellatrix—the name of another cousin—is the twenty-second brightest star in the sky. Other star-related names feature on a Black family tree.[12] We find family members named Orion (who was the father of Sirius and Regulus), Cassiopeia, Cygnus, and Pollux.

Regulus's middle name of Arcturus is also significant,[13] for Regulus, who despite his unpromising origins and past proves in fact to have been unexpectedly brave and right-minded, has as a middle name not only the name of a star but also the Latinized form of the name Arthur (as found for instance in the final line of Malory's *Morte d'Arthur*, "Hic jacet Arcturus rex quondam et futurus.") This is, of course, wholly typical of Rowling's refusal to offer easy pigeonholing or to divide the whole world into two camps, one of unequivocally good people and one of bad: as Sirius puts it, "the world isn't split into good people and Death Eaters."[14] Umbridge may be foul but she is no Death Eater, just as Barty Crouch, Sr., and Horace Slughorn may also be in some ways unattractive but are ultimately committed to much the same values as characters who are more obviously "good."

As well as echoing Merlin and Arthur, Dumbledore is also reminiscent of Tolkien's Gandalf, not least in that his first name of Albus translates as "white," the color that Gandalf ultimately adopts as his own. There are other echoes of Tolkien's work. Harry, Ron, and Hermione are captured by vulgar, poorly spoken Death Eaters as Sam and Frodo are captured by largely inarticulate orcs.[15] The giant spiders in *Chamber of Secrets* recall those found in *The Hobbit* and Shelob in *The Lord of the Rings*. The concept of the Horcrux bears some remarkable similarities to the function of the One Ring as explained by Gandalf to Frodo in *The Fellowship of the Ring*. Both incorporate some of the power of their dark rulers; both must be destroyed before Sauron and Voldemort can fall. The invisibility-giving heirloom cloak that turns out to be a Deathly Hallow recalls the invisibility-giving heirloom ring that turns out to be the One Ring. Dumbledore's ongoing contest with Fudge resembles that of Gandalf with the similarly defeatist and ineffectual Denethor. In *Half-Blood Prince*, Dumbledore and Harry go through a magically guarded and concealed door into the cave as Gandalf and Frodo enter Moria and, as in Moria, something menacing in the water is disturbed and emerges; later, there are dead bodies lying in the water as in the Dead Marshes.[16] There are also clear similarities between the Burrow and the Last Homely House, between the Black Riders and the dementors, between the tree that apparently swallows Ron and the tree that threatens to swallow a hobbit in the Old Forest, and above all between Harry Potter and Frodo Baggins, both presented as ordinary people on whom an extraordinary destiny has been thrust. In *Half-Blood Prince*, a further similarity emerges in that Neville, like Sam, is revealed as an alternative potential bearer of the burden, suggesting that what ultimately happens is not what automatically had to happen.

At the same time as the two epic narratives of *The Lord of the Rings* and the Arthurian legendarium are evoked, however, they are also repeatedly, and determinedly, marginalized, because the differences prove to be as important as the similarities. Harry is no Hobbit, and he is accompanied not by eight male companions but by one male and—in a distinctly un-Tolkienian manner—one female friend, with the female proving the more determined and resourceful of the two. It is also intriguing that at the absolute climax of her narrative Rowling's imagination turns not to Tolkien but to his imaginative opposite, C.S. Lewis, since Harry's lone walk to a death that is ultimately negated by the workings of a deep magic so clearly recalls Aslan's. The influence of Lewis is also apparent in the appearance of the first name "Harfang" on the Black Family Tree because Harfang is the name of the giants' castle in Lewis's *The Silver Chair*, and Cedric Diggory's surname may point to Digory Kirke, the hero of *The Magician's Nephew*, who grows up to be the Professor of *The Lion, The Witch and the Wardrobe*. (Later, one of the Gryffindor Beaters is called Andrew Kirke.)[17] Finally, in *Prince Caspian*, the young prince is taken up on top of a tall tower to be given a lesson in astronomy by his tutor, the half-dwarf Dr. Cornelius.[18] In a recent book on Lewis, Michael Ward argues that a different planet governs each Narnia book.[19] As mentioned above, Rowling too has apparently interested herself in astronomy—the study of stars—and notably *not* in the unscientific astrology, which purports to be the study of the way in which stars affect human lives. Her books may be larded with names of constellations, but they are notably much less interested in the signs of the zodiac, and the centaur Firenze is firm in his rebuttal of the idea that there is any direct link between what is "written" in the stars and individual human actions, saying, briskly, "That . . . is human nonsense."[20] Indeed, Firenze shares his name with the city in which Galileo invented the telescope, so that in some sense he stands as a living emblem of astronomy rather than astrology. In each of these three cases—Arthurian allusions, Tolkienian echoes, and the language of stars—it seems indeed as if paradigms are being evoked only in order that they may be disabled.

It is particularly important in this respect that it is not Harry himself who extracts the sword from the water, but Ron, who then stabs the locket with the sword.[21] Arthurian motif there may be, but it is displaced from the hero onto his friend, whose father is indeed called Arthur, and whose eldest brother has Arthur as a middle name.[22] Elsewhere in the books, there are strong signs of Rowling's policy of deliberate dislocation of markers of "specialness" and fatedness firmly away from Harry. Professor Trelawney guesses that Harry was born in midwinter, but actually it was in July,[23] in a neat double illustration both of the fallibility of Divination and the extent to which Harry conspicuously fails to map on to the template of the Christ-figure. In fact, it is *Voldemort* who was born on New Year's Eve to a mother who had been given shelter in the snow.[24] Similarly, when Peeves wonders whether Harry has been speaking in tongues,[25] as in the miracle of Pentecost, the possibility is clearly presented as ridiculous; the iconography of Christianity, a belief system heavily dependent on ideas of destiny and preordination, is here evoked only to be disabled, as it is again when a character named Dolores, a name evocative of Mary of the Sorrows, turns out to be wholly unpleasant.

Nor are Christian echoes the only ones to be simultaneously evoked and marginalized. Harry, like the fate-driven Oedipus, meets a sphinx, but the answer to this sphinx's riddle has nothing to do with the ultimate destiny of man, as Oedipus's had,[26] and the Oedipus parallel is even more comprehensively disabled when it is dislocated onto Barty Crouch, Jr., who notes that both he and Voldemort killed their fathers.[27] Another potential paradigm is also disabled: Harry's name is shared with the younger of the two British royal princes, who is often known as the "spare" to Prince William as the "heir," but though Cedric is explicitly identified as the spare, being openly called so—"Kill the spare"[28] — Harry is equally explicitly identified as *not* the heir of Slytherin, or indeed of anything else. In every case, then, the effect is to present Harry as ordinary rather than as special or marked out by destiny.

Harry's own literary and narrative affiliations are in fact significantly different from either the Arthurian or the Tolkienian paradigm. One of them is Shakespeare. The Forbidden Forest echoes the world of *A Midsummer Night's Dream*: the centaurs recall the transformation of Bottom into a half-equine creature, the spiders remind us of *"Hence, you long-legg'd spinners, hence!"*[29] and most of all, the Forbidden Forest stands in the same relation to Hogwarts as the wood does to Athens, as a place of truth and danger close to hand. In *Prisoner of Azkaban*, there is a chapter called "Cat, Rat and Dog," which echoes *Richard III*, a play also echoed when the ghosts of those killed by Voldemort appear to encourage Harry.[30] Most importantly, the Hogshead recalls the Boar's Head tavern of the Henriad, and the connection with the Henriad is confirmed by the revelation in *Half-Blood Prince* that Voldemort's mother was a member of the House of Gaunt: John of Gaunt was the father of Henry IV and the grandfather of Henry V, while Harry himself shares a first name with both Hotspur and Hal. Although these are all relatively small details in the great overall scheme of the books, it is necessary to pay attention to details because that is the essence of Rowling's method: little things mentioned only once turn out to be significant.

There is a fundamental difference between these two sets of narratives. The stories of Arthur and of Tolkien's hobbits are ones of appointments with destiny, but the story of Prince Hal is one of an individual's choice and growth. In some children's books, destiny rules. In Stuart Hill's *Blade of Fire*, for instance, Sharley "knew he'd be allowed to ride a horse when it was necessary for him to do so. Obviously there were powers at work beyond his understanding," while Krisafitsa says to Tharaman, "I somehow feel the One has other plans for our demise."[31] This is also a marked emphasis of children's fantasy books that draw on the Arthur stories. Alan Garner's *The Weirdstone of Brisingamen* (1960) could be read as a parallel text to the Harry Potter books: Cadellin is tall with long white hair and a beard; spells are in Latin; owls understand human speech and take messages; Colin and Susan are trapped by a plant that seems to work much like Devil's Snare; and the tall, hooded figure of Grimnir has something of the same effect as a dementor, especially because dark thoughts come out of his lake. However, everything Cadellin does is in the service of a prophecy, and the Stromkarl sings another old prophecy that is soon fulfilled.[32] In the sequel, *The Moon of Gomrath*, Susan rides with living stars, paralleling Rowling's interest in star names, and a big black dog appears as a warning of death, but there too Angharad Goldenhand assures Susan that "Little of this is chance."[33]

The same emphasis is also found in a book that may not look like either a source for Harry Potter or an Arthur story but is, I think, both. In *Dracula*, the Count has a scar on his forehead, which Jonathan gave him, and he is soon joined in this by Mina, who is scarred on her forehead by the Host and is subsequently able to see into Dracula's mind when in trance and report back on his location; the novel, like the Harry Potter sequence, ends with the deactivation of the scar and then fast forwards several years, and a possible influence might also be apparent in the way that Van Helsing's preferred form of address of "Madam Mina" is echoed in the titles of Madam Pince, Madam Hooch, and so on, while Mina's full name of Wilhelmina is also that of Professor Grubbly-Plank. The Arthurian nature of the narrative (and its interest in the power of certain woods) is suggested by the name of Arthur Holmwood and his title of Lord Godalming, with the obvious pun on god-arming, and its status as narrative of destiny is spelled out for us when Jonathan declares that "There is something of a guiding purpose manifest throughout, which is comforting. Mina says that perhaps we are the instruments of ultimate good."[34]

In Rowling, however, the idea of destiny is presented as explicitly fallacious when Scrimgeour tries to persuade Harry to help the Ministry on the grounds that "The idea that there is somebody out there who might be able, who might even be *destined*, to destroy He-Who-Must-Not-Be-Named—well, naturally, it gives people a lift."[35] It is the distinction between destiny and choice that Dumbledore tries so hard to explain to Harry, starting with his insistence that "It is our choices, Harry, that show what we truly are, far more than our abilities,"[36] and culminating in his warning to Harry, "never forget that what the prophecy says is only significant because Voldemort made it so."[37] Dumbledore consistently insists that if Voldemort had never known of the prophecy, it, like many others, would have remained unfulfilled; indeed the prophecy might originally have referred to either Neville or Harry, and it was Voldemort's actions that ensured that it could ultimately apply only to Harry.[38] When Harry finally grasps this point,[39] the understanding makes his position not only tolerable but survivable: despite the prophecy, despite his past, Harry still has a choice, and, Aslan-like, it is because he exercises that choice that he ultimately escapes death, in Rowling's equivalent of the Stone Table cracking and the Deep Magic reversing the workings of the more superficial magic.

A number of other aspects of the later books work to stress the importance of individual choice rather than of any preordained patterns or structures. One particularly notable thread that runs throughout the books, but only really emerges in its full force and clarity in the very last, is a concern with the differences between siblings—people who have been brought up in the same houses, by the same parents, and come of the same stock, but make very different choices in life, demonstrating that the future is not dictated or preordained by the past. Because Harry himself is an only child (as apparently is Hermione), this emphasis is not noticeable at first, and even when we meet the many-siblinged Ron, the stress is precisely on the difficulty he has in establishing any individuality with such a quantity of brothers. Nevertheless, from the very beginning we have the understated but powerful contrast between Aunt Petunia and her sister, and the more we find about that sister, the stranger and more intriguing the differences and indeed the whole relationship become, not least when we unexpectedly learn, late in the final book, of Aunt Petunia's frustrated longing to be a witch herself. As the series of books progresses, we also learn of the differences between Padma and Parvati Patil, who are twins, but in different houses; of the apparent difference and yet underlying similarity of Sirius and Regulus Black, who are both prepared, in the end, to die for what they think is right; and of the very different attitudes and yet ultimately shared values of Percy Weasley and his siblings.

Most notably, the last book of all is structured around groups of very different siblings. It is this underlying logic which helps explain the otherwise odd-seeming structure of this last book, because at the same time as we feel we should be pushing full speed ahead to reach the end of the story and finally discover what will happen to Harry, Ron, and Hermione, we find the forward thrust of the narrative repeatedly delayed by an impulse to delve back into the past. Harry would sooner know about Dumbledore's long dead sister and mother than find another Horcrux, and at a crucial moment of the final battle he chooses not to join in the action, but instead to view Snape's memories.

Indeed we learn notably more about the past histories of characters in this final book than about their future lives: despite all the emphasis in previous books on what Harry, Ron, and Hermione might do when they grow up, we never do find out, but we do learn of the early friendship between Snape and Lily, that Sirius gave Harry his first broomstick, and that Mrs Weasley's entirely unexpected talent for dueling aligns her with the two heroic members of the original Order of the Phoenix, Gideon and Fabian Prewett, whom we only now learn to have been her brothers. And in fact these are not distractions, for although there may initially seem to be a tension between these excursions into the past and our wish for knowledge of the characters' futures, the two turn out to be fundamentally linked, because what all these narratives of the past work to reveal is that family is not destiny. The Grey Lady might have been Rowena Ravenclaw's daughter, but she all too clearly inherited none of her mother's wisdom; Aunt Petunia might have been Lily's sister, but she did not share her magical powers.

Looming largest in these family portraits is the troubled group of Albus, Aberforth, and Ariana Dumbledore. Although we have heard tantalizing mentions of Aberforth in previous books (and have in fact, albeit unknowingly, actually encountered him on the occasion of the formation of Dumbledore's Army), there has been no previous hint of the existence of Ariana, and yet knowledge of her story proves crucial to finally understanding Dumbledore's own story. The three Dumbledore siblings have strikingly different lives, which in turn work to illustrate the complex relationship in Rowling's world between what was always bound to happen and what might not have done: if Ariana had not been seen and tormented by Muggles she might perhaps have grown up to reveal as much talent as Albus, and yet Aberforth's difference from his brother seems to have been as much a matter of temperament as a response to any external circumstances, and he shows no signs of equaling Albus's talent.

Sirius's three cousins, Andromeda, Bellatrix, and Narcissa offer an equally interesting set of contrasts. Bellatrix is purely evil, an obsessive follower of Voldemort who worships purity of blood; Andromeda so much resembles her physically that Harry at first thinks that she *is* Bellatrix, and yet she married a Muggle and turned her back on her family; she also tolerates, even if she does not particularly approve, the marriage of her daughter to a werewolf. The third sister, Narcissa, is different again both in appearance—she is blonde where the others are dark, she is named after a flower where the other two are named after stars or constellations—and also, ultimately, in character, because she finally puts her son before her loyalty to her cause, falsely assuring Voldemort that Harry is dead because he has given her information about Draco. Draco Malfoy is also in his own right a telling illustration of the extent to which family is not destiny. Unlike his aunt, he is no sadist; he cannot stomach the torture of the Muggle Studies teacher, and prevaricates when asked to confirm the identities of Harry, Ron, and Hermione, saving them from the possibility of Voldemort being instantly summoned to dispose of them.

The three Peverell brothers (who seem to derive their name from the Norman nobleman Payn Peveril, to whom King Arthur's domain is said to have fallen after the Conquest, and who is sometimes said to have had the Grail in his possession) also offer an object lesson in siblings making different choices, so much so indeed that their story is uncertainly positioned between being real-life historical narrative and emblematic, morally oriented fable. Were they really Ignotus, Cadmus, and Antioch Peverell, or are they personifications of three radically different values and perspectives on life—or is there, in fact, a crossover rather than a tension between these two ostensible binaries? Certainly, although their story features in what is clearly the wizarding equivalent of the Brothers Grimm, the Peverell brothers do seem to have been real since we see the grave of one of them, and the Hallows that they are said to have been given certainly do exist. Nevertheless, their story smacks so much of the logic and atmosphere of legend that it has passed into legend and has been received as such. Their very different choices—which are interestingly echoed by Harry, Ron, and Hermione when each plumps for a different preference for the best among the three Hallows—seem to be followed through in the very different histories of their descendants, since it seems clear that the brother who chose the Resurrection Stone was the ancestor of the Gaunts and hence ultimately of Voldemort, whereas the brother who chose the Cloak was the ancestor of Harry. The Peverell brothers too thus prove that family is not destiny.

Equally noteworthy is the fact that in the final book Dumbledore says to Snape, "I sometimes think we Sort too soon."[40] From the very start of the series, the distinct character of the houses, and of the fierce interhouse rivalry, have been central to the story and to Harry's experiences at school. From his first encounter with Draco Malfoy, Harry fears being in Slytherin and is dogged throughout the early books by the knowledge that the Sorting Hat considered putting him there. The Hat itself, however, becomes more and more insistent on the need for interhouse cooperation, even going so far as to wonder whether it should have refused to collaborate with the original founders' plans for subdividing the school into houses, and when in the epilogue Harry's younger son Albus voices his own fear that he might be put in Slytherin, Harry offers a spirited defence of the house that once contained all his worst enemies: "you were named for two headmasters of Hogwarts. One of them was a Slytherin and he was probably the bravest man I ever knew."[41] Both Harry's tribute to his old adversary and Dumbledore's earlier words clearly imply that the fact of being in Slytherin does not of itself simply tell us all we need to know about Snape, any more than it did about Regulus Black, Horace Slughorn, or indeed Draco Malfoy, because at least two of these, Snape and Regulus Black, showed courage worthy of a Gryffindor. Houses too, it seems, are not destiny.

The importance of the motif of individual choice is further underlined by Harry's checkered career as a student of Divination. Although Bane is angry that Firenze saves Harry in apparent contradiction of what is decreed by the planets,[42] in fact Divination is systematically discredited. It is the careerist and pompous Percy who recommends Divination to Harry on the grounds that "It's never too early to think about the future";[43] the sensible Professor McGonagall, by contrast, has no patience with the subject,[44] and even Firenze, who teaches it, effectively dismisses it.[45] When Harry and Ron invent their Divination homework, they receive top marks, and Dumbledore is not surprised that Harry should fall asleep in Divination.[46]

This sense of the importance of choice operates on an extra-diegetic level, too. Although Rowling famously had the last sentence of the final book written down and stored in an Edinburgh bank vault, she is on record as saying that she changed her mind in at least one respect, reprieving a character whom she had originally intended to kill off (my own guess would be that that character was George Weasley, but the actual identity is immaterial). Indeed the extent to which the ending of the narrative was *not* a foregone conclusion was amply illustrated by the fevered prepublication speculation about whether Harry would die: Daniel Radcliffe, the actor who plays Harry, went on record saying, "I've always had the suspicion that he might die. Harry and Voldemort have the same core. The only way Voldemort could die is if Harry dies as well."[47]

Instead of dying, however, Harry grows up. Rowling said from the outset that she wanted her characters to age realistically, and her insistence on adhering to this provides another strand of the books' emphasis on choice and avoidance of destiny because the structure is thus that of a Bildungsroman, a journey into one's own psyche, rather than that of a narrative of destiny. One strongly marked element of this is that fact that many of the tasks that Harry and his friends face involve penetrating into tunnels or otherwise forbidden and often subterranean interiors, in an obvious emblem of interiority. At the end of *Philosopher's Stone*, Harry and his friends go down a tunnel, at the end of *Chamber of Secrets* down a pipe, in *Prisoner of Azkaban* down two secret passages, and in *Goblet of Fire* into the lake. It is not surprising that in *Goblet* Fleur guesses (albeit wrongly) that the last task will involve underground tunnels.[48] Most telling is the fact that in the first two books Harry, on each occasion, finds out something about himself and something about Voldemort, underlining the extent to which the motif is bound up with the idea of self-discovery.

For Harry, then, far more than for most heroes—and certainly more than for Tolkien's—to learn about his enemy is to learn about himself. It is consequently not surprising that, despite his closeness to Ron and Hermione, he goes to what he thinks will be his death alone, and although his parents and Sirius in some sense accompany him some of the way, even they have disappeared by the end, because as Harry has now come to understand, nothing external to himself has any control over his choices and actions. The only meaningful battle is with the self, something that has already been illustrated by the extent to which his greatest fear, the dementors, are readable as that great internal enemy, depression, from which Rowling has recently revealed that she has suffered herself.[49] This stress on the importance of self-discovery is further underlined by the repetition of the name "Harry Potter" in the titles of all seven books: the books are, in a sense, exploring aspects of Harry's personality and the influences and history that have helped shape it almost as much as they are telling the story of the battle against Voldemort, for the two prove to be intimately interwoven.

And this, ultimately, is their most Arthurian aspect. Rowling's books are not, like the Arthur myth, a collective epic narrative of nation formation, and still less do they offer the inevitable working-out of an already ordained destiny; nor are they even narratives of heroic knightly adventure, despite the occasional gesture in that direction such as Ron's becoming a knight in the chess match which closes *Harry Potter and the Philosopher's Stone* or the mention of chivalry as a Gryffindor characteristic. Rather they share a less obvious but no less important quality of Arthurian legend, which is the extent to which success in a quest, despite all the trappings of external adventure, depends ultimately on internal qualities: only the one most worthy of it will find the Grail, just as Sir Gawain can be wounded by the Green Knight only in the same measure that he himself has transgressed against him. King Arthur may be a figure of destiny, but for his knights, it is personal choices which count above all, and that, I think, is why Rowling simultaneously evokes the Arthurian myth but is careful to detach it from Harry himself, for he too is an illustration of the importance of personal choice.

## NOTES

With thanks to Sam Hopkins and Matt Steggle for their very helpful observations.

1. J.K. Rowling, *Harry Potter and the Deathly Hallows* (New York: Scholastic, 2007), 366. All further quotations will be taken from the same edition.

2. See for instance the popular retelling by Roger Lancelyn Green, *King Arthur and His Knights of the Round Table* (Harmondsworth: Penguin, 1953), 52–53. This book was regularly reprinted throughout Rowling's childhood and she might well have known it.

3. Rowling, *Hallows*, 367.

4. William Shakespeare, *King Lear*, edited by Kenneth Muir (London: Routledge, 1972), III.ii.91 and 95.

5. Rowling, *Hallows*, 720.

6. Sir Thomas Malory, *Le Morte d'Arthur*, 2 vols. (Harmondsworth: Penguin, 1969), Vol I, 112.

7. See Geoffrey Ashe, *King Arthur's Avalon* [1957] (London: Book Club Associates, 1974), 156.

8. See http://www.mugglenet.com/books/name_origins.shtml.

9. Ashe, *King Arthur's Avalon*, 52.

10. Notably, we discover in the last few pages of *Deathly Hallows* that Draco's son is named Scorpius, also a constellation.

11. See http://www.regulusastro.com/regulus.html.

12. Created by J.K. Rowling for the International Book Aid Charity Auction in 2006 and reproduced at http://www.hp-lexicon.org/wizards/blackfamilytree.html.

13. Rowling, *Hallows*, 186.

14. J.K. Rowling, *Harry Potter and the Order of the Phoenix* (New York: Scholastic, 2003), 302.

15. Rowling, *Hallows*, 446–48.

16. J.K. Rowling, *Harry Potter and the Half-Blood Prince* (New York: Scholastic, 2005), 558–60, 561, and 505–06.

17. Rowling, *Phoenix*, 453.

18. The name of Dr. Cornelius may conceivably have influenced that of Cornelius Fudge.

19. Michael Ward, *Planet Narnia* (Oxford: Oxford University Press, 2008). It is also worth remembering the importance of planets in the *Out of the Silent Planet* sequence.

20. Rowling, *Phoenix*, 603.

21. Rowling, *Hallows*, 372–73.

22. Ibid., 145.

23. J.K. Rowling, *Harry Potter and the Goblet of Fire* (New York: Scholastic, 2000), 201.

24. Rowling, *Prince*, 266.

25. Rowling, *Phoenix*, 246.

26. Rowling, *Goblet*, 628–29.

27. Ibid., 690.

28. Ibid., 638.

29. William Shakespeare, *A Midsummer Night's Dream*, edited by Harold F. Brooks (London: Methuen, 1979), II.ii.20.

30. Rowling, *Goblet*, 665–67.

31. Stuart Hill, *Blade of Fire* (Frome: The Chicken House, 2006), 329 and 450.

32. Alan Garner, *The Weirdstone of Brisingamen* [1960] (London: Lions, 1971), 82, 194, 72, and 83.

33. Alan Garner, *The Moon of Gomrath* (London: William Collins, 1963), 72, 153, and 118.

34. Bram Stoker, *Dracula*, edited by A. N. Wilson (Oxford: Oxford University Press, 1983), 282, 296, 378, and 316.

35. Rowling, *Prince*, 345.

36. J.K. Rowling, *Harry Potter and the Chamber of Secrets* (New York: Scholastic, 1998), 333.

37. Rowling, *Prince*, 509. For further discussion of the prophecy, see Patricia Donaher and James Okapal's chapter in this volume.

38. Rowling, *Phoenix*, 842.

39. Rowling, *Prince*, 512.

40. Rowling, *Hallows*, 680.

41. Ibid., 758.

42. J.K. Rowling, *Harry Potter and the Sorcerer's Stone* (New York: Scholastic, 1997), 257.

43. Rowling, *Chamber*, 252.

44. J.K. Rowling, *Harry Potter and the Prisoner of Azkaban* (New York: Scholastic, 1999), 109.

45. Rowling, *Phoenix*, 603.
46. Rowling, *Goblet*, 233 and 599.
47. http://news.bbc.co.uk/cbbcnews/hi/tv_film/newsid_3755000/3755513.stm.
48. Rowling, *Goblet*, 550.
49. *The Daily Telegraph*, 24 March 2008, 2.

# 6

# The Good, the Bad, and the Ugly:
## Lies in Harry Potter

*Chantel M. Lavoie*

J.K. Rowling's orphan hero spends a decade living a lie—from the age of one to eleven—fittingly mirrored by his spending much of that time in a closet under the stairs. This lie is the story told to him that his parents' death and his own lightning bolt scar resulted from a car crash, a story that in turn denies what and who he is: an extraordinary wizard. This lie about a murder is the first of many falsehoods on which Rowling's battle between good and evil is predicated, yet lies themselves are variously good, bad, and ugly in this series—some prove hurdles to the child Harry, others have him hurtling toward manhood. There are impostures, the Imperius Curse that traps the bewitched in falsehood, political propaganda, and malicious lies leading to suffering and to death. On several occasions Harry shouts "That's a lie"—chiefly in defense of his parents' memory—as well as "It is NOT a lie" to the sadistic Professor Umbridge, when she tells her class that Lord Voldemort, the darkest wizard in 1,000 years, has *not* risen again.[1] The punishment set for Harry by Umbridge is to carve into his own hand the indelible lesson: "I must not tell lies."[2] He bravely defies the spirit of this professor's rule, while following it to the letter by making public unwanted truths.

Yet lie Harry does: lies of the schoolboy code told to teachers and enemies in other houses, white lies told to friends, countless lies of omission, some foolish and even self-defeating. Lying—a vehicle for evil, is by no means *de facto* evil in the Harry Potter books, and some of the most important lies in the series are demonstrably reasonable and moral responses to unreason and evil. Truth may be absolute in Rowling's magical world, but it is also, as headmaster Albus Dumbledore tells Harry, "a beautiful and terrible thing, and should therefore be treated with great caution."[3] Which truth? How much truth? Who might be hurt by it? By the conclusion of book VII, Dumbledore's already complicated statement about truth, beauty, and terror is exploded further as the headmaster's own troubled past comes to light. Like some potions—brewed to embody a lie or to reveal one—lies have a place, and are represented as needing to be used in moderation in Rowling's magical world. The same holds true, by implication, in our own, muddled, Muggle world.

From the outset Rowling has made it clear that there is real evil, and real consequences to evil, in her books, and the conclusion of the series, set for the most part in a state of wizard fascism, follows through on her promise. Gradually, the lies that litter Harry's past move into the present, indeed to the very center, of Harry's world, such that in the regime we encounter in *The Deathly Hallows* two plus two equals five, and the all-seeing magical eye wrenched from a fallen warrior is now put to insidious use at the Ministry of Magic. At Hogwarts, the code that one can lie to one's teachers but not to one's mates is mostly realized, and guilt does not often accompany rule-breaking unless such transgressions actually hurt another (good) person or disappoint an adult whom Harry respects, such as gamekeeper, Rubeus Hagrid, or teacher Remus Lupin. And it certainly seems understandable, even forgivable, that the Weasley children regularly lie to their mother—matter-of-fact, what-can-we-get-away-with lies told by the enterprising and mischief-making twins, Fred and George (and the Marauder's Map fittingly passes through their hands on its trajectory from father—James Potter—to son, Harry). Harry's best mate, Ron Weasley, regularly lies, as well as cheats by copying Hermione's homework, and so does Harry. Ginny appears to have picked this duplicity up effortlessly, as if it is a family trait, along other lessons from her six brothers, from skill astride a broomstick to toughness in the face of danger. The one stickler about such things as rule-breaking is Percy Weasley, who chooses to embrace the biggest, most dangerous lie of all in his sycophantic role at the Ministry of Magic—again, that Voldemort, father of lies, has not returned.

Lies tear families apart, yet lying is a skill, like any other that can be put to the service of good or ill. When the false Professor Moody dismantles his Dark detectors at Hogwarts, the prevalence of lying of all types is underscored: "no use here [for the detectors], of course, too much interference—students in every direction lying about why they haven't done their homework.... I had to disable my Sneakoscope because it wouldn't stop whistling. It's extra sensitive...."[4] A lie well told is presented by Rowling as an aesthetic accomplishment, and therein lies another shade of gray. When given a glimpse into the young Tom Riddle's careful smooth-talking of a professor fifty years before, we learn this: "It was very well done, thought Harry, the hesitancy, the casual tone, the careful flattery, none of it overdone. He, Harry, had had too much experience of trying to wheedle information out of reluctant people not to recognize a master at work."[5]

Important to note is that Hermione Granger, who rarely lies, is not inherently good at it. Nor has she had enough practice to master the skill, which the novels establish that, like flying, is a talent that doesn't come from books. Hermione fails to convince Mr. Borgin, the proprietor of a shop for dark objects, in her sidling questions to ascertain what Lucius Malfoy has bought, and Ron is dismissive of her attempts at duplicity: "Worth a try, but you were a bit obvious."[6] Clearly, she is not aligned with the manipulative, silver-tongued Riddle, but, although she is very like Percy in her strict adherence to most rules, she—a heroic character—sees that lies can be valuable. The lifetime bond between Hermione and Harry and Ron begins with her lie to protect them from punishment when they attack the troll: "I went looking for the troll." Harry's mental reaction—"Hermione Granger, telling a downright lie to a teacher?"[7]—shows that she has her priorities "straight." Most significantly, Hermione is able to lie, and keep lying, even under torture in the final book, to which Harry's praise testifies: "You were amazing—coming up with that story when she was hurting you like that."[8] Rowling's life-changing experiences working for Amnesty International come strongly to the fore here, as they have, increasingly, informed the novels; people suffer and die for the truth—to reveal it and to suppress it—every day.

The dark spells and incantations that Hogwarts students learn to combat are predicated upon ugly lies. As David and Catherine Deavel note, both

boggarts and dementors make use of deceit to paralyze their victims. Boggarts take on false forms to confuse and overwhelm opponents through fear, and dementors take away not only happiness and peace, but hope—the virtue that allows one to be open to peace and happiness in the future. This offense against hope is essentially an offense against truth. Whether Harry's happy thoughts and feelings have been sucked away or not, it is simply not true that Harry's past and present life have not contained the happiness and peace which are the results of love that Harry has been given and has given to others.[9]

The way to fight such deceit is with truth—the *Ridikulous* spell, which reveals that the boggart's form is not more substantial than any other, and the Patronus, which is conjured up by recalling a forceful, good memory—a "truth" from the past. Additionally, among the Unforgivable Curses, the Imperius Curse is important because, although it traps the bewitched in a lie, it is also the one that some wizards, such as Harry Potter, *can* fight off. Succumbing to a lie, therefore, is often an indicator of weakness; deflecting or detecting one reveals strength. In *Half-Blood Prince*, we learn that in order to conceal a shameful moment in his own past, Professor Slughorn lied to Dumbledore by tampering with his own memory. Slughorn is weak and requires liquid courage—alcohol— whereas Harry needs liquid luck—Felix Felicis—to bring the truth into the light.[10]

In embracing the dark, others freely choose to live harmful lies—Professor Quirrell in book I, who has allowed Voldemort into his heart and—quite literally—his mind, conceals this with a turban; the Death Eaters, who cover their faces with masks when meeting and perpetrating crimes. Most notable is Lucius Malfoy, a favorite of the Dark Lord. Voldemort says of Malfoy that he "present[s] a respectable face."[11] Respectability and money also mask the darkness within for many of Voldemort's followers. The name Death Eaters suggests the swallowing of darkness, of lies—chiefly in order to preserve their parasitic leader.[12] Rowling makes plain the argument that nonresistance, too, perpetuates violence. When countless "good" wizards refuse to believe that Voldemort has returned, they become in some sense Death Eaters themselves; they swallow a lie that hearkens back to and foretells death. You are what you eat.

And, with their morning toast and kippers, readers of the *Daily Prophet* are fed lies at different points in the series as well. The biases of this mainstream wizarding newspaper are significant. Whereas the name "The Daily Prophet" emphasizes truth (as well as the ever-questionable foretelling of the future) it also serves as a homonym for "profit." Money talks in the Harry Potter books, and in doing so, money frequently inspires lies. An irritated reporter Rita Skeeter tells Hermione "*The Prophet* exists to sell itself, you silly girl."[13] What sells is sensationalism, hyperbole, reassurance (when the truth is too objectionable) and downright falsehood. Harry's childhood spent in a closet is re-enacted in the scene where Skeeter takes him into a broom cupboard for her interview upon his becoming Triwizard champion; as her acid green Quick Quill flourishes across the page, we know no truth can come from her reportage. She also keeps referring to him as a twelve-year-old, although he is fourteen—a cramped and regressive lie, as well as sensationalistic. Skeeter spies on people ("bugs" them) in order to obtain juicy gossip and has no compunction about reproducing *or* producing lies.

Like this unscrupulous journalist, the spy is another kind of expert, professional liar, key to the plot of each novel and series as a whole. At the beginning of *Goblet of Fire*, the old Muggle Frank Bryce overhears Voldemort and Wormtail mention "Ministry of Magic," "wizards," and "Muggles," and he "could think of only two sorts of people who would speak in code: spies and criminals."[14] Although he is wrong about the code, he is right about the nature of the speakers: they are spies as well as criminals. Near the end of the same book, Harry must answer a riddle in a maze, posed by a Sphinx. It is an image of layers of confusion, and the first couplet leads to the word "spy":

> First think of a person who lives in disguise,
> Who deals in secret and tells naught but lies.[15]

This spy, although Harry does not yet know it, describes the person who has been responsible for Harry's place in this deadly maze—the false Mad-Eye Moody, a disguised Bartemius Crouch, Junior, spy for Voldemort.

The rest of the riddle gives clues that, when the answers—"spy," "d," and "er"—are strung together spell "spider," an animal that makes an appearance in each book in this series about webs of lies. In book I, when Harry keeps asking his uncle about the mysterious letters addressed to him, Vernon Dursley lies that they were "addressed to you by mistake." Harry's confrontation results in Vernon yelling, "SILENCE," at which point "a couple of spiders fell from the ceiling."[16] Spiders, Ron's worst fear, turn up elsewhere: small ones scuttle out of the castle to flee the basilisk, and huge and hairy maneaters reside in the Forbidden Forest. Harry thinks of Professor Slughorn, the name-dropping professor whose pride is his influence on generations of students, as "a great swollen spider, spinning a web around it, twitching a thread here and there to bring its large and juicy flies a little closer."[17]

Professor Quirrell, Rita Skeeter, Barty Crouch Junior—these more or less serious players in the spy game are caught and fittingly punished. But the arch-spy in the series is Severus Snape. The most complicated character is also the most complicated liar, and his own power to deceive and avoid detection, as is confirmed in *Deathly Hallows*, is remarkable. As a double agent, Snape lives lies within lies for seventeen years, risking everything for good as he once did for evil as a Death Eater. Working for Dumbledore, Snape must tell ethically sound lies; however, his lies to Harry and other students he doesn't like are also ugly. He tells Harry cruel part–truths about his father in order to wound him— that the sins of the father may be visited upon the son. Harry, unknowingly, automatically, accuses him of lying. They are both wrong. As it turns out, James Potter *was* an arrogant, often foolish, and even cruel teenager; but he *was* a teenager—one who changed into a responsible adult, a theme repeated when we learn Dumbledore's story in the final book. It is from Potions Master Snape that Harry learns about Polyjuice Potion—a concoction to incarnate a lie, to turn the self into a lie. He and his friends use it for good in *Chamber of Secrets* and *Deathly Hallows*, whereas it is used for evil by the younger Barty Crouch in *Goblet of Fire*. Outside of class, in an outrageous threat, Harry learns from Snape about Veritaserum—the most powerful truth potion known to humankind; Veritaserum reappears in order to wrench the truth from Barty in *Goblet of Fire* but also in *Phoenix* when Umbridge attempts to learn the whereabouts of Dumbledore and Sirius Black from Harry.

In *Half-Blood Prince*, Snape makes an unbreakable vow to Narcissa Malfoy, which results in Dumbledore's death. In this instance Snape *cannot* tell a lie; to do so would mean his own death. We learn that he would prefer this to the difficult task he must perform, but he must remain true to his word for the greater good, and to an earlier vow to Dumbledore himself. He lies to many people, and lies constantly once Voldemort returns to power, yet he breaks neither one of his major promises.

In contrast to Snape, the most deceptively simple character at the beginning of the series is Neville Longbottom, who in one way begins living a lie just as Harry steps out of the shadow of another. Neville enters Hogwarts when Harry does. Whereas everyone knows Harry's story, and the fact that he was brought up by Muggles because his parents were killed by Lord Voldemort, almost no one appears to know that Neville was raised by his grandmother because his own parents were tortured to the point of insanity by Voldemort's followers; as a result, as Harry learns in book IV, Mr. and Mrs. Longbottom do not recognize their own son. Because of evil associated with swallowing lies, Harry's parents have stepped out of time: Neville's, out of truth.

Neville's lack of magical talent, his clumsiness, and poor memory make him little more than a joke in the first few books. Interestingly, we do not see him lie in the series. Neville's bravest moments, however—defying a corrupt regime at Hogwarts and his destruction of Voldemort's last Horcrux with Godric Gryffindor's sword—confirm his rightful place among the courageous students of Gryffindor House. The Horcrux Neville destroys, Voldemort's snake Nagini, represents a living lie: not only does she keep murdering—causing/eating death—but the image of the snake evokes Judeo-Christian iconography and the deceitful serpent in the Garden of Eden. Correspondingly, Voldemort's eyes have become snake-like slits, not only because of his relationship with Nagini, his ability to speak Parseltongue, and his inheritance from Salazar Slytherin, but because the eyes are windows to the soul, and Voldemort has severed his soul into parts.

Harry is told repeatedly that he has his mother's eyes, and it is to this that Dumbledore calls Snape's attention to awaken the Potions master's conscience, and love: "Her son lives. He has her eyes, precisely her eyes. You remember the shape and color of Lily Evans' eyes, I am sure?"[18] The revelation of this lifelong love follows upon Harry's witnessing of Snape's death, hearing Snape's last words, and fulfilling a dying wish: "'Look . . . at . . . me . . . ' The green eyes found the black, but after a second something in the depths of the dark pair seemed to vanish, leaving them fixed, blank and empty."[19] What leaves them is the soul. This moment, with its meeting of Snape's soul and that of Lily Evans, looking out through Harry's eyes, is the beginning of the revelation of a crucial truth, which Harry has yet to discover in the Pensieve. The truth does set Harry free, yet it is a freedom that Voldemort would not see as such: the freedom to choose death.

Voldemort himself is particularly skilled at detecting falsehood, being a master of it. He says this to Frank Bryce, who *is* frank, yet tries to get away with inventing a wife who will call the police if he does not return from his encounter with Voldemort. The precise wording of this exchange is worth noting:

"Do not lie to Lord Voldemort, Muggle, for he knows . . . he always knows . . . "

"Is that right?" said Frank roughly. "Lord, is it? Well, I don't think much of your manners, *My Lord*."[20]

Contrast this with the exchange between the Death Eaters and Professor Albus Dumbledore, minutes before his own inevitable death, in *Half-Blood Prince*:

"Good evening, Amycus," said Dumbledore calmly, as though welcoming the man to a tea party. "And you've brought Alecto too . . . Charming . . . "

The woman gave an angry little titter. "Think your little jokes'll help you on your deathbed, then?" she jeered.

"Jokes? No, no these are manners," replied Dumbledore.[21]

What they are, too, are a part of a lie. And the nature of it—either as joke or as manners—highlights Dumbledore's superiority, his control of self despite having lost control of the situation. He is preparing for what he once described to Harry: "to the well organized mind, death is but the next great adventure."[22] Dumbledore's death, like his life, represents sacrifice for the sake of others, and he has repeatedly asserted that there are worse things than death. As Lana A. Whited and M. Katherine Grimes note in "What would Harry Do," "Rowling has made clear . . . that immortality [Voldemort's goal to conquer death] is to be subverted to higher principles" with the destruction of the Philosopher's Stone and Nicholas Flamel's sacrifice of life.[23] The life-giving properties of this kind of sacrifice, this kind of love—to lay down one's life for one's friends—comes to its fullest realization in Harry's own acceptance of death. He follows his many mentors in taking this step, and meets Dumbledore in the space in-between life and death, which also is one of both obscurity and revelation.

As a model up to the point of his death, Dumbledore accords truth the dignity which giver and recipient deserve. He tells outright lies to the Ministry when necessary, for instance, and every lie he tells seems to be a good one—that is, necessary for the greater good. Prior to book VII, the headmaster does encourage lies, as when Harry is caught escaping the meeting of the secret (and illegal) Defense Against the Dark Arts Society. Here the Minister of Magic, Cornelius Fudge, asks: "Well, Potter . . . I expect you know why you are here?"

Harry fully intended to respond with a defiant "yes": His mouth had opened and the word was half formed when he caught sight of Dumbledore's face. Dumbledore was not looking directly at Harry; his eyes were fixed on a point just over his shoulder, but as Harry stared at him, he shook his head a fraction of an inch to each side.

Harry changed direction mid-word.

"Yeh—no."

"I beg your pardon?" said Fudge.

"No," said Harry, firmly.[24]

As a response to a ministry fraught with self-deception and deception of the public, based upon personal ambition and a Dursley-like obsession with normalcy, lies are evidently right and proper. Umbridge, a spy for the Ministry, represents a real challenge to children reading these books—Rowling proposes that authority and tyranny must be questioned, resisted, and even fought. All adults do not deserve respect by mere virtue of age, just as all teenagers do not deserve whole-scale exoneration for their mistakes because they are young.

Largely because of Dumbledore's circumspection, Harry labors under, and suffers because of, a number of half-truths, the other halves of which are revealed from book to book. One of the frustrations of the boy's ongoing trial (and a source of suspense for the reader) is how often a fuller comprehension of the truth might have benefited him—facts and educated guesses that Dumbledore does not share with him, or tells him too late: for example, why Voldemort killed his parents, or why he might lure Harry to the Department of Mysteries in *Order of the Phoenix*. "I cared about you too much. . . . I acted exactly as Voldemort expects we fools who love to act. . . . What did I care if numbers of nameless and faceless people and creatures were slaughtered in the vague future, if in the here and now you were alive, and well, and happy?"[25]

Surely, and clearly, love is better than its absence. Although Voldemort, like Dumbledore, also lies, his belief system is so different from the headmaster's that he does not *think* he is lying when he disputes the latter's repeated assertion that "there are things worse than death." Love has power greater than destruction, Rowling tells us, again and again. It is the old conflict between Eros and Thanatos—love and death. Each has its own room in the Department of Mysteries. What Voldemort does not accept is that death is not separate from, but part of life, and in *The Deathly Hallows* much attention is afforded to the universal resistance to this very mystery. The most important truth cannot be comprehended while we live, and we are all subject to this absence of information. Voldemort despises his given name—the first because "a lot of people are called Tom," and the last, Riddle, because it came from his "filthy Muggle father"—because he rejects all things common, including death, the great leveler, and thinks magic can prevent it. He does not merely commit and spread lies; he deceives himself. This is his great weakness, why he could not kill the infant Harry, and this is how Harry finally kills him: by giving up his life for his friends and embracing the truth about death.

The terrifying scene near the end of *Goblet of Fire*, when Voldemort rises again, echoes every mythic battle between good and evil—it is a reincarnation, paid for with the bone, flesh and blood of others—a parody in which a Satan-figure inverts Christ's sacrifice. However, while Rowling's work has been compared to C.S. Lewis's Narnia chronicles, *Harry Potter* is not as straightforward an allegory of Christianity, and the opportunity to join forces with evil here is not as tempting as the Turkish Delight in *The Lion, The Witch and the Wardrobe*. In Lewis's world of children called into magic and battle, *every* lie is wrong. Not so in the wizarding world. Rowling almost never uses the words child or children; her books are more about growing up than most series, and Rowling's maturity imperative grows with Harry; he must "fight like a man" and finally die like one.

A life worth living, and a good death, are both predicated on free will in Rowling's work. Free will is also the grounding of Immanuel Kant's Categorical Imperative, which has provoked one of the most debated responses to the act of lying in philosophical history. Kant's advice: "Act only according to that maxim where you can at the same time will that it should become a universal law."[26] Being a moral agent, then, means guiding one's conduct by universal laws—moral rules that hold, without exception, in all circumstances. We could not *will* that it be a universal law that we should lie, because it would be self-defeating; people could not trust or depend on one another. Kant proposed an extreme example: the case of the inquiring murderer, where the moral dilemma is whether to answer truthfully to a murderer who asks where his intended victim has gone—when that intended victim has fled past you and told you he is going home to hide. Kant's argument—in brief—is that even in such a case, "[t]o be absolutely truthful (honest) in all deliberations . . . is a sacred and absolutely commanding degree of reason, limited by no expediency."

Naturally, many philosophers have suggested expediencies that should limit absolute truthfulness. In Rowling's work, Kantian absoluteness is also rejected, and absolution certain for those who lie to the inquiring murderer. Although Rowling does not suggest that truth is relative, Kant's Categorical Imperative—and the case of the inquiring murderer most specifically—is a key component to Rowling's depiction of good and evil. Voldemort is the inquiring murderer, and Peter Pettigrew (a.k.a. Wormtail), the sniveling coward who quite literally "rats" on his best friends—Harry's parents—is arguably the most *despicable* character in the books. He told the truth to save his own life, but mostly to curry favor as a spy to that murderer. To this same inquiring murderer, Severus Snape also gave truthful information leading to the Potters' deaths. He did not intend that Voldemort cause the death of his beloved Lily (Evans) Potter, but the truth killed her just the same. Furthermore, the important spell of "the secret keeper" seems very much a direct response to Kant; this person is required to occlude the truth to protect the innocent who are in hiding from Voldemort—Harry's parents in Godric's Hollow, and the brave wizards in the Order of the Phoenix at Grimmauld Place. In book III, Sirius and Lupin tell Peter Pettigrew he should have died instead of betraying his friends. Had Pettigrew lied to Voldemort, he probably would have died; the narrative proposes that he should have done both. These are not easy requirements. Yet the importance—indeed, the imperative—to lie in the Harry Potter books seems itself a response to the extent to which Voldemort lays waste to the ethics behind Kant's second formulation of the Imperative: "Act in such a way that you treat humanity, whether in your own person or in the person of any other, always at the same time as an end and never merely as a means to an end."[27] Every human, and humanity itself, are means to an end in Voldemort's tyranny.

Any lie is a gamble, because things might come out wrong despite the best intentions, and this does happen in Harry Potter. But there are, Rowling argues forcefully, morally good lies. Like Polyjuice Potion and Veritaserum, the ability to lie can be used for good or for evil. Similarly, Pareseltongue—snake language—is assumed by most in the wizarding world to be intrinsically evil because Lord Voldemort and Salazar Slytherin—and not many other wizards

in history—can speak it, but so can Harry and he has used it to liberate—first a
snake, then Hufflepuff student Justin Finch-Fletchley, then Ginny Weasley.[28]
The inquiring murderer, the inquiring torturer, and the inquiring spy should
be lied to, because goodness and truth must at times fight fire with fire. Harry
Potter must, after all, reach the understanding that Severus Snape imparts:
"The Dark Arts . . . are many, varied, ever-changing and eternal."[29] Responses
to such arts must also be protean. Voldemort—née Tom Riddle—is a riddle
because all mass murderers are. Ultimately, solving such a riddle is not as
important as stopping it. And so he dies with "a mundane finality . . . the snake-
like face vacant and unknowing."[30] And as Riddle's name suggests, lies are not
black and white in these books, but puzzling and complicated. Necessary evils,
perhaps, but not necessarily evil.

## NOTES

1. J.K. Rowling, *Harry Potter and the Order of the Phoenix* (New York: Scholastic,
2003), 245.

2. Ibid., 266.

3. J.K. Rowling, *Harry Potter and the Sorcerer's Stone* (New York: Scholastic, 1997),
298.

4. J.K. Rowling, *Harry Potter and The Goblet of Fire* (New York: Scholastic 2000),
300.

5. J.K. Rowling, *Harry Potter and the Half-Blood Prince* (New York: Scholastic
2005), 497.

6. Rowling, *Prince*, 127.

7. Rowling, *Stone*, 127–28.

8. J.K. Rowling, *Harry Potter and the Deathly Hallows* (New York: Scholastic,
2007), 485.

9. David and Catherine Deavel, "A Skewed Reflection: The Nature of Evil." *Harry
Potter and Philosophy: If Aristotle Ran Hogwarts.* Ed. David Baggett, Shawn Kein and
William Irwin (Chicago: Open Court, 2004): 132–147, 139–40.

10. Rowling, *Prince*, 469–91.

11. Rowling, *Goblet*, 650.

12. Horrible as they are, the Death Eaters are eerily childish with Voldemort, abasing
themselves for his favor, choosing him before their own families. All those who embrace
falsehood in these books evidence some form of arrested development—the solipsistic
Dursleys, Wormtail, Fudge, Voldemort—each is driven by fear of the dark; yet in some
sense they swallow and regurgitate lies—they eat death—so as not to face it. Bellatrix
Lestrange is somewhat exceptional in that she is a kind of sexualized pet in relation to
Voldemort. She is no less a case of arrested development, however, than he is in his
problematized father-son relationship with other Death Eaters.

13. Rowling, *Phoenix*, 567.

14. Rowling, *Goblet*, 8.

15. Ibid., 629.

16. Rowling, *Stone*, 37.

17. Rowling, *Prince*, 75.

18. Rowling, *Hallows*, 678.

19. Ibid., 658.

20. Rowling, *Goblet* 14.

21. Rowling, *Prince*, 593.

22. Rowling, *Stone*, 297.

23. Lana A. Whited and M. Katherine Grimes, "What Would Harry Do? J.K. Rowling and Lawrence Kohlberg's Theories of Moral Development," in *The Ivory Tower and Harry Potter: Perspectives on a Literary Phenomenon*. Ed. Lana A. Whited (Columbia: University of Missouri Press, 2002): 182–208.

24. Rowling, *Phoenix*, 610–11.

25. Ibid., 838–9.

26. Immanuel Kant, *Grounding for the Metaphysics of Morals; with, on a supposed right to lie because of philanthropic concerns* [1785]. Trans. James W. Ellington, 3rd ed. (Hackett 1993), 30.

27. Kant, 30.

28. And at least two of the Horcruxes are dealt with by using Parseltongue as well.

29. Rowling, *Prince*, 177.

30. Rowling, *Hallows*, 744.

# II

## The Politics of Harry Potter: Issues of Gender, Race, and Class

# 7

# Happily Ever After: Harry Potter and the Quest for the Domestic

*Ximena Gallardo C. and C. Jason Smith*

It is our choices, Harry, that show what we truly are, far more than our abilities.

—Albus Dumbledore

In our *Reading Harry Potter* chapter "Cinderfella: J.K. Rowling's Wily Web of Gender," we examined the depiction of gender in the first four books of the *Harry Potter* series and concluded that, despite its rather stereotypical portrayal of female and male characters, the series challenged standard constructions of gender and gender roles in significant ways. First, the cyclical portrayal of Harry Potter as passive subject at home and active subject at Hogwarts School of Witchcraft and Wizardry closely aligns Harry with the female protagonists of many fairy tales, particularly stories of the Cinderella archetype. Second, Harry must constantly decide between what we deemed "masculine" and "feminine" choices, typically espoused or embodied by his best friends Ron, as the masculine principle, and Hermione, as the feminine principle. Whenever Harry chooses the "feminine" side of the binary, he is rewarded.[1] Third, the series' obsession with understanding "otherness" (represented by witches, giants, Muggles, house-elves, etc.) opens the narrative structures to a critique of binaries, including the most essential: sex/gender difference. We concluded that while the first four books of the series do not support strong feminist readings, overall they are progressive as children's literature and, therefore, have ample material to support feminist positions and provide positive role models for young readers.

As we began reading the books following *Goblet of Fire*, however, we started to believe that our initial assessment of Harry's identification with the feminine would be undermined in the aggregate. The narrative seems to connect Harry more and more to his father, James Potter, and Harry's hetero-masculinity is underscored by his second, this time very serious, attraction to a girl, Ginny Weasley.[2] Furthermore, the recursive Cinderella narrative structure of "home to school to home" we had identified in "Cinderfella" is dismantled when Harry leaves his abusive stepfamily for good, drops out of Hogwarts, and goes forth with his trusted friends on a typical hero quest to destroy Voldemort's Horcruxes.[3] Once we finished the series with *Deathly Hallows*, however, we realized that our original arguments from "Cinderfella" still applied, regardless of the surface changes in the narrative. In terms of gender, the issue is not whether Harry is radically different from the myriad heroes, male and female, who have come before, but whether the series as a whole challenges in any meaningful way what it *means* to be identified as male or female, masculine or feminine. We shall argue that Rowling's creation actively troubles the culturally defined binaries that divide us all. So, we begin our final look at gender in the Harry Potter series by examining three of the witches who transgress gender expectations and cause a little trouble themselves.

## WITCHES JUST WANT TO HAVE FUN

The first section of "Cinderfella," significantly entitled "Girls Just Aren't Any Fun," argued that the *Harry Potter* series was not particularly progressive in its gender representations, partly because it reinforced traditional categories of labor by presenting the female characters primarily as wives, mothers, and "spinster" teachers, and partly because it portrayed women as generally emotional, irrational, and gossipy. In all, we felt the surface message of these books was "men are interesting, women are good."[4] The final three books of the series see this good wife and good mother tradition continue, most notoriously in the image of a domesticated Fleur Delacour, who is transformed from a Triwizard Tournament competitor and dangerously captivating beauty to Bill Weasley's doting wife and homemaker. However, shortly after we worried in "Cinderfella" that the female characters were limited in both number and scope, Rowling introduced three powerful females in *Order of the Phoenix*: the punky Auror Nymphadora Tonks, Minister Fudge's toady Undersecretary Dolores Umbridge, and Lord Voldemort's mad lieutenant Bellatrix Lestrange, each of whom challenges traditional notions of femininity as displayed in the previous four volumes.[5]

Nymphadora Tonks is anything but conventional. A progeny of the ancient pureblood Black family, Tonks is a hip, spirited young Auror whose punkish hair and "Weird Sisters" T-shirt invoke counterculture movements such as Punk, Goth, and, more recently, Emo as well as the erotic postfeminist "Suicide Girls" subculture. Each of these styles combine hyperbolized elements of femininity and fetish such as frilly dresses, gaudy fingernail polish, and heavy makeup with overt transgressive body modifications—including radical hairstyles and colors, tattoos, and body piercings, to name a few. In each case, the overall implication is of a culturally enacted commentary on notions of "masculinity" and "femininity" ironically performed in an unusual or even unsettling way. Because her very name, Nymphadora Tonks, implies the same ironic juxtaposition as that of Tank Girl of comic-book fame (a beautiful young woman who is tough as nails),[6] we are not surprised to learn that Tonks has never been very good at household spells and gets annoyed if people call her by her girly first name.[7] Like Tank Girl, Tonks is the "sexy tomboy" of the story, a teenage boy's fantasy whose first noteworthy magical act is to change her hairstyle in front of Harry without any thought of the effect this otherwise intimate act might have on an adolescent boy.

Although there are clear parallels between Nymphadora Tonks and Fleur Delacour—exotic beauty, magical prowess, and eventual heterosexual marriages, to name a few—Tonks's function in the narrative of *Harry Potter* is quite different from that of Delacour's. Whereas Delacour's primary roles in the series are to be an object of desire for teen boys and of envy for girls, a victim in need of rescue in the Triwizard Tournament, and a loyal wife to Bill Weasley, Tonks is a forceful, opinionated, and independent woman who rolls her eyes jokingly at the lectures of the daunting Mad-Eye Moody and eventually marries a known werewolf. However, where readers might assume that a strong, rebellious female like Tonks would be portrayed as an example for female characters, and thereby for *Harry Potter's* many female readers, within the narrative Tonks primarily serves as a role model for Harry because, as an Auror, she holds the very job that Harry dreams of, yet unlike the crippled Mad-Eye Moody and the insane Longbottoms, she is young, spirited, and unconventional—a position with which Harry can easily identify regardless of gender difference. Also like Harry, one of Tonks's parents was Muggle-born and she suffers insults and persecution from pureblooded witches and wizards, including her own family, the Blacks—an ironic turn on Harry's position with the Dursleys where he is mistreated for his magical blood.

Overall, Tonks seems to embody the very notion that being different and complex is not necessarily a bad thing. She is descended from a noble family and yet is a "cop"; she is beautiful and a tad vain but also tough in battle; she is concerned and brave; she is a woman who speaks bluntly with men, and so on. In all, Tonks seems to live a constructive, happy life in juxtaposition, and this gives us hope for Harry's increasingly grim future. A radically different female than we have previously seen in Rowling's magical world, Tonks embodies a liminal position that is nonetheless powerful—like Harry, she is in between.

Tonks is at her most transgressive in her pairing with the werewolf Remus Lupin, for while she enters a conventional heterosexual marriage arrangement, she cares little for the societal intolerance she and her husband will have to face from the wizarding community; she even has a child with him, although there is a chance the child will carry his father's affliction.[8] Similarly, her death challenges expected roles: when she joins the final battle against Voldemort, we are to understand that her active role in the fighting is appropriate even though she is a new mother. In fact, the end of *Deathly Hallows* shows her, along with the underage Ginny Weasley and grandmother Augusta Longbottom, rejecting the cultural imperative that certain classes of persons—mothers, children, the elderly—must be hidden away from danger while others (usually men) fight.[9] Thus, Tonks's actions remind us that all responsible individuals are at war with phallogocentric power mongers, and that "staying at home" is simply not an option because home is ultimately no more safe than the rest of the world when faced with a tyrant, as James and Lily Potter found out. Tonks is, in her life and untimely death, a good Auror and a good mother who makes the ultimate sacrifice as both: she takes positive action to help save the world and thereby saves her son.

Despite her hip attitude, Tonks still can be read within the wife-mom pattern we outlined in "Cinderfella." In contrast, senior Undersecretary Dolores Umbridge—later the High Inquisitor and Headmistress of Hogwarts—exerts power untempered with the nurturing previously associated with Rowling's maternal females and paternal males such as Molly Weasley and Albus Dumbledore. Umbridge may come across at first as a hard-working, albeit quirky, career woman bent on suppressing news of Lord Voldemort's comeback by discrediting Harry and his advocate, Dumbledore. As her last name implies, however, she is not what she appears to be.[10]

Umbridge's most obvious pretense is her disquieting performance of femininity. Her soft, "girlish" voice, demure manners, feminine attire, and collection of plates decorated with mewling kittens are all props in her crusade for power and control. Tricked out in fluffy pink sweaters and hair bows, Umbridge mimics the ideal of the proper, ultraconservative woman who consolidates her power behind the scenes—a type epitomized in history by powerful political wives such as Nancy Reagan. What lies beneath Umbridge's performance of the feminine is an obsessive need to enforce institutional order coupled with a methodical malice when opposed. Like the castrating female villain in Ken Kesey's *One Flew Over the Cuckoo's Nest*, Big Nurse Ratched (as in "ratchet" and "wretched"), who is described as "a real veteran at adjusting things," Umbridge seems to believe that the evil she perpetrates, such as torturing students with a pen that writes with their own blood, is for the ultimate good of an orderly society.[11]

Umbridge is so malevolent that readers would have every right to expect her to be one of Voldemort's Death Eaters. Besides forcing children to write using their own blood, a short list of her underhanded villainy includes booby trapping Harry into breaking the magical law by ordering two dementors to attack him in a public space, actively keeping Hogwarts students from learning real defensive magic that might be able to save them in the event of attack, abusing the students and staff with her stifling "educational decrees" and

"Inquisitorial Squads," and, of course, attempting to use the illegal Cruciatus Curse on Harry.

Moreover, just because Umbridge does not turn out to be a proclaimed follower of Voldemort does not mean she cannot help carry on, however unwittingly, the Dark Lord's eugenics agenda. In *Deathly Hallows*, she is proud to head the Ministry of Magic's newly formed Muggle-born Registration Commission, a racist organization that "monitors" witches and wizards born of nonmagical parents.[12] The zeal that Umbridge exhibits in her new position is complicated by her own behavior concerning the purity of her lineage; we learn that the antique silver locket that she wears is not, as she well knows, from her Selwyn family ancestors (if, indeed, she has such blood ties). While the text does not reveal Umbridge's true lineage or motives, her actions clearly indicate that she believes that terms such as "pure blood" and "lineage" are convenient political fictions (again, referencing the meaning of her last name) from which she, the politically savvy *auteur*, can generate power.

The combined effect of Umbridge's genteel, moralistic mannerisms and perverse methods makes her one of the downright nastiest and creepiest adversaries of the whole series. Interestingly, her sheer excessiveness in both femininity and wickedness compel her beyond the very gender stereotypes she embodies. Thus, in his review of *Order of the Phoenix*, the master of horror Stephen King identified Umbridge with villainy beyond simple considerations of sex by comparing her to a male serial killer when he labeled her "the greatest make-believe villain to come along since Hannibal Lecter."[13] Umbridge, then, unravels the conventional gender boundaries we identified in "Cinderfella" and, since she seems to believe she is a moral person in spite of her wicked acts, she also complicates the series' heretofore binary of "good" and "evil." In all, this is one female character in *Harry Potter* who is certainly not good, though she is certainly interesting. One other such character is the female Death Eater, Bellatrix Lestrange.

Reminiscent of Shakespeare's "fiend-like" Lady Macbeth, Bellatrix Lestrange of the Black lineage focuses all her energy and talent on fulfilling Voldemort's ambition to rule over both the magical and mundane worlds. Her first name, Bellatrix, which in Latin means "female warrior," indicates the presence of phallic aggression in the female body, which again echoes the character of Lady Macbeth, who in her only soliloquy asks for "spirits" to "unsex" her and fill her with the presumably masculine "direst cruelty" so that she can help her husband commit murder without remorse.[14] Certainly, Lestrange is as bellicose and talented a warrior as her name suggests. She delights in dueling other witches and wizards and is capable of defeating even the most accomplished Aurors. During the battle at the Ministry's Department of Mysteries, she even deftly deflects one of Dumbledore's attacks.[15]

Still, what makes Lestrange particularly scary is her mad glee in inflicting pain on others. We learn, for instance, that she tortured the Aurors Alice and

Frank Longbottom by means of the Cruciatus Curse until they went insane.[16] By way of comparison, when Harry attempts the same curse on Lestrange after she has killed his godfather Sirius Black, he barely hurts her. She, in turn, mocks his righteous indignation, explaining that an Unforgivable Curse such as the Cruciatus results in injury only if the caster *enjoys* causing pain to others.[17] Interestingly, the series does not link Lestrange's delight in agony to a desire for absolute power, as in the case of Lord Voldemort, but to her insanity. Lestrange's extended stay in Azkaban Prison is partially the cause of this instability; however, the text also makes oblique references to potential inbreeding problems in the Black family. The descriptions of the Black house and the reference to the "top-down" style of the Black family tree, for example, invoke the nearly branchless tree of Edgar Allan Poe's "The Fall of the House of Usher" and thereby prefigure the congenital madness present in another ancient pureblood wizarding family, the House of Gaunt.[18] Having already been introduced to Sirius Black's recklessness and ferocity in *Prisoner of Azkaban*—his incarceration, too, led to instability—we are to read Lestrange through Black: she is the female version of Sirius, an "evil twin" of sorts. Even Harry worries about the similarities between them when he notes that Lestrange gives "the same exhilarated laugh" before dying that Black made just before Lestrange killed him.[19]

Certainly, Lestrange's pureblood fanaticism seems to have been inherited from previous generations of Blacks, best represented by the dark mother, Walburga Black, whose magical portrait hangs permanently in the hallway of Number Twelve, Grimmauld Place. From the portrait, the seemingly insane image of Mrs. Black screams vicious insults at any visitor to the house whom she deems impure—most obviously Remus Lupin, the werewolf, her grand-niece Tonks whose father is Muggle-born, and her own son, Sirius, whom she deems a blood traitor. We also learn that Mrs. Black has literally blasted relatives off of the family tree for associating with impure families—the ancient tapestry that serves as a record of the Black family has several burnt holes where relatives' names should be.[20] Mrs. Black's policing of her own bloodline is typical of the strong-willed woman who—being limited by society to the household and family affairs—becomes the overbearing mother who manifests power, and expresses that power, through control over the one thing that is truly hers: her offspring. Accordingly, Mrs. Black (or what is left of her) is represented as trapped in the house, locked inside her picture frame. As a less restricted version of her aunt, Lestrange will seek to further "prune" her family tree by killing her cousin, Sirius, and her niece, Nymphadora Tonks.

Still, the most important piece of Lestrange's depiction as a monstrous female is that she, like Umbridge, does not display the motherly feelings commonly associated with women. In *Half-Blood Prince*, for instance, her callous attitude toward the fate of her nephew Draco is purposefully contrasted to that of her sister Narcissa, who is almost out of her mind for worrying about her son. Lestrange's rebuke to her sister—"If I had sons, I would be glad to give them up to the service of the Dark Lord"—again echoes the ruthlessness of Lady Macbeth:

> I have given suck and know
> How tender 'tis to love the babe that milks me:
> I would, while it was smiling in my face,
> Have plucked my nipple from his boneless gums
> And dashed the brains out, had I so sworn as you
> Have done to this.[21]

It is fitting, then, that Lestrange's final duel is against the super-mom of the series, Molly Weasley, who gains extra strength of purpose because she is defending her youngest child, Ginny.[22] Interestingly, Molly's exclamation to Lestrange, "NOT MY DAUGHTER, YOU BITCH!" is clearly meant to reference Lt. Ellen Ripley's "Get away from her, you bitch!" from the 1986 film *Aliens*. This moment in *Aliens* has thrilled generations of moviegoers and has become iconic of the last stand between the good mother and the monstrous female.[23] Mrs. Weasley's use of the curse word "bitch," which in the Muggle world is used to demean and disempower women, marks the end of Lestrange's ascendancy. We are to understand that Lestrange does not stand a chance against Molly Weasley because the latter is fighting for more than herself: She is fighting for her children. Most importantly, Lestrange's death causes Voldemort to turn in fury on Mrs. Weasley, an act that forces Harry Potter to reveal that he is alive so that he can cast a forceful Shield Charm to protect her—his surrogate mother—from the Dark Lord's curse.[24] For, as we will see in the next section, Harry must follow and defend the good mother at all costs.

## A MOTHER'S LOVE

As Harry is reminded repeatedly, he survived Lord Voldemort's Killing Curse as an infant because his mother, Lily, sacrificed her life to save his. Thus, as we pointed out in "Cinderfella," the celebrated lightning-shaped scar on Harry's forehead serves as the outward symbol of this first clash between the masculine principle and the feminine principle,[25] and also points to Harry's inner conflict when choosing between might and right. As both the occasion and site of this conflict, Harry becomes the living embodiment of Voldemort and Lily's struggle.

As the ultimate manifestation of Tom Riddle's angst, Lord Voldemort is the extreme expression of aggressive masculinity in the series. To signal his role as the narrative's grand tempter and emasculator, Voldemort is associated with the image of the snake. As the Heir of Salazar Slytherin, whose symbol is a "serpentine" letter "S,"[26] Voldemort can talk to serpents and thus command the poisonous Basilisk in *Chamber of Secrets*. His familiar, Nagini, is a giant snake, and the sign that he uses to rally the Death Eaters is a skull with a serpent as a tongue.[27] Even his body becomes snake-like, signaling his internal phallic aggression, which is articulated in his signature spell, the lethal curse *Avada Kedavra*.

Voldemort's one fear is death, as indicated by his name, which translates from the French as "flight from death."[28] Interestingly, the series connects this fear of death with the death of his mother, the witch Merope Gaunt. During his first meeting with Dumbledore in the Muggle orphanage where he was raised, the young Riddle wonders which of his parents was magical, and concludes that it could not have been his mother because she died when, he believes, magic would have saved her.[29] Because Riddle believes being a wizard means being able to conquer death, it is easy to see, then, that he would reject his mother's illogical end and strive to be the opposite of the weak, vulnerable, feminine principles she seems to represent.

As Klaus Theweleit argues in *Male Fantasies*, a treatise on the psychology of the German Freikorpsmen who would later become Nazis, this desire to reject or purge the threat of the feminine is one of the central fantasies of the fascist. Such a man must remake his body into an armor not only to fight the messiness of the feminine outside but also to contain the messiness inside.[30] Riddle creates a similar, yet infinitely more effective, magical armor by saving portions of his soul into six magical objects called Horcruxes, which shield him from death. Thus, Riddle divests himself of that part of his being that he believes can be wounded—the feminine soul that he associates with his mother's decline and eventual death.[31]

Riddle's contemptuous rejection of the power of love can also be traced to the fear of what happened to his mother. After all, Merope's unrequited love for the Muggle Tom Riddle, Sr., an inferior being in Riddle's mind, was what caused her ruin and her death. In all, Riddle's actions indicate that he feels he must not, by any means, end up like his mother. He rejects those who gave him life as unworthy, and discards the Muggle name that ties him to his father. Both acts start him on the path as a destroyer of families. He creates a persona that will clearly set him apart as being different—especially from his biological families—better than others, and more powerful, as his adopted title, "Lord," indicates.

While Voldemort's immediate foe is Harry, and vice versa, it is Lily Potter's eternal power of love that thwarts Voldemort throughout the series. In *Sorcerer's Stone*, for example, Harry is saved from Professor Quirrell's attack because Quirrell (who is sharing his body with Voldemort) cannot stand to touch someone who has been so deeply marked by Lily's goodness.[32] In *Order of the Phoenix*, we learn that Lily's sacrifice for her son enabled Dumbledore to produce a powerful blood spell that was sealed when Lily's sister took Harry into her house as an infant. As long as Harry considers the house of a blood relative as his home, however much he detests living there, he will be protected from Voldemort's attacks.[33] As the series moves forward, Dumbledore struggles to impress Lily's lesson of love and sacrifice on Harry with increasing immediacy, as this knowledge is what will finally give Harry the ultimate advantage in his last stand with Voldemort.

As we pointed out in "Cinderfella," the structure of Harry's story is closely connected to the classic Brothers Grimm's story "Ashenputtel" (and other Cinderella tales) where the protagonist is guided and protected by her dead mother whose spirit inhabits a tree that grants the girl's wishes.[34] In an interesting twist on this classic formula, Rowling *internalizes* the feminine principle within the protagonist, and, in this case, within a *male* protagonist. Instead of inhabiting a magical tree, or, as in the Disney version, appearing as a fairy godmother,[35] Lily's love and goodness are literally inside of Harry, shining through the striking green eyes he inherited from her. The importance of Harry's green eyes is underscored throughout the series. He is repeatedly told that he physically looks just like his father, James, but that his eyes are his mother's, implying that his "soul" is his mother's.

Other characters' recollections of the green-eyed Lily illustrate her remarkable power to contain masculine aggressiveness. Her most obvious achievement is to charm the young James Potter away from the destructive impulses that he indulges in with his friend Sirius Black, such as torturing an awkward fellow student, a young Severus Snape.[36] However, her striking impact on others is illustrated most poignantly in the life of said Severus Snape. One of the mysteries of the series is why Professor Snape hates Harry so much and yet works so hard to keep him alive. Only when Harry becomes privy to his professor's memories toward the end of *Deathly Hallows* do we realize that Snape had been deeply in love with Lily since childhood.[37] His memories also show that Lily's presence in Snape's life counters his normal inclinations. As a young man, Snape speaks poorly of Muggle-borns yet desires the Muggle-born Lily intensely. He is also attracted to Dark magic, which, even after he insults Lily by calling her a "Mudblood," she warns him against.[38] Once he becomes a Death Eater, the hope of saving Lily's life drives him away from Lord Voldemort to Dumbledore. Finally, her murder and his unwitting part in it compel him to pledge to protect her newborn son and to become Dumbledore's double agent.[39] In the end, however, Snape proves to be much more than an agent of either man; when Snape is dying by Voldemort's hand, his final wish is to look into Harry's eyes to remember his saving grace, Lily, once again, proving that Snape's commitment is to *her*.[40] Thus, Snape redeems himself through Lily's memory and keeps a part of her alive by being as much of the person she might have wanted him to be.

## OF HALLOWS AND HORCRUXES

Harry is not only inhabited by his mother's goodness; he also harbors a piece of Voldemort's soul.[41] The fact that Harry is a Horcrux—a piece of information that Harry will learn and Voldemort will not—will be the base on which Voldemort's defeat is built. But *how* Harry comes to this knowledge is just as important as the fact itself. As Harry looks for Horcruxes and then, for a time, fixates on beating Voldemort to the Elder Wand, the first of the Deathly Hallows, he is not so much pursuing *things* as engaging with *competing narratives*: the first being the "closed" masculine narrative of the Deathly Hallows as related in the tale of "The Three Brothers," and the second being the unfolding "open" feminine narrative of Voldemort's Horcruxes.

Of the two tales, the Deathly Hallows are most obviously tied to an actual story, "The Tale of the Three Brothers," which Hermione reads out loud at Xenophilius Lovegood's house.[42] In the story, the said brothers incidentally cheat Death at a dangerous river crossing by using magic to make it through. Stymied, Death decides to trick the brothers back into his clutches by offering each a prize of their choosing for having "beaten" him. The oldest brother asks for a wand that "will always win duels for its master." The middle brother requests the power to "recall others from death" and receives a magical stone. The youngest, wisest brother, who does not trust Death, asks for something that will allow him to leave the river without being followed by Death and Death gives him his own Cloak of Invisibility. Predictably, the first two items backfire on their wielders, as the eldest brother is murdered in his sleep by a wizard who wants the wand, and the middle brother goes "mad with hopeless longing" after recalling his beloved from the dead; he ends up killing himself to be reunited with her. It is only the humble and wise younger brother who escapes Death with the cloak.[43]

The purpose of this kind of tale is to serve as a template to help the audience apply the lessons learned to similar instances in the future. It is, in effect, a "closed," or masculine, narrative whose conclusion is well known and foregone—as evidenced by Ron's recollection of it due to repeated telling in his youth—and whose only use beyond entertainment is its moral. The point of "The Tale of the Three Brothers," then, is to warn the audience about the folly of seeking to master Death through the aggressive, clearly phallic power represented by the Elder Wand or through the power to break the cycle of birth and death represented by the Resurrection Stone. Only by making himself inconspicuous (invisible) does the youngest brother get to live a long life without constantly fearing Death. The lesson of the tale—reject power, accept the inevitableness of death, and endeavor to have a quiet life—is what Dumbledore hopes Harry will learn in time for his battle with Voldemort, and it is why he bequeaths the storybook that contains the tale to Hermione.

In his desperation to defeat Voldemort, Harry ignores the meaning of the tale and fixates on uniting the Hallows and becoming the Master of Death. Believing himself in possession of the Cloak of Invisibility and the Resurrection Stone, he obsesses about finding the Elder Wand—the object of phallic power—before Voldemort does.[44] This obsession with gaining the wand is exactly the same mistake Voldemort makes when he seeks it, as Harry will eventually come to realize. As Dumbledore indicates, Voldemort never cared for the Hallows or the tale,[45] and therefore does not understand the narrative or the magical rules of each object. However, as Voldemort ultimately learns, to possess the thing is to enter its narrative and thus he enters the masculine "closed tale" whose end is foretold: those who seek possession of first two Hallows, be it the eldest brothers of the story, the Dark wizard Grindelwald, or even Dumbledore, have ensured their own death. (Dumbledore, of course, through his understanding of the narrative, consciously manipulates this foregone conclusion by orchestrating his own death.) Only readers and interpreters of the tale can learn from it and avoid temptation altogether, as Hermione suggests *she* would do when discussing the tale with Harry and Ron.[46]

Unlike the tale of the Deathly Hallows, the story of the Horcruxes represents an unfolding "feminine" narrative whose end is not known; therefore, its conclusion is "open" and subject to a wider range of choice. The tale of the Horcruxes is, of course, the tale of Tom Riddle and his transformation into Lord Voldemort. By pursuing the Horcruxes themselves, Harry grows in understanding of his enemy's history, his strengths, weaknesses, and motivations. Just as importantly, Harry learns about his own past and, in a moment of epiphany, learns that he is one of Voldemort's Horcruxes. In order to ensure that Voldemort can be defeated, Harry realizes he must die to destroy the shard of Voldemort's soul within him. Finally freed of the destiny to be the great hero of the final battle, Harry surrenders his life to Voldemort to save his community.

Harry's sacrifice is repaid with new life and new understanding: since Voldemort has previously used the young protagonist's charmed blood for his own resurrection in *Goblet of Fire*,[47] Harry cannot necessarily be killed as long as his blood runs through the Dark Lord's new body.[48] Furthermore, as a consequence of understanding the meaning of "The Tale of the Three Brothers" and choosing instead to enter the "open" tale of the Horcruxes, Harry becomes the master of both narratives—he has actively destroyed the Horcruxes and through *inaction* become the master of the Hallows—and thereby of the masculine/feminine duality the narratives represent. Thus enlightened and newly empowered, Harry dons Death's cloak and, wrapped securely in the folds of invisibility, heads for the final battle with Voldemort. Tellingly, because Harry has learned the lesson of the mother and sacrificed himself for love of others, his very presence safeguards those he loves from the Dark Lord. He explains his new powers of protection to Voldemort after revealing himself:

"You won't be killing anyone else tonight," said Harry as they circled, and stared into each other's eyes, green into red.... "*I have done what my mother did*. They're protected from you. Haven't you noticed how none of the spells you put on them are binding? You can't torture them. You can't touch them." [italics added][49]

Since Harry has no need to wield the phallic wand that will destroy his enemy, he attempts to be Voldemort's redeemer instead. Like Goethe's Eternal

Feminine lures the otherwise doomed, power-hungry Faust toward perfection,[50] so Harry offers Voldemort one last chance. As he says, "it's all you've got left.... I've seen what you'll be otherwise.... Be a man... try... Try for some remorse.... "[51] However, unlike Faust, Voldemort rejects the call of the feminine with a final *Avada Kedavra*!

Having learned Dumbledore's lesson that it is the *choice* more than the *ability* that shows "what we truly are," Harry, true to himself, chooses to respond with his signature spell, the protective *Expelliarmus*, one last time. The choice to disarm proves true—the Killing Curse rebounds off Harry's defensive spell, the Elder Wand leaps from Voldemort's hand into Harry's, and Lord Voldemort dies a "mundane" death, as we all must do in the end.[52]

## THE BOY WHO LIVED HAPPILY EVER AFTER

It is not uncommon for heroes in mythology and fairy tales to long for hearth and home. In Homer's *Odyssey*, for example, the forlorn Odysseus, trapped for years on the island of the nymph Calypso, sits every day on the rocky shore and cries while he scans the horizon toward his kingdom.[53] However, the tale of Odysseus and those like it tend to either focus on the hero's adventures on his journey home—much of the *Odyssey* is occupied with such feats—or to equate domestic bliss with "making it big": after many tests, the poor farm boy marries the wealthy princess. Seldom is making a home the *actual goal* of the male narrative. Odysseus, for example, may miss his faithful wife Penelope, but it is the threat posed by the suitors who would steal his property, kill his son, and take his place next to his wife that provides him with the impetus to take his household back by force. In the male narrative, domestic bliss, if achieved, is simply a fringe benefit of the overall drive for power and glory. So strong is the impulse to have the male hero avoid domesticity that the poet Alfred, Lord Tennyson saw it necessary to send the "idle" Odysseus back out to sea "to strive, to seek, to find, and not to yield" in his famous poem "Ulysses."[54] A male who *likes* home is, by traditional logic, clearly no hero.

Virtually all girls' tales, on the other hand, are based on domestic themes. Desiring and achieving a good marriage and a happy home are the signs of maturity in a young female protagonist, as epitomized in the Cinderella tales and even dark domestic stories such as "Bluebeard."[55] In fact, the Cinderella tales purposefully set up a "bad home" where the female protagonist is maltreated so that she can transcend it by founding her own "good home." Thus, Cinderella's "happily-ever-after" ending does not just signal the protagonist's move from ashes and rags to riches and nobility, but also her achievement of what women supposedly desire most: a happy home they can call their own.

*Sorcerer's Stone* promptly establishes the Dursley household on Privet Drive as the "bad home" that Harry must escape. Dull, intolerant, abusive, and full of themselves, the Dursleys are a caricature of respectable suburban normalcy that

Harry learns to despise. They, in turn, treat Harry not so much as a stepchild but as an unwanted indentured servant whose strange powers and "freaky friends" assault their bourgeois, White, Anglo-Saxon sensibilities. Harry's escape to the magical castle of Hogwarts gives him, for a time, a family of sorts with close friends such as Ron and Hermione and parental figures such as Professor McGonagall and Headmaster Dumbledore. But Hogwarts also proves to be less a happy home than a place of trials and tribulations as Harry is engaged in confrontations with fellow students, abused by professors, attacked repeatedly by dire monsters, and almost killed by Voldemort more than once. Considering his abysmal life with the Dursleys, Harry has no other option than to think of Hogwarts as his home; he is soon to discover, however, that his nemesis Voldemort has exactly the same desire.[56]

Other homes in the series prove just as frustrating for Harry. The home of the Weasley clan, The Burrow, whose name invokes the cozy hobbit-holes of Tolkien's fantasy world, is a "mother's domain," a sort of externalized womb full of warmth, food, and hugs through which the Weasleys and their friends pass as they are ordered about by Mrs. Weasley. But, while Harry is always welcome in The Burrow, he is painfully aware that his presence brings perennial trouble to his friends. Likewise, though Harry hopes that he might be able to live a bachelor's life with his godfather, Sirius Black, in Number Twelve, Grimmauld Place, Black seems unstable, often confusing Harry with his father, James, and he does not seem to worry sufficiently about Harry's age and welfare, as Molly Weasley points out.[57] In any case, Harry's hopes of forming a family with his godfather are dashed when Bellatrix Lestrange kills Black.

Perhaps the most pitiable representation of a "home" in the Harry Potter series is the cold, musty tent that Harry shares with Hermione and Ron in *Deathly Hallows* as they simultaneously flee from Voldemort's forces and attempt to find a way to vanquish him.[58] Their constant shifting of the tent's location and the need to protect it with charms represent their precious yet precarious friendship during dangerous times. Once they begin to feel the psychological effects of Slytherin's locket (one the Horcruxes), the real impact of Voldemort's insidious effect on families, homes, and communities becomes clear. Lord Voldemort is not so much a "person" as an "idea" that penetrates secure homes full of love and reduces them to temporary lodgings in unsafe surroundings and alters positive communal feelings such as loyalty, mutual respect, and camaraderie to paranoia, deceit, jealousy, and betrayal. That Harry, Ron, and Hermione—and many of their friends and family in the underground movement—ultimately survive the ordeal as friends speaks to the strength of their commitment to the group and the achievement of collective goals.

The failure of each of these households points to Harry's aching desire for the absent home, the cottage he shared as an infant with his parents in a village called Godric's Hollow. But when Harry and Hermione finally visit the village in *Deathly Hallows*, the cottage has been left in ruins as a reminder of

Voldemort's cruelty and the Potters' sacrifice.[59] As the inscribed sign on the cottage's gate and the statues of Harry and his parents in the center of the village indicate, Harry's birth home is literally history. Harry cannot go back to being a child, no matter how much he may desire to.[60] Rather, the narrative continually reminds us that Harry's dream of being reunited with his parents is unhealthy and even dangerous. From the first book to the last, the message is always the same: just as Dumbledore advises a very young Harry after his third visit to the Mirror of Erised, where he sees himself surrounded by his family, that "it does not do to dwell on dreams and forget to live,"[61] so "The Tale of the Three Brothers" serves as a warning against the unnatural desire to bring the dead back to life.

The resolution of the series sees Harry moving beyond infantile desire when he leaves the Resurrection Stone behind in the Forbidden Forest. In so doing, he gives up the concept of "home" as defined by a child ("me and my parents") and instead chooses a broader sense of community and collective responsibility. Harry also rejects the hero's life by relinquishing the Elder Wand, which he dubs "trouble." Instead, our protagonist hopes for the long life and attendant domesticity represented by the Invisibility Cloak. Tellingly, this last unconventional decision confuses Ron—as a boy more fully entrenched in boy culture, Ron has difficulty imagining anyone who would not want to wield the phallic power of the Elder Wand. Certainly, Harry's desire for domesticity is unusual for a male hero, but for us what makes this moment extraordinary is that Harry chooses domesticity at so very young an age and that the narrative portrays his choice in such an overwhelmingly positive light: both Hermione, who is perennially right about what constitutes the correct thing to do, and the portrait of Dumbledore approve of his decision.[62]

And, then, of course, there is the epilogue. We have two views of the final paragraphs of the Harry Potter series, a sort of double vision, neither of which we seem to be able to put away; therefore, we have chosen not to resolve the binary, although we certainly prefer the latter reading. In our first reading, we see the epilogue as defining the idea of "happily ever after" by focusing on a domestic Harry who, nineteen years after defeating Voldemort, has married and had children with Ginny Weasley, finally becoming part of the Weasley clan. The indomitable Hermione Granger has also been domesticated and integrated into the Weasley family via her marriage to Ron. Although this ending fills in the lack left by the loss of "Lily and James"[63]—the heterosexual couple at the center of all events in *Harry Potter*—it has unfortunate repercussions for the otherwise subtly transgressive nature of the series, as it suggests that the real quest of the main characters was to restore the traditional nuclear family.

Significantly, however, Rowling forgoes the traditional wedding scene with all the accompanying symbolism of patriarchal authority: the white virginal dress, the rings indicating possession, the "giving away" of the bride from one man to another, the statements of servitude, and so on. Instead, by jumping years ahead, Rowling chooses to focus on the family as part of an extended community. The epilogue, then, is not as much about the hero as about the *future* this hero, Harry Potter, has helped to create.

Thus, Rowling repeats the expected "happily-ever-after" pattern of heteronormativity—Harry does get married to a woman and have children—but as Judith Butler argues in *Gender Trouble*, "the task is not whether to repeat" since repetition, even in opposition, is inevitable, "but *how* to repeat or, indeed, to repeat and, through a radical proliferation of gender, to *displace* the very gender norms that enable the repetition [of compulsory heterosexuality] itself."[64] In other words, Harry as an adult is a "man" and "heterosexual," but by consciously and actively performing these positions *differently* he shifts, however slightly, what being "a man" means within the sex/gender system. As a model for young readers, this small difference could have significant wide-ranging impact on future generations who may consciously choose to reject strict binaries as social fabrications—including "male" and "female" and "masculine" and "feminine"—and oppose individual phallic power in favor of collective thought and action for the good of all.

This interpretation of the epilogue gives us a sense of important growth in Harry. For while Ron continues to emphasize the traditional antipathy between the school houses of Gryffindor and Slytherin to his children, Harry has come to understand that it is the binary divisions that we create among ourselves (Purebloods vs. Mudbloods, Wizards vs. Muggles, Gryffindor vs. Slytherin) that allowed for the rise of Voldemort in the first place, and he is determined to teach his children something different. Thus he has meaningfully named his son "Albus Severus" for two Hogwarts headmasters: Albus Dumbledore of Gryffindor House and Severus Snape of Slytherin. When young Albus tremulously reveals to Harry that he is scared that the Sorting Hat will place him in Slytherin House, Harry explains the meaning of his name to him and stresses that his House placement is irrelevant to those that love him. Albus Severus Potter, then, represents a future where being "other"—a Slytherin, for example—will not be grounds for contempt or rejection, but a difference to be explored and enjoyed. This resolution of the Gryffindor–Slytherin binary has underlying repercussions for the masculine–feminine dichotomy as well: though the series is about a boy, its narrative shows that in the world of Harry Potter gender may matter, but—like one's school-age House—it is not, in the end, destiny.

## NOTES

1. Ximena Gallardo C. and C. Jason Smith, "Cinderfella: J.K. Rowling's Wily Web of Gender," in *Reading Harry Potter: Critical Essays*, ed. Giselle Liza Anatol (Westport, CT: Preager, 2003), 199.

2. See, for example, J.K. Rowling, "Chapter 24: Sectumsempra," in *Harry Potter and the Half-Blood Prince* (New York: Scholastic Press, 2005).

3. For a full description of the Hero's Quest, or monomyth, see Joseph Campbell's *The Hero with a Thousand Faces* (Princeton: Princeton UP, 1949).

4. Gallardo C. and Smith, "Cinderfella," 194.

5. Harry gets a glimpse of Bellatrix Lestrange in "Chapter 30: The Pensieve" of *Harry Potter and the Goblet of Fire* (New York: Scholastic Press, 2000), but we do not learn much about her until *Harry Potter and the Order of the Phoenix* (New York: Scholastic Press, 2003).

6. For the origins of Tank Girl as well as her appeal to female readers, see, for example, Roger Sabin, *Comics, Comix & Graphic Novels: A History of Comic Art* (New York: Phaidon Press, 2001, 142–45).

7. Rowling, *Phoenix*, 47–53.

8. Rowling, *Prince*, 624.

9. J.K. Rowling, *Harry Potter and the Deathly Hallows* (New York: Scholastic Press, 2007), 603–6 and 624.

10. "Umbrage" may mean "appearance" or "semblance" in the noun form and "disguise" or "offend" in the verb form, all of which apply to Umbridge's actions and personality. See, for example, "Umbrage, v." and "Umbrage, n." in *The Oxford English Dictionary Online* (Oxford UP, 2008).

11. Ken Kesey, *One Flew Over the Cuckoo's Nest* (1962; New York: Penguin, 1996). See, for example, 180–81 and 188.

12. Rowling, *Hallows*, 209.

13. Stephen King, "Potter Gold," *EW.com: From Entertainment Weekly*, 11 July 2003, http://www.ew.com/ew/article/0,,462861,00.html [Accessed 3 May 2008].

14. William Shakespeare, *The Tragedy of Macbeth*, 1.5.37–53.

15. Rowling, *Phoenix*, 809.

16. Ibid., 515.

17. Ibid., 810.

18. Rowling, *Prince*, 212.

19. Rowling, *Hallows*, 736.

20. Rowling, *Phoenix*, 98–120.

21. Rowling, *Prince*, 35; William Shakespeare, *The Tragedy of Macbeth*, 1.7.54–59.

22. Rowling, *Hallows*, 735–36.

23. See, for example, our extended discussion in Chapter 2 of *Alien Woman: The Making of Lt. Ellen Ripley* (New York: Continuum, 2004).

24. Rowling, *Hallows*, 737.

25. Gallardo C. and Smith, "Cinderfella," 197. As we suggest, the scar is phallic in shape, but as a "wound," it is also a vaginal opening, now closed.

26. Rowling, *Prince*, 437.

27. Rowling, *Goblet*, 117–28.

28. "Voldemort" is a combination of "vol" meaning "flight," "de" meaning "from," and "mort" meaning "death." See, for example, *Harper Collins Robert French College Dictionary* (New York; Collins, 2002).

29. Rowling, *Prince*, 275.

30. Klaus Theweleit, *Male Fantasies: Vol. 1: Women, Floods, Bodies, History*, Stephen Conway, trans. (Minneapolis: U of Minnesota P, 1987) and *Male Fantasies: Vol. 2: Male Bodies: Psychoanalyzing the White Terror*, Stephen Conway, trans. (Minneapolis: U of Minnesota P, 1989). For an extended discussion of the "messy body"

and its repression in literature see Mikhail Bahktin's *Rabelais and his World*, Helen Iswolsky, trans. (Bloomington: Indiana UP, 1984).

31. The hidden soul or heart theme is common in mythology and folk tales. For a discussion of the mythology behind the Horcruxes, see, for example, Sir James George Frazier's *The Golden Bough: A Study in Magic and Religion* (New York: Macmillan, 1951), particularly "Chapter LXVI: The External Soul in Folk Tales" and "Chapter LXVII: The External Soul in Folk Custom." Although the word "soul" has a long and complicated tradition of usage in the West, in the *Harry Potter* world the term "soul" is clearly used as one-half of the dichotomy of body–soul. The soul is that which is present in a living person and that which is absent in a dead body. In Western literature, this essence of the living person is traditionally represented as being metaphorically "feminine" to the "masculine" body (thus in Greek "psyche" is represented as a goddess and in Latin "anima" is in the feminine form as opposed to the body, "corpus," in the masculine form). This notion is echoed in literature in the likes of Goethe's "Eternal Feminine" and in psychology in C.G. Jung's adoption of the term "anima" for the male's "feminine side" (women have an "animus" or "male side" to their personality). Following this tradition, Rowling further emphasizes that Voldemort's soul is metaphorically feminine by portraying him as increasingly phallic in body as he divests himself of pieces of his soul.

32. J.K. Rowling, *Harry Potter and the Sorcerer's Stone* (New York: Scholastic Press, 1997), 299.

33. Rowling, *Phoenix*, 836.

34. Gallardo C. and Smith, "Cinderfella," 195.

35. *Cinderella*, Clyde Geronimi, Wilfred Jackson, Hamilton Luske, dir. (Disney Studios, 1950).

36. Rowling, *Phoenix*, 644–49.

37. Rowling, *Hallows*, 662–65.

38. Rowling, *Phoenix*, 648; *Hallows*, 673–76.

39. Rowling, *Prince*, 545–50; *Hallows*, 676–79.

40. Rowling, *Hallows*, 656–58.

41. That Harry is a Horcrux explains the eerie similarities Harry has with Voldemort, such as being a Parselmouth, a person who can speak the language of snakes (Rowling, *Chamber*, 332–33), and why Harry can sometimes see what Voldemort sees and hears his thoughts. See, for example, *Goblet*, 15–16; *Phoenix*, 462–65; and *Hallows*, 500–01.

42. Rowling, *Hallows* 406–09.

43. Ibid., 407–10.

44. Ibid., "Chapter 22: The Deathly Hallows."

45. Ibid., 721.

46. Ibid., 414.

47. Rowling, *Goblet*, 642.

48. Rowling, *Hallows*, 709.

49. Ibid., 738.

50. Johann Wolfgang von Goethe, *Goethe's Faust*, Walter Kaufman, trans. (New York: Doubleday, 1961), ll. 12094–111.

51. Rowling, *Hallows*, 741.

52. Ibid., 743–44.

53. Homer, *The Odyssey*, Book V, ll. 159–66.

54. Alfred, Lord Tennyson, "Ulysses," ll. 1, 70.

55. See, for example, Andrew Lang's 1889 version of "Bluebeard" in *The Blue Fairy Book* (New York: Dover, 1965), 290–95.

56. Rowling, *Prince*, 431; *Hallows*, 500.

57. Rowling, *Phoenix*, 87–97.

58. Rowling, *Hallows*, 425.

59. Ibid., 332–33.

60. Harry's infantile desire is for what Lacan would term *jouissance*, for the pre-individuated state before the experience of individuality and suffering. See, for example, Judith Butler's summary in *Gender Trouble: Feminism and the Subversion of Identity* (New York: Routledge, 1990), 43–49.

61. Rowling, *Stone*, 214.

62. Rowling, *Hallows*, 748–49.

63. See, for example, Isabelle Cani's discussion of the centrality of the absent couple, Lily and James, in "Lily et James Potter, ou les visages morcelés de l'unité perdue," *Belphégor: Littérature Populaire et Culture Médiatique*, 6.1 (November 2006): n.p. http://etc.dal.ca/belphegor/vol6_no1/fr/main_fr.html [Accessed 15 June 2008].

64. Butler, *Gender Trouble*, 148.

# 8

# The Replication of Victorian Racial Ideology in Harry Potter

*Giselle Liza Anatol*

In *Reading Harry Potter*, I mapped the neocolonial and Eurocentric impulses of the first four novels in Rowling's series. I argued that although one might at first read the wizarding world as a realm of ethnic, racial, and cultural difference quite distinct from the "real world" of nonmagical Britain, it simultaneously serves as an accurate reflection of British society—a space where racism and xenophobia might be officially declared counterproductive and outdated, but proliferate nonetheless. In this chapter, I will continue my interrogation of racial ideology in the wizarding world, particularly in Rowling's representations of magical nonhumans. In the end, I believe that her inconsistent rendering of what it means to be an Other to society's hegemonic forces weakens the explicit antiracism theme of the books. Thus, as David Roediger discusses, although overt forms of racial prejudices in contemporary society have been largely erased from political discourse, they still hold sway in many cultural arenas.[1] Furthermore, I propose that the resonance of racialized imperialist tropes in the Potter novels might provide one explanation for the books' tremendous popularity: the narratives replicate the adventure and accompanying values of classic tales from centuries past, from Daniel Defoe's *Robinson Crusoe* to Charles Dickens' *Oliver Twist* to Robert Louis Stevenson's *Treasure Island* and *Dr. Jekyll and Mr. Hyde*, rather than present a compelling account of twenty-first century globalization. The familiarity of—and possibly nostalgia for—the conventional stories of civilizing missions, established hierarchies, and settled truths sit so comfortably with readers that they do not notice the racism that lurks beneath the surface of the stories.

## HARRY POTTER'S ANTIRACISM MESSAGE

As has been discussed extensively in interviews, blogs, websites, and Harry Potter scholarship, an overarching theme of Rowling's series is the battle between the purebloods and those who believe in equality for all magical humans—regardless of bloodline—as well as peaceful coexistence with non-magical humans. The Gaunts, for example, maternal ancestors of Tom Riddle/ Lord Voldemort, are so obsessed with maintaining their pureblood status that Marvolo and his children appear to suffer genetic defects associated with in-breeding. Both Morfin and Merope have eyes that gaze in opposite directions; Marvolo is strangely proportioned, with overly broad shoulders and elongated arms, "which . . . gave him the look of a powerful, aged monkey."[2] Rather than witnessing evolution *from* primates, the reader sees a *de*-evolution to an apelike creature; Rowling thus connects racism to regression, not progress.

The Gaunts' bigoted perspective is interestingly written on the body. The internal character is physically coded onto the exterior of the subject.[3] Similarly, Voldemort's insistence upon the superiority of purebloods and its connection to White racial supremacy in the "real" world is conveyed in part by the references to the whiteness of his skin, made more and more explicit as the series progresses. Whiteness is not rendered in positive terms, with its connotations of purity and innocence; rather, it comes across as eerie and disturbing. Harry often sees Voldemort's hands when he becomes vulnerable to the Dark Lord's thoughts: they are "long-fingered and white as though they had not seen sunlight for years."[4] In *Phoenix* Harry also witnesses "[a] face whiter than a skull" and a "terrible snakelike face white and gaunt."[5]

Although whiteness is definitely not made desirable, Voldemort's humanity is strongly de-emphasized, making his complexion less connected with a race of people than with animals like snakes and spiders and objects like skulls, all of which are rendered frightening in Western iconography. Whiteness becomes associated with death, and not the identity of the living. In other words, the Dark Lord's complexion takes on an unnatural tinge, not the color of "real" White people. With a face that "shone through the gloom," and a pallor that makes him appear to give off "a pearly glow," he looks as if he is "gleaming" in the dark, and thus resembles a ghost more than a human being.[6]

This whiteness in connection with pure evil is sharply different from the whiteness of characters—both good and bad, positive and negative—whose color is emphasized primarily when they are frightened, angry, tired, or ill. Draco's mother Narcissa panics over the likely fate of her son in *Deathly Hallows*, and her face turns "paper-white."[7] When Harry mentions Voldemort's name Ginny's face blanches; Hermione claims to know when Harry is in pain because he is "white as a sheet."[8]

Just as Voldemort's whiteness becomes of a physical manifestation of his evil character, throughout the series Harry's lightning bolt-shaped scar is "read" by other characters as well as by Harry himself. Harry comes to use the scar to warn him of Voldemort's increasing strength, approach, and/or emotions. The mark also identifies Harry to others, much like the title of a book, conveying his early experience with the Dark Lord so that he is often not even given the chance to speak the story. In book V, for instance, Kreacher states: "Kreacher can see the scar . . . that's that boy who stopped the Dark Lord"; the eyes of a security guard at the Ministry flicker from Harry's visitor's badge to his forehead; the gaze of the barman at the Hog's Head—Aberforce Dumbledore—also pauses for a moment on the wound.[9] Professor Slughorn's eyes fly to the mark when they are introduced, and upon meeting Harry at the Burrow, Xenophilius Lovegood's eye "slid straight to the scar on Harry's forehead."[10] One might read Rowling's construction of the mark as an apt metaphor for race: an obvious physical trait, like the color of one's skin, the shape of one's nose, and/or one's epathalmic eye folds, that makes one the object of others' gazes and assumptions, whereas one's actual experiences tend to be ignored. The scars on the back of Harry's hand, inflicted during one of Dolores Umbridge's brutal punishments, also serve as text on the protagonist's body, parallel to complexion and race in that all work as physical emblems of past experiences. This correlation can be seen in other ways, too: the locket Horcrux leaves an impression burned on the skin over Harry's heart, and Nagini's fangs leave puncture marks on his forearm in the last novel of the series. The problem with this metaphor is that when Harry finally hears the prophecy explicating his connection to Voldemort, he views himself as "a marked man" and wishes that he could disappear:[11] being marked is seen as being undesirable. Rather than attempt to change the system where one is rendered "invisible," akin to the lack of social recognition, access, and power of Ralph Ellison's Invisible Man, Harry wishes to *become* invisible and blend into the crowd.[12]

## OTHER RACIAL ALLEGORIES: GIANTS, CENTAURS, AND GOBLINS

Rowling repeatedly seeks to establish that judging others based on appearance is unwise. Tom Riddle is dashingly handsome; Gellert Grindelwald's blonde curls and mischievous grin are also portrayed as deceptively appealing. The approach that Harry, other witches and wizards, and the series narrator take to other magical beings, however, actually echoes the European writing of colonial expansion and the ensuing ethnographic impulses from the sixteenth through the nineteenth centuries.[13] As Joan Pau Rubiés explains:

Although the emergence of an academic discourse based on comparison, classification, and historical lineage called ethnology is a nineteenth-century phenomenon, in reality both ethnography and ethnology existed within the humanistic disciplines of early modern Europe in the primary forms of travel writing, cosmography, and history, which often informed specific debates—about the capabilities and origins of the American Indians, the definition of "natural man," the influence of climate on national characteristics, or the existence of stages in the history of civilisation.[14]

The travels of various British subjects outward in the name of the Empire required a certain flexibility and porousness of England's borders. Not only could explorers, merchants, missionaries, and settlers travel *out*, but, in later years, multiracial, multicultural, and multinational subjects could travel back *in*. The borders between the nonmagical and magical worlds in the Harry Potter series are equally porous, making Hogwarts a pluralistic society, not only in terms of its pureblood and Muggle-born students, but also, ostensibly, in terms of other types of diversity.

Historically, British imperial projects had goals that were religious, commercial, and scientific; in book V, we find an example of the financial aspect as Harry and his classmates begin the exciting yet anxiety-producing process of planning their future careers. A pamphlet from Gringotts reads: *"Are you seeking a challenging career involving travel, adventure, and substantial, danger-related treasure bonuses?"* The bank advertises at Hogwarts in order to recruit the brightest of the graduating classes to work as Curse-Breakers;[15] their older employees, as can be seen through the example of Bill Weasley, tend to leave these jobs as they grow older and settle down back in England. At the beginning of *Phoenix*, Bill has returned home from Egypt, taking a desk job although "he misses the tombs" and his job as Charm Breaker for the bank.[16] This move represents his growing up, maturing, and readiness to start a family in addition to his dedication to fighting Voldemort through the Order of the Phoenix: he accepts a "safe," although boring, job and commits to protecting the home front, where he and future wife Fleur will marry and raise children.

Readers see other evidence of an international magical community—the International Confederation of Wizards is mentioned in Harry's fifth-year History of Magic exam; we learn that Albus Dumbledore was once the first-place winner of a prize at the International Alchemical Conference in Cairo, and that after graduation, he and Elphias Doge were scheduled for a grand tour of the world, starting with Greece;[17] Minister of Magic Cornelius Fudge explains to a newly elected British prime minister that there are "witches and wizards still living in secret all over the world"[18]—but true involvement between these populations seems lacking. In fact, Fudge claims that the British Ministry holds "responsibility for the whole Wizarding community,"[19] suggesting a reincarnation of the historic British Empire, with London as the seat of power and control. Dumbledore might have repudiated his youthful argument for wizard dominance "FOR THE MUGGLES' OWN GOOD"[20]—an idea that mimics the rhetoric of the European "right to rule" colonized countries in Africa, Asia, and the Caribbean—but his rejection of a system that proposes "responsible" domination of another people does not translate to the larger worldview that Rowling paints with her pen.

Most telling is the false symbolism of the Ministry of Magic's Fountain of Magical Brethren. Its name suggests equality between magical beings: a community where the bonds between the species parallel those of an intimate family. However, Harry observes that the centaur, goblin, house-elf, and witch are all "grouped around" a wizard, who stands taller than the rest, and the expressions on the faces of the nonhuman beings are "adoring."[21] The hierarchy of power is not at first evident to Harry, partially because, perhaps, as is true in "real" life, he benefits most from it. The wizard's height and central position suggest the sculptor's perception of his position of authority, both as a man and a magical human. Harry's awareness of the constructedness of the image comes after his Hearing: "up close, Harry thought [the wizard] looked rather weak and foolish," the witch's smile makes her seem like a "vapid . . . beauty contestant," and the goblin's and centaur's "soppily" ingratiating gaze is improbable. "Only the house-elf's attitude of creeping servility looked convincing."[22]

Dumbledore, too, calls attention to the statue's false image of magical brotherhood when recalling Kreacher's betrayal of Sirius Black and the rest of the Order of the Phoenix: "We wizards have mistreated and abused our fellows for too long, and we are now reaping our reward."[23] However, one should not ignore the fact that Harry merely grins when initially thinking of Hermione's response to the statue of the house-elf. Although she has founded an organization to fight for elf rights, Harry clearly has not been swayed by her arguments. And by the end of the Potter series, an exhausted Harry is thinking only about sleep in his "four-poster bed . . . and wondering whether Kreacher might bring him a sandwich there."[24] Thus, the closing line of the main body of the novel—and the body of the seven-book saga—embraces slavery, rather than firmly rejecting it.

Even more significant than a compellingly flawed protagonist's perspective, however, is the way that the author uses the magical beings to attain her own narrative ends. In the battle between Dumbledore and Voldemort near the conclusion of *Phoenix*, Harry gets caught in the middle. When the Dark Lord tries to inflict a Killing Curse on Harry, his headmaster animates the figures from the statue to come to his protégé's aid. The wizard, now headless, springs to life and leaps between Harry and Voldemort, where the spell bounces off its torso as it flings out its arms to protect Harry. The witch statue charges Bellatrix and pins her to the floor, and the centaur, now only one-armed, charges Voldemort. Both reveal bravery similar to the wizard's. The goblin and elf, however, display only cowardice, and a certain smallness of heart as well as of physical size and stature: they "scuttled toward the fireplaces set along the wall."[25]

Furthermore, when, in book VII, Kingsley Shacklebolt urges the listeners of the resistance radio program to fight against the dangerous ideology of "Wizards first," reasoning that "Every human life is worth the same, and worth saving"[26]—Rowling's use of the word "human" has significant implications for her construction of the antiracist agenda. Clearly, various types of *human* life are valued, but what about nonhuman magical beings? How are readers to think about characters like the giants, centaurs, goblins, elves, mermaids, and leprechauns, to name only a few?

In *Phoenix*, Hagrid identifies himself and Harry Potter as kindred spirits. He states they are both outsiders and both orphaned.[27] As a half-giant, twice the height and thrice the width of a "normal" man, Hagrid has been derided and shunned by many wizards and witches in his life. His immense size and lack of social status make him a physical Other in wizarding society, an apt metaphor for being a racial Other in the Muggle world. He is continually cast as not very bright, as when under the scrutiny of Dolores Umbridge, he keeps glancing toward Harry, Ron, and Hermione's hiding spot as if imploring them for help.[28]

Given that Hagrid is a close friend, one might think that Harry would make an effort to learn about giants, a group to which those in the wizarding world have little exposure; however, when the fifth years learn about giant wars in Professor Binns' fifth-year History of Magic class, Harry finds the lesson boring and doesn't pay attention. His attitude seems to replicate that of most other magical humans (although Rowling strives in other cases to make Harry a model of tolerance). For example, although Harry and his friends think that giants' locations throughout Europe are secret, Hagrid reveals this to be a falsehood born of wizarding arrogance: "It's jus' that mos' wizards aren' bothered where they are, s' long as it's a good long way away." Rowling demonstrates how the wizards' fear and self-importance lead to segregation rather than understanding and integration of the two communities, and the racial allegory is strengthened by her naming the different giant groups as "tribes": Hagrid claims that of the 100 different tribes from around the globe, twenty have been eradicated, and all have been "dyin' out fer ages."[29]

Rowling does not, however, render these tribes as culturally and politically distinct units; instead, they are all represented as unique only against the backdrop of the wizarding world, which is made comparable to settler cultures. In this way, the depiction echoes the description of American Indians as one lumped group of "uncivilized barbarians . . . important for the English colonial enterprise in modern North America."[30] Hagrid continues:

mostly [the giants] killed each other. . . . They're not made ter live bunched up together like tha'. Dumbledore says it's our fault . . . who forced 'em to go an' made 'em live a good long way from us an' they had no choice but ter stick together fer their own protection.[31]

Their fate parallels that of the indigenous Americans, New Zealanders, and Australians who were forcibly relocated to reservations and in the nineteenth and twentieth centuries, but the language of biological determinism—that they are "not made" to alter their behavior and adapt in order to survive—places blame at their feet and weakens Dumbledore's charge that responsibility for cultural extinction lies with the magical human community.[32] As Elaine Ostry argues in Reading Harry Potter, Rowling's portrait of Hagrid as one who essentially lacks self-control suggests that he and his people "therefore seem to deserve . . . lower status."[33]

Dumbledore instructs Hagrid to give the giant chief—the Gurg—presents to convey respect, furthering the image of giants as foreign and "exotic" rather than indigenous to the European magical landscape and "normal." When Hagrid describes the Gurg as "the biggest, the ugliest, an' the laziest," weighing as much as two bull elephants, with "[s]kin like rhino hide" and roaring at his subjects for food, Rowling shifts the imagery away from a sympathetic portrait of Native Americans, Maori, or Aboriginal peoples to a grotesque rendition of the stereotypical savage native.[34] The Gurg is not just one lazy individual but "the laziest"; he is not simply ugly but the most hideous of a generally ugly group. Like the rest of his community, he exhibits no self-control, whether it comes to consumption of food or to killing. The giants are thus cast as the complete opposite of the reserved wizards—to be read, in this case, as the British or Euro-Americans who are threatened by their existence yet seek their assistance, bringing civilization, or magic, in the form of Gubraithian fire.[35] Even though, as scholars such as Jeffrey Sissons point out, issues such as indigenous education, the complexity of indigenous identity, land rights, and self-determination are among the most crucial in contemporary First Nations politics, these concepts are not raised in Rowling's fiction. Rather, as is common throughout the nineteenth and twentieth centuries where the *images* of indigenous peoples are "treated as the common property of post-settler nations,"[36] Rowling freely appropriates the "native" for use as a symbol necessary for the construction of a more "civilized" wizarding nation. Witches and wizards thus come to represent a modern, cosmopolitan perspective, whereas Rowling's portrait of the giants "seems to imply a romantic reification of non-European cultures as static, isolated systems."[37] Like those who focus on cave drawings, totem poles, scalpings, teepees, and bows and arrows, Rowling employs the imagery of the vicious giant to establish a romanticized culture that the wizards long ago rejected and transcended.

Back at Hogwarts, attention is called to the obnoxiously self-important behavior of those wizards who believe themselves to be superior: when Umbridge speaks to Hagrid, she increases in volume and decreases in speed as if talking to someone "both foreign and very slow" and she pantomimes what she is trying to convey as if someone of giant ancestry would not have any facility with a spoken language.[38] Pansy Parkinson takes advantage of Umbridge's prejudice and claims not to be able to understand her teacher because he always sounds like he is grunting. Both Umbridge and Pansy participate in the animalization of giants, corresponding in many ways to the racist beastialization of non-European people—in this case, indigenous populations. Hermione notes that Umbridge has particular distaste for beings of mixed "race"; her anti-miscegenation ideology comes through when she calls Hagrid a "half-breed oaf."[39] This disgust for the mixing, more than against the Other itself, could be linked to her obsession with racial purity: if giant blood is mixed with human, this means human blood has been "corrupted" in the process. A good deal of nineteenth-century American literature, for example, expressed panic at the thought of interracial couples, which could lead to "mongrelization" and "race suicide"—the end of "pure White"/"Nordic" supremacy in the United States.

Albus Dumbledore, the voice of moral authority throughout much of the series, understands the "racial" bias that pervades the wizarding community. When giving Hagrid instructions on how to act most effectively as an envoy to the giants, he advises the half-giant to go slowly and allow the giants to see that promises will be kept—he knows, it seems, that wizards have proved themselves to be deceitful, untrustworthy, and unreliable. However, an insult lies just beneath the surface: Hagrid intuits that giving the giants too much—in terms of material gifts and reasons for joining in the fight against Voldemort—will be too taxing on a people with limited intellect: "overload 'em with information an' they'll kill yeh jus' to simplify things."[40] He has absorbed the racism of the society of his upbringing and perpetuates it; he is unable to observe and convey an empirical description without considering that the giants might have their own rules and agendas. He becomes the "cross-over" traveler who "has made the European discourse his own."[41]

Hagrid's internalized racism is also evident in his dealings with his half-brother, the full-giant Grawp. Hagrid brings Grawp to the Forbidden Forest against his will, believing that if he just gets him "back" and teaches him manners he will be able to prove him "harmless"—in other words, his suitability for wizarding society.[42] He has engaged in a civilizing mission, much like the child abductions throughout the Americas, Australia, and New Zealand,[43] as well as a way of proving his own worth in the wizarding world, although Hagrid argues that it was more of a rescue action, since other giants bullied Grawp for his small size. And even though Grawp kept desiring to return home,[44] Hagrid forces him to stay on the Hogwarts grounds, believing that he—one who is significantly half human, and has grown up in human society—knows what's better for the giant than the giant himself. Hagrid has adopted the perspective of the "settler culture" that deems itself rational and superior, with "a gendered and rugged individualism that views land and the natural world as needing to be brought under control."[45]

And although the reader might not trust Hagrid's perspective on giants, given his lack of judgment when it comes to many living things, from men selling dragon eggs to the safety of hippogriffs in the classroom, Harry's and Hermione's negative reactions to Grawp serve to reinforce a particular hierarchy of magical beings. When the centaur Firenze warns that Hagrid's attempts to train and civilize Grawp are pointless, Harry wonders how Hagrid could delude himself about Grawp's potential to "mix with humans."[46] Harry's first observations of the "strangely misshapen" giant are also telling:

What Harry had taken to be a vast mossy boulder . . . he now recognized as Grawp's head. It was . . . almost perfectly round and covered with . . . hair the color of bracken. . . . The back, under what looked like a dirty brownish smock comprised of animal skins sewn roughly together, was very broad. . . . [He had] enormous, filthy, bare feet.[47]

As a mossy, "earthen mound" wearing a grimy smock, he comes across as sounding filthy and unconcerned with bodily hygiene; this is emphasized several pages later when his "misshapen yellow teeth" and "dirty knuckles" are described.[48] Grawp lacks the markers of a "true" civilization as it has been constructed in Eurocentric paradigms—his feet are bare and his body is clothed in a roughly sewn covering of pelts. The imagery simultaneously reinforces the notion of indigenous peoples as possessing an innately close kinship to the earth and natural environment. Rowling seems to engage in a type of eco-indigenism—"a discourse that seeks to revalue primitivism and tribalism in relation to destructive western rationality and individualism," making the focus of the representation closeness to nature instead of reactions to/relationships with settler cultures and colonization.[49] Because of the parallelisms between giants and First Nations peoples, the largely vacant expressions on Grawp's face are additionally disturbing. When he rescues Harry and Hermione from the centaurs, for example, his "lopsided mouth" gapes "stupidly" and his eyes appear "dull."[50]

Also damning are the associations between Grawp and a young child: Rubiés classifies the stereotypes in Victorian England as wavering between "carefree noble savages [and] childish, sexually weak American Indians,"[51] and although Hagrid might be interpreted as the embodiment of the former, Grawp clearly represents the latter. He holds his knuckles to his eyes like an overgrown baby; he grabs out for Hermione as if he is a toddler, both when he meets her and during the rescue effort; he yells for "Hagger"—Hagrid—like a child who has lost its mother.[52] Harry's first impulse when Grawp reaches for Hermione is a violent one; he thinks only of protecting himself and Hermione, and compassion for the confused Grawp never enters his mind. And when the centaurs release their arrows and the whole group goes smashing into the woods, Hermione worries that Grawp might slaughter the entire bunch. Harry replies with bitterness that he's not "fussed."[53] Hermione's words tellingly suggest more concern for the centaurs than the giant, although the former were on the verge of killing her and Harry, and Harry shows no sympathy for either side. In book VI, when Harry recalls his involvement with Grawp from book V, he remembers "a vicious giant with a talent for ripping up trees by the roots, his vocabulary had comprised five words."[54] Emphasis falls on the giant's violence and his apparent stupidity, not on the way he was abducted from his people or his frustrations over his inability to communicate. Grawp, and by extension, indigenous peoples everywhere, are rendered through Harry's eyes—those of the character with whom readers are most likely to relate—as "savages" completely incapable of and "uninterested in progress."[55]

It should be noted that Hagrid does not escape the animalizing strokes of Rowling's pen. As in the cases of Columbus, Cook, and others who conveyed sympathy for indigenous peoples only when they were "friendly" and lived up to European assumptions and expectations of behaviors, readers are placed in the position of finding this character likeable but still somewhat unpredictable as a tamed savage. In *Phoenix*, he roars repeatedly when he is fired from Hogwarts. He wears a "horrible, hairy brown suit" to Bill and Fleur's wedding, its texture giving him the appearance of having fur.[56] Indeed, he and his dog Fang are

indistinguishably large and furry as they burst through a window and land in
Hogwarts for the final battle against Voldemort's forces near the conclusion of
*Deathly Hallows*.[57]

Where giants can be read as metaphors for a stereotyped indigenous people
at several points in the text, centaurs seem to fulfill this role as well. They
live in harmony with the natural landscape of the Forbidden Forest, and carry
only bows and arrows. The leader, Magorian, tells Hagrid: "Our ways are not
yours, nor are our laws."[58] Whereas Bane's hotheaded and aggressive nature
would seem to link him with the stereotype of the scalping Indian Savage,
Magorian's diplomacy and sense of honor render him according to the trope of
the Noble Brave. Late in book V, when Hermione confesses that she and Harry
have brought Dolores Umbridge into the Forbidden Forest in hopes that the
centaurs would chase her away, the binaries of violent versus peaceful, human
versus centaur, and, by extension, "white" versus "red" become acute. One irate
centaur roars that the teens "have the arrogance of their kind." He rejects being
viewed as "obedient" animals, either "hounds" or "pretty talking horses." In a
statement that oozes with the language of the "proud Indian brave," he asserts,
"We are an ancient people who will not stand wizard invasions and insults!
We . . . do not acknowledge your superiority."[59]

Hagrid, who appreciates nature and nonhuman creatures more than most
other witches and wizards, greatly respects the power and intellect of the centaurs. He calls them the "[c]leverest creatures" in the Forbidden Forest.[60] The
fact that he refers to them as "creatures" rather than "beings," however, reveals
a human-centered perspective that relegates nonhumans lower down a hierarchical chain of living things. When angered, his true feelings appear to rise to
the surface: he calls them "a bunch of mules" to their faces and then, to Harry
and Hermione, refers to them as "Ruddy old nags."[61] The centaurs, however,
view themselves as another *race*, and not a separate *species*. While teaching the
Divination class, the centaur Firenze tells the students that by looking at the
patterns of stars, one can read the destiny of both races, and one of the centaurs
in the confrontation with Hermione identifies the group as "a race apart."[62]

The prejudice that other magical humans hold against the centaurs can be
seen elsewhere in the series. Professor Trelawney's jealousy over Firenze's
continued presence on the Hogwarts faculty causes her to complain about
"the horse."[63] When she loses her temper, Umbridge, an obvious bigot, calls the
centaurs "Beasts! Uncontrolled animals!" She insists that they are only in the
forest because the Ministry allows them to occupy allotted land, suggesting a
parallel to the situation of American Indians and various indigenous groups
who were forced onto reservations set out by governments they did not recognize. However, the fact that the angered centaurs react more like animals than
humans at the end of the novel seems to support Umbridge's claim: when she
insults them in the Forbidden Forest, the herd "roared with rage and pawed
the ground," and this is one of the last images with which readers are left in
book V.[64]

Rowling does attempt to reveal the offensive nature of racial ignorance during Harry's first Divination class with Firenze. Lavender gets confused when their new professor refers to his community as a herd, and is shocked by the thought that there are more centaurs in the woods. The author appears to be interrogating the exoticism of single members of larger racial or ethnic groups who enter into the dominant culture. Lavender's reaction suggests that she found one centaur enthralling, but more than one might pose a threat. Dean asks whether Hagrid has bred the centaurs, suggesting that they have no agency, no intimate social, emotional, or intellectual relationships. He quickly apologizes, realizing his mistake almost immediately, but Firenze still chides that centaurs are not "servants or playthings" for magical humans. He clearly sees himself as superior, identifying certain beliefs as "human nonsense." He states that humans are "blinkered and fettered by the limitations of your kind," suggesting that *they* are the animals, and the inferior species.[65] The class session thus reads like the students' awkward attempt at ethnography. They eagerly pursue information about

topics like political order, including kingship, aristocracies, warfare, and justice; national, or racial, temperaments; economic activities, including (when applicable) cities and trade; religion; . . . marriage, women, and sexuality; dress, or nudity, and ornamentation; habits of eating and hygiene; language and oral rhetoric; literature and science; technology, navigation, and other arts.[66]

Instead of easily gaining the details from a passive informant, however, they are confronted by a self-possessed subject who resists the overly familiar bent of their questions and their assumptions of superiority. He resists having himself or his culture appropriated and manipulated by those in social power.[67]

In her article on travel writing and ethnography, Rubiés describes how George Anson's *A Voyage Round the World in the Years 1740–4* served to depict the Chinese "as deceitful, cowardly, and corrupted by an innate addiction to lucre, in an almost literary caricature of national temperament that served to present the intrusive English in an heroic light."[68] Edward Said's expansive definition of Orientalism—false assumptions underlying the West's attitudes about the East, which create the East as well as the West—details the collapsing of regional, national, and cultural distinctions in Asia and the Middle East. He describes how in the British mind, "the Orient" comes to represent inherent inferiority, silence—linked to stealth and sneakiness—weakness and passivity, which contributes to a perceived absence of masculinity in men and sensual excess and seduction in women (one that undermines rational thought and Western control), innate duplicity, at once tied to shrewdness, cutthroat business sense, greed, and love of money. Because of all of these factors, the Asian subject was conceived as an inherent danger for the West, or "Occident." And "European culture gained in strength and identity by setting itself off against the Orient as a sort of surrogate and even underground self."[69]

Frank Wu contributes to this dialogue by describing the variety of stereotypes that have hounded him and other Asian people in the United States in
more contemporary times, from railroad laborer to violin prodigy, philosophical
karate master to Chinatown gangster to ping-pong champion:

> I was given many masks to wear. I could be ... a gardener trimming the shrubs while
> secretly planting a bomb; ... a kamikaze pilot donning his headband somberly, screaming
> "Banzai" on my way to my death; a peasant with a broad-brimmed straw hat in a rice
> paddy on the other side of the world, ... an obedient servant in the parlor, ... a sniper
> camouflaged in the trees of the jungle, training my gunsights on G.I. Joe; a child
> running with a body burning from napalm ...; a chef serving up dog stew, a trick on
> the unsuspecting diner.... [70]

The list seems to go on and on. Despite the length of the catalog, however,
themes of mysterious silence and treachery abound—an element disturbingly
present in Rowling's Orientalist portrayal of goblins in Harry Potter.

Although at least one reader has connected Rowling's depictions of the
greedy, duplicitous goblins to caricatured stereotypes of Jews,[71] the repeated
references to the goblins' "dark, slanting eyes" create an obvious resonance between goblins and Asian peoples.[72] Griphook has glittery "slanting black eyes"
that appear to have "no whites."[73] His face is initially described as "swarthy,"
making skin tone the bodily "text" that one reads to identify the goblin's difference: his racial or ethnic identity.[74] Harry later observes finer details: in addition
to the black eyes and "sallow skin," Griphook possesses "long thin fingers,"
dirty, elongated feet, and a "domed head ... much bigger than a human's."[75]
He is clearly marked as a fascinating exotic Other.

Bill Weasley explains to Harry—and, by extension, the reading audience—
that goblins do not simply have just a different physical form: they belong
to a completely separate culture. He claims that their ideas of ownership and
payment are not the same as "human" conceptions of these ideas.[76] In other
words, they live in Said's notion of "a world with its own national, cultural, and
epistemological boundaries and principles of internal coherence,"[77] but Rowling
specifies that their world is distinctly alien, and nonhuman. Bill refers to wizards
and goblins in terms of "us" versus "them," with the goblins occupying a
stereotypical space of inscrutability. Having no other goblin to contrast to
Griphook as is the case with Dobby and Kreacher, the reader is left with a
one-dimensional view of this "different breed."[78]

Rowling portrays Griphook as infinitely sneaky. He looks at Harry out of the
corners of his eyes instead of directly, head-on. At one point he "sidle[s] into the
room without Harry noticing," and at another he "slunk back to the bedroom."
The goblin is cowardly as well; hearing a bang at the front door of Shell Cottage,
he hides under the table instead of standing with the others.[79] He contributes yet
another figure to the "imaginative demonology of 'the mysterious Orient.'"[80]

As in the first half of the Potter series, goblins occupy an uneasy place in larger magical Britain as well. In *Reading Harry Potter*, I recalled Rowling's reference to a 1612 Goblin Rebellion and the presence of the Goblin Liaison Office at the Ministry of Magic. During Harry's fifth-year History of Magic exam, readers also learn about eighteenth-century goblin riots. And during this academic year, we see how the anxiety of witches and wizards in regards to goblins resurfaces and intensifies: rumors spread about "subversive goblin groups" and the fact that Fudge might have had goblins assassinated.[81] A parallel can easily be drawn to Western fears of Asian takeovers, especially in the United States. Wu cites Jack London, author of *The Call of the Wild* and *White Fang*, as crucial to perpetuating notions of the "yellow peril" in the nineteenth century: one of his essays warned of "the 'menace' to the Western world from 'millions of yellow men' (Chinese) under the management of 'the little brown man' (Japanese)."[82] At the turn of the twentieth century, U.S. labor organizer Samuel Gompers incited fear with his essay, "Meat versus Rice: American Manhood Against Asiatic Coolieism—Which Shall Survive." And in the late twentieth century, anxieties about Asians bumping White Americans out of their valedictory and prestigious college spots raged.[83]

Adults in Harry's own inner circle wonder whether the goblins—a largely separatist community—will take sides with Voldemort. Mr. Weasley, the eternal optimist, opines that the goblins would never align with Voldemort, who has murdered some of their population. Lupin, however, more of a pragmatist, responds that their allegiances will depend on whether they're offered the liberties that wizards and witches have been withholding "for centuries."[84] As a werewolf who is discriminated against in wizarding society, Lupin can intuit the resentments that might be fomenting in other "racial" communities. Rowling thus provides some material that enables readers to avoid simply stereotyping: carefully examining the textual details leads one to see that the goblins did not riot unexpectedly, but rather in response to laws that prohibited their carrying of wands. In book VII, Griphook uses the demeaning phrase "wand-carriers" to refer to witches and wizards, and Ron defensively argues that goblins do not need wands to perform magic. Griphook dismisses this fact as irrelevant, because wizarding insistence on controlling the situation—and thus, the current social hierarchy—and refusing to share the intricacies of wand work denies goblins the ability to augment their powers. He asserts: "As the Dark Lord becomes ever more powerful, your race is set still more firmly above mine!"[85] However, because of his lack of interest in the subject of history, Harry cannot usually make these connections on his own.[86] As Dana Goldstein argues, Rowling "critiques, yet ultimately hews to, a fantasy script dependent on stereotypes culled from real-life racism."[87] Thus, Harry's androcentric perspective on goblins gets transmitted as a Eurocentric perspective on other races and cultures—one that is not challenged through the course of the books. Harry describes the goblins' language as "a rough and unmelodious tongue, a string of

rattling, guttural noises," and later identifies the language as "Gobbledegook"—
an insulting term that suggests a lack of organizational patterns, grammar, and
logical progression.[88] When he comes to view Griphook as "unexpectedly blood-
thirsty, [one who] laughed at the idea of pain in lesser creatures, and seemed
to relish the possibility that they might have to hurt other wizards" to get to
the correct vault,"[89] the information comes across as objective and unbiased.
Griphook arrogantly refuses to eat what Fleur prepares for the group, and Harry
is disgusted by his insistence on eating "lumps of raw meat, roots, and various
fungi"—a diet that many young readers will find equally repulsive.[90] In other
words, because of the reader's close identification with the boy hero, it is unlikely that these perspectives will be questioned. Thus, although the perspective
is definitely Harry's, the narrative reinforces the idea that goblins—like giants
and elves—are not only unassimilable but also subhuman.

Some readers might find my chapter provocative; others might claim that
it is nothing but exotic, abstract theory, exploiting recent trends in cultural
studies; still others might complain that it unfairly alleges racism where none
was overtly intended. In *Colored White*, Roediger argues that while at one time
antiracism critics were called "impatient" and "too little aware of the weight
of history and tradition," the accusation has shifted to calling us "atavistic—so
eager to dwell on the bleak past that we miss the glorious future." I hope,
however, as he does, that studies such as this one allow us to see the role that
an "astonishingly diverse" range of sources play in "spreading and challenging
ideas about race."[91] I hope that the readings provided here will, at the very
least, cause readers to pause and consider the possibilities of what Rowling's
characters and storylines contribute to contemporary ideas about race, and
possibly stimulate some much-needed dialogue on that topic. What we must
continually strive for is a more comprehensive understanding of the fact that
"learning to understand *ourselves, our* history, *our* environment, *our* language,
*our* political system" requires an equal understanding of the "thems" in our
midst.[92] Since discovering one's identity can only be worked out in a social
context, through interactions and comparisons and contrasts with others, only
when a full understanding of society is gained can a full understanding of the
individual Self be achieved.

## NOTES

1. David R. Roediger, *Colored White: Transcending the Racial Past* (Berkeley: University of California Press, 2002.)

2. J.K. Rowling, *Harry Potter and the Half-Blood Prince* (New York: Scholastic,
2005), 212.

3. This case and others challenge Karin Westman's assertion that "The body can bear
marks of difference that confer authority—remember Albus Dumbledore's comment to
Professor McGonagall that 'scars can come in useful' (*Philosopher's Stone*, 17)—but the
series' emphasis on choice . . . continues to argue against the determinism of materialist

ideologies." Karin E. Westman, "Specters of Thatcherism: Contemporary British Culture in J.K. Rowling's Harry Potter Series." *The Ivory Tower and Harry Potter.* Ed. Lana A. Whited (Columbia: University of Missouri Press, 2004): 305–28, 328.

4. J.K. Rowling, *Harry Potter and the Order of the Phoenix* (New York: Scholastic, 2003), 584. On another occasion, as Harry begins to mentally merge with Voldemort, he notices the whiteness of his own hand; its color is emphasized when, as if disembodied, it pulls out a wand. Rowling, *Harry Potter and the Deathly Hallows* (New York: Scholastic, 2007), 232 and 343.

5. Rowling, *Phoenix*, 586 and 812.

6. Rowling, *Hallows*, 3 and 653.

7. Ibid., 35.

8. Ibid., 89 and 233.

9. Rowling, *Phoenix*, 109, 128, and 337.

10. Rowling, *Prince*, 65 and *Hallows*, 399. The scar also gives Harry's identity away when he, Ron, and Hermione are apprehended by Fenrir Greyback. The werewolf and his gang of Snatchers discover who Hermione is and then hypothesize who the spell-disguised Harry might be. Greyback stares at Harry's face and whispers, "What's that on your forehead, Vernon?" (Rowling, *Hallows*, 452). When Harry is subsequently taken to Malfoy Manor, Lucius's eyes "raked Harry's forehead" to see if there is "something there" (458).

11. Rowling, *Phoenix*, 856.

12. The very first page of *Phoenix* reveals Harry's impulse to choose invisibility: he hides himself in a hydrangea bush to avoid being seen by the Dursleys's neighbors, and when Tonks asks if he wishes he could sometimes hide his scar to conceal his identity, he turns his back on her to keep her from staring at his forehead. In a similar way, the Death Eaters' Dark Marks—the physical signs of their allegiance to Voldemort that give them a group identity and sense of common purpose—act as a stigma in the larger society and so are typically hidden.

13. I choose to use the word "beings" rather than "creatures" because I believe the latter animalizes rather than acknowledges the more human qualities of the subjects. For instance, critic Peter Dendle presents a compelling argument about how the novels use interspecies tension to work through issues of interracial tension, but how "*[l]esser creatures* are systematically exploited by wizards for utility, recreation, and ornament, and Rowling regularly introduces these elements casually for comic effect" [italics added] (166). By calling house-elves, goblins, and other magical beings "lesser creatures," Dendle replicates Rowling's framework, relegating magical beings to inferior social status. His thesis relies on this shift, as he is concerned with wizarding and human readers' negative attitudes toward animals and animal welfare, but his recognition that magical beings also embody "issues of both race and class" (165) comes dangerously close to aligning non-White races with animals. Peter Dendle, "Monsters, Creatures, and Pets at Hogwarts: Animal Stewardship in the World of Harry Potter," *Critical Perspectives on Harry Potter*, 2nd ed. Ed. Elizabeth E. Heilman (New York: Routledge, 2009): 163–76.

14. Joan Pau Rubiés,"Travel Writing and Ethnography." In *The Cambridge Companion to Travel Writing.* Ed. Peter Hulme and Tim Youngs (New York: Cambridge UP, 2002), 243.

15. Rowling, *Phoenix*, 657.

16. Ibid., 70.

17. Rowling, *Hallows*, 353.

18. Rowling, *Prince*, 5.

19. Ibid.

20. Rowling, *Hallows*, 357.

21. Rowling, *Phoenix*, 127.

22. Ibid., 156.

23. Ibid., 834.

24. Rowling, *Hallows*, 749.

25. And after the battle, Harry sees the elf and goblin statues "leading a stunned-looked Cornelius Fudge forward" (*Phoenix*, 816). Even the statues are in positions of service.

26. Rowling, *Hallows*, 440.

27. Rowling, *Phoenix*, 563.

28. Ibid., 436.

29. Ibid., 425–26.

30. Rubiés, "Travel Writing and Ethnography," 245.

31. Rowling, *Phoenix*, 426–27.

32. Hagrid repeats this belief, giving it even greater emphasis: *"They can' help themselves*, they half kill each other every few weeks." [italics added] Rowling, *Phoenix*, 429.

33. Elaine Ostry, "Accepting Mudbloods: The Ambivalent Social Vision of J.K. Rowling's Fairy Tales." In *Reading Harry Potter*. Ed. Giselle Liza Anatol (Praeger, 2003), 96.

34. Rowling, *Phoenix*, 427.

35. Ibid., 428.

36. Jeffrey Sissons, *First Peoples: Indigenous Cultures and Their Futures* (London: Reaktion Books, 2005), 8.

37. Rubiés, "Travel Writing and Ethnography," 256.

38. Rowling, *Phoenix*, 447–48.

39. Rowling, *Phoenix*, 752.

40. Ibid., 429.

41. Rubiés, "Travel Writing and Ethnography," 255.

42. Rowling, *Phoenix*, 691.

43. The name for the myriad Australian aboriginal children separated from their families from 1883 to 1969 is "The Stolen Generation." Phillip Wearne's *The Return of the Indian: Conquest and Revival in the Americas* (1996) and Theresa McCarty's *A Place to Be Navajo: Rough Rock and the Struggle for Self-Determination in Indigenous Schooling* (2002) address separations in the American context. As Sisson notes: "The loss of children from indigenous communities was often physical and symbolic; physical, in that children were abducted by state authorities or forced to attend distant boarding schools, and symbolic, in that children became culturally alienated from their families and home communities" (28–29).

44. Rowling, *Phoenix*, 692.

45. Sissons, First Peoples, 33.

46. Rowling, *Phoenix*, 697.

47. Ibid., 693.

48. Ibid., 696.

49. Sissons, *First Peoples* 23. Sissons also argues that "[p]erhaps the most serious omission from international debates on the future of indigenous cultures is inadequate recognition of the fact that most indigenous people now living in settler states are urban" (28).

50. Rowling, *Phoenix*, 757.

51. Rubiés, "Travel Writing and Ethography," 249.

52. Rowling, *Phoenix*, 695–96.

53. Ibid., 759.

54. Rowling, *Prince*, 170.

55. Rubiés, "Travel Writing and Ethography," 250.

56. Rowling, *Hallows*, 119.

57. As Julia Park details in her chapter in *Reading Harry Potter*, Rowling constructs Hagrid as a (lower-class) figure of comic relief rather than as in any way frightening. Exceptionally weepy, he carries a flowery pink umbrella and is magically incompetent.

58. Rowling, *Phoenix*, 698.

59. Ibid., 756–57.

60. Ibid., 687.

61. Ibid., 699. In *Deathly Hallows*, while carrying Harry, whom he believes to be dead, Hagrid strikes out against the centaurs by calling them "yeh cowardly bunch o' nags" (728) because they refused to take up arms in the battle against Voldemort. The centaurs do, however, eventually join in the war, revealing their own self-perception as a part of a larger world struggle between the forces of good and evil.

62. Rowling, *Phoenix*, 602 and 756.

63. Rowling, *Prince*, 317 and 544. She also refers to him as "the usurping nag" (426).

64. Rowling, *Phoenix*, 754.

65. Ibid., 602–3.

66. Rubiés, "Travel Writing and Ethnography," 251.

67. Because the institution of slavery presents a somewhat different set of considerations, and because the connection between enslaved house-elves and enslaved Africans is discussed at length in Brycchan Carey's compelling chapter in *Reading Harry Potter* and his work in this volume as well, I do not address it here.

68. Rubiés, "Travel Writing and Ethnography," 256.

69. Edward W. Said, *Orientalism* (New York: Vintage/Random House, 1979), 3. Said identifies the late 1700s as the time when Great Britain and France began their sustained and extensive political control over the geographical region as well as the idea of "the Orient"; he locates the moment of shift to American domination as World War II.

70. Frank H. Wu, *Yellow: Race in America beyond Black and White* (New York: Basic Books/Perseus, 2002), 5–6.

71. Matt Zeitlin, "Harry Potter and the Jewish Goblins," *Matt Zeitlin: Impetuous Young Whippersnapper* (24 July 2007). http://whippersnapper.wordpress.com/2007/07/24/harry-potter-and-the-jewish-goblins/ (accessed November 15, 2008).

72. Rowling, *Goblet*, 446.

73. Rowling, *Hallows*, 486 and 505.

74. Ibid., 466.

75. Ibid., 485.

76. Ibid., 516.

77. Said, *Orientalism*, 40.

78. Rowling, *Hallows*, 516.

79. Ibid., 512, 515, and 513.

80. Said, *Orientalism*, 26.

81. Rowling, *Phoenix*, 308 and 395.

82. Wu, *Yellow*, 13.

83. Wu reports on some anxiety-produced jokes among non-Asian college students: MIT stands for "Made in Taiwan" instead of "Massachusetts Institute of Technology"; UCLA stands for "United Caucasians Lost Among Asians"; UCI (University of California at Irvine) stands for "University of Chinese Immigrants" (48).

84. Rowling, *Phoenix*, 85.

85. Rowling, *Hallows*, 488.

86. Tellingly, Harry "skipped question four" about how wizarding wand laws affected eighteenth-century goblin relations (*Phoenix* 725). Philip Nel argues that like Lewis Carroll, Rowling critiques the Victorian educational model that requires memorization without inspiring questions or thought about what has been learned. Nel, *J.K. Rowling's Harry Potter Novels: A Reader's Guide* (New York: Continuum, 2001), 29–30. I would counter, however, that Professor Binns's lessons still contain invaluable information.

87. Dana Goldstein, "Harry Potter and the Complicated Identity Politics." *The American Prospect* (July 24, 2007), web only. http://www.prospect.org/cs/articles?article=harry_potter_and_the_complicated_identity_politics (accessed 19 September 2008).

88. Rowling, *Hallows*, 294 and 296. I am reminded of Frank Wu's stories of running into young boys who "see me and suddenly strike a karate pose, chop at the air, throw a kick, and *utter some sing-song gibberish*" [italics added] (8).

89. Rowling, *Hallows*, 509.

90. Ibid., 510.

91. Roediger, *Colored White*, 14 and 137.

92. Susan Wolf, "Comment," *Multiculturalism and "The Politics of Recognition": An Essay by Charles Taylor* (Princeton: Princeton University Press, 1992): 75–85, 84.

# 9

# A Marxist Inquiry into J.K. Rowling's Harry Potter Series

*Shama Rangwala*

As phenomenally popular novels, the Harry Potter books might be dismissed as a poor quality manufacture of a culture industry. However, the use of conventions in the series is not a limiting force, but rather a framework through which Rowling uses her highly realist prose to construct an allegorical universe. Just as the magical world is in many ways a rewriting of the very real world of late capitalist Britain, Rowling evokes and then revises the often simplistic generic conventions of the traditional folk tale in order to create a deceivingly complex narrative. Yet by focusing on the suspense and intricate plot twists of the story, we may often overlook the cultural implications of the novels. This chapter examines the specific ways in which the text reflects current social and economic conditions of late-capitalist Britain, arguing that the text functions as "an ideological act in its own right"[1] and works to produce and reproduce ideology in the neo-Marxist sense.

In *The Political Unconscious*, Fredric Jameson posits that every narrative is a socially symbolic act, gesturing to the Marxist meta-narrative and providing "imaginary or formal 'solutions' to unresolvable social contradictions."[2] Through this lens, we can read Harry Potter as promoting a particular ideology. With Jameson's text as a theoretical framework, the work of Barbara Ehrenreich in *Fear of Falling: The Inner Life of the Middle Class* provides a substantive description of the defining characteristics of the middle class in relation to the aristocracy and the working class. Ehrenreich outlines the evolution of an older middle class into a new consumerist class obsessed with social mobility—"one that begins with a mood of generosity and optimism and ends with cynicism and narrowing self-interest."[3] My reading of Harry Potter is primarily as class allegory, designed to school its readers in traditional middle-class values by privileging the academy and the intelligentsia in opposition to the unbridled consumption of this newer middle class.

## HARRY AS HERO

Harry, an orphan who lives with relatives who persecute him, suddenly finds himself in a literally magical world that remedies the deficiencies of his former life. He becomes the locus of the imaginary resolution: both orphan and hero, Harry must reconcile the two positions and find a middle ground between being the juvenile delinquent and the overconfident champion. Throughout the series, he combines the values of the moderate and fiscally responsible middle class with the economic capital of the consumerist class. Harry's different positions in the magic and nonmagic worlds speak to his identity as an economic subject. In the magic world, Harry realizes the economic position for which the Dursleys strive: effortless wealth and unlimited power of consumption. One of the primary fantasies Harry fulfills by entering the magic world is an economic one, in which he is able to participate on a higher level in the capitalist system than in the "real," nonmagic, world.

Harry's life of deprivation with the Dursleys prepares him for responsible management of his newfound wealth so that his privilege does not instigate a degeneration into Dudley-like vacuity. In this way, Rowling combines the fantasy of economic power with the pedagogic message of temperance. Harry is still a child with natural desires of consumption, but he does not indulge them to excess. During his first ride on the Hogwarts Express, Harry meets Ron Weasley, a poorer student who eventually becomes his best friend. As the candy trolley rolls past, Harry "leapt to his feet, but Ron's ears went pink again and he muttered that he'd brought sandwiches. . . . He had never had any money for candy. . . . Not wanting to miss anything, he [Harry] got some of everything and paid the woman eleven silver Sickles and seven bronze Knuts."[4] In the magic world, not only does Harry finally have the requisite capital, but the products available are also much more exciting than the prosaic Mars Bars. Rowling's description of the trolley emphasizes the fantastical nature of this new world— Harry is in a better position for consumption than Dudley both on the side of purchasing power and access to goods. Furthermore, unlike Dudley, Harry enjoys sharing his wealth: "'Go on, have a pasty,' said Harry, who had never had anything to share before or, indeed, anyone to share it with. It was a nice feeling, sitting there with Ron, eating their way through all Harry's pasties, cakes, and candies (the sandwiches lay forgotten)."[5] Privileging the purchased goods over the homemade sandwiches, Harry's pleasure comes equally in having the ability to acquire goods as from sharing them with another. The magic world thus remedies his deficiencies in both human and financial interactions.

Although Harry's economic status is more upper class—he inherits his wealth—his values are of the early, pre-Dursley middle class, whose "emphasis on discipline and deferred gratification goes back to its emergence as a class near the turn of the [twentieth] century."[6] In the third novel, *Harry Potter and the Prisoner of Azkaban*, Harry spends a few weeks living in a pub above Diagon Alley, the wizarding high street of London. Idle and alone, Harry roams the streets looking in all the shops, particularly the broom shop with a new Firebolt in the window. "He had never wanted anything so much in his whole life";[7] however, although he strongly desires the broom, he defers gratification until that time when he can afford to spend such an amount. Unlike the Weasleys' economising, Harry's restraint does not deprive him of a popular high-quality commodity; he already has a working broom and can technically afford a new one. Indeed, it takes discipline to resist something one can afford but *should not buy*—the lesson would be meaningless if his desire could not possibly be fulfilled.[8] Furthermore, Harry's restraint is always magically rewarded; when his Nimbus breaks during a match, a mysterious package arrives with a new Firebolt.

Indeed, we can read Harry's very attendance at Hogwarts as a reward for years of good behavior with the terrible Dursleys. Instead of rebelling against his relatives, Harry submits to the cruelest treatment. Hogwarts is not a place for the Dudleys of the world: although magic is typically a fantasy of production without labor, one that would appeal to commodity fetishists, the magic at Hogwarts entails a specifically middle class sort of labor. In order to perform magic, one must endure years of difficult schooling, both theoretical and practical. Rowling's series teaches young readers that if they persevere through bad situations, good fortune will eventually come their way. This good fortune is not the kind of easy consumerism for which the Dursleys strive, but rather the ability to manipulate the codes of an abstract type of labor; in other words, the desire fulfilled is one of a typical professional managerial class (PMC) subject.

If, as Louis Althusser writes, "ideology interpellates individuals as subjects,"[9] then Harry is interpellated in entirely different ways in the two worlds. However, although Althusser argues that we are subjects entirely constituted by interpellations, Rowling's text—while acknowledging and exploring this conception—ultimately emphasizes the role of individual agency, choice, and experience in transcending external imposition. In the nonmagic world, Harry's family—the most immediate ideological state apparatus—hails him as a troublemaking leech. Rowling uses Dudley as a foil for Harry's valorized qualities while simultaneously emphasizing the importance of the subject's ideological interpellation, rather than any innate nature, in identity formation. The Dursleys never call Harry by name, preferring "the boy" or "you," thus denying Harry's individual subjectivity. When Vernon's sister, Aunt Marge, visits the Dursleys in *Prisoner of Azkaban*, Vernon directs Harry to play the role of the deviant nephew who attends "St. Brutus's Secure Centre for Incurably Criminal Boys." After Marge maligns the memory of Harry's parents, he allows his anger at her to overcome his better judgment and inflates her like a balloon. Thus, Harry becomes exactly what his relatives label him—a criminally dangerous delinquent. Indeed, whenever Harry is with his relatives, he is more similar to their perception of him than he is to the wizard hero of Hogwarts; from their perspective, the Dursleys are perfectly justified in viewing Harry not only as ungrateful for all they provide him but also as an active menace.

In the magic world, Harry is hailed—both in the colloquial and Althusserian senses—as a hero. As Professor McGonagall says, somewhat meta-textually, "He'll be famous—a legend . . . there will be books written about Harry—every child in our world will know his name!"[10] In the nonmagic world, no one ever calls Harry by name, but in the wizarding world, one of the first changes Harry notices is the overwhelmingly positive attention his name and presence garner. Harry grows accustomed to this position and playing the hero progressively becomes an integral part of his identity, the extent to which is a key problem in *Harry Potter and the Order of the Phoenix*. Harry wholeheartedly takes on the role into which the wizarding masses interpellate him. When he wants to rush to the rescue of his godfather Sirius, he disregards Hermione's cautions. Just as he took on the negative interpellations of his relatives on Privet Drive, in the wizarding world Harry takes on the positive interpellations of the hero; however, being molded in this way has a hazardous effect. Harry's heroism in *Order of the Phoenix* becomes reckless and creates the conditions for his godfather's death.

At the end of *Harry Potter and the Half-Blood Prince*, Harry achieves a reconciliation between the two extremes. He learns that his entire life was predetermined by a prophecy—echoing Althusser's contention that "individuals are always-already interpellated by ideology as subjects.[11] Although Harry believes that he does not have choice, that his fate is predetermined by the prophecy, Dumbledore explains, "The prophecy does not mean you *have* to do anything! . . . You are free to choose your way, quite free to turn your back on the prophecy! But Voldemort continues to set store by the prophecy. He will continue to hunt you . . . which makes it certain, really, that . . . one of [you] is going to end up killing the other."[12] Harry gains from Dumbledore an ideological stake in bourgeois individualism and understands his personal role: "It was, he thought, the difference between being dragged into the arena to face a battle to the death and walking into the arena with your head held high."[13] However, Harry's realization is problematic when viewed in the larger context of the Althusserian conception of ideology. The Potter series—as a fantasy fairy tale—valorizes individual agency, but in this case agency has more to do with choosing to accept a predestination rather than having actual choice. The prophecy sets in motion a series of events that leads to the construction of Harry's identity and moral code. Voldemort's decision "to mark [Harry] as his equal" is a form of interpellation and because of this always-already determined identity, Harry chooses to fight. His personality is such that he truly desires to fulfill the prophecy, but Rowling codes this in the language of individual agency.

In *Harry Potter*, the issue of choice is not quantitative, but qualitative: only one real choice is available, but acknowledging this limitation represents courage for Harry, not capitulation. This message is part of a larger agenda in Rowling's series: we should want to accept a role within a larger structure and value temperance over excess. Moreover, this acceptance should not stem from resignation; the way in which ideology has always-already interpellated us as subjects creates the desire to be that subject. With this realization at the end of *Half-Blood Prince*, Harry reaches a middle ground between his two identities. Sobered by the experience of contributing to his godfather's death, his sense of self as hero is not a reckless one as in *Order of the Phoenix*. Although he could opt to become what his relatives think he is (a juvenile delinquent), Harry instead follows the difficult path of the prophecy. The contradiction between the two identities is reconciled in a developed awareness of himself as ideological subject—not hailed by the wizarding masses or his relatives but by the privileged character of Dumbledore and the prophecy. In other words, what the text articulates is a binary: oppressed and delinquent orphan on one side and famous and beloved hero on the other. Harry reconciles these positions by finding a third way, through the middle-class ideology of the academy and its representative, Dumbledore. The text also privileges *how* the headmaster shapes Harry's identity: instead of nomination, Dumbledore orchestrates experiences for his student. For instance, Harry must confront Voldemort through Professor Quirrell and battle the Basilisk, endeavours Dumbledore could have easily undertaken himself. Because Harry performs these tasks and actually enacts "hero" rather than being labeled as such, he is in a better position to make informed choices about his actions in the future. Through diversity of experience, his identity is no longer confined to one specific interpellation or another.

To fulfill his ultimate task of defeating Voldemort, Harry rejects Scrimgeour and the Ministry and uses the skills and information he has learned from Dumbledore. He demonstrates the most privileged trait of the novel—individual courage in the face of a "losing battle"[14]—a characteristic lacking in Dudley Dursley or Draco Malfoy. Harry evolves from a boy who needs institutional recognition—good grades, winning the House Cup—to a young man who does what is right regardless of external support. In *Deathly Hallows*, Harry undergoes another evolution. Faced with the decision to pursue the Hallows, which he strongly desires, or the task Dumbledore gives him to destroy the Horcruxes, Harry chooses to defer gratification, perhaps indefinitely, and follow the trajectory set out for him by his headmaster. Rowling presents this choice as one between an immature and selfish course—although Harry may believe the Hallows will benefit the greater good, it is a tertiary justification—and a difficult pursuit farthest from personal gain. The imaginary resolution involves Harry fulfilling both and eventually choosing to forgo being master of the Hallows, content in a relatively more modest position as a government employee.

## NARRATIVE AS ALLEGORY

In Harry Potter, the overarching battle against Voldemort functions as an allegorical enactment of a class struggle between an aristocratic elite and a predominantly middle- and working-class democracy. Rowling inscribes the ideology of Voldemort in different ways: using the words of Karl Marx, she "conjure[s] up the spirits of the past to their service, borrowing from them names, battle slogans, and costumes in order to present this new scene in world history in time-honored disguise and borrowed language."[15] Voldemort and his followers, the Death Eaters, are dressed alternatively in feudal, fascist, and Thatcherite ideologies. Just as Harry finds a third way between his contradictory interpellations, the actor emerging ideologically triumphant in this struggle is neither the aristocratic elite nor the welfare state, but rather the academy and the intelligentsia represented by Dumbledore and Hogwarts. In this way, the Battle of Hogwarts embodies the struggle for signification of Hogwarts as Castle or Academy.

At the beginning of the series, we have a superficial idea of Voldemort and his Death Eater followers as absolutely evil villains, in the mold of Tolkien's Sauron or other fairy-tale and mythological characters. However, as the story progresses, we learn more about Voldemort's past and the motivations behind his actions and must complicate our earlier assessment—an example of Rowling's commitment to realism. Growing up in an orphanage, Voldemort develops a hatred for nonmagic people as he was ostracized for the unusual accidents he would cause; when Dumbledore brings him to Hogwarts, he is finally at home with others of the same persuasion. After gathering a group of pureblood followers, Voldemort attempts to bring about a return to the old ways when non-purebloodwizards and Muggles were persecuted.

Voldemort surrounds himself with the aristocracy of the magic world to the exclusion of all others. Few of his followers work, apart from those who sell dark-magic artifacts or use their occupations as a cover for espionage. In *Goblet of Fire*, the terror tactics used by the Death Eaters at the Quidditch World Cup are deliberately reminiscent of the Ku Klux Klan: "A crowd of wizards, tightly packed and moving together with wands pointing straight upward, was marching slowly across the field. Harry squinted at them. . . . They didn't seem to have faces. . . . Then he realized that their heads were hooded and their faces masked."[16] The inclusion of this scene at a sporting event analogous to the World Cup of Soccer emphasizes the historical connection: Rowling includes signifiers such as strong nationalism and spectacle that make the event recognizable to contemporary readers. That the Death Eaters engage in the sport of drunken Muggle-baiting by literally "puppeteer[ing]"[17] their victims points to Voldemort's fascism. His entire project is to take absolute control by reverting power to the elite classes and violently oppressing all others. Voldemort's name translates roughly as "flight from death" and his biggest fear is death, which signifies a loss of control over the self; he thus tries to transcend this inevitable state through his Horcruxes. He also copes with his fear through an ideological emphasis on bloodlines and legacies. Voldemort's putative immortality derives from this focus on lineage. He divides his soul into seven Horcruxes, objects that have particular significance for him and no one can kill him completely while these objects are intact. His choice of Horcruxes is telling, all connected to old wizarding blood, including Hogwarts' founders. Voldemort's fascism stems from personal fear; he is not truly an ideologue, although he dresses his desire for control over death in the rhetoric of pureblood supremacy and social engineering. To have ambitions for class ascension, in order to facilitate his self-preservation, is a desire that can never be satisfied—no upper limit exists. By contrast, the privileged middle class in the series requires only reaching an equilibrium between vocation and compensation. Banal bourgeois labor—the privileged category in this text—has an actuality in a way that the infinite upward aspirations of Voldemort do not.

On the other side of this conflict is the Ministry of Magic, an apparent allegory of the New Labour government. The magic world is a capitalist welfare state, with free health care and public transportation. Hogwarts School accepts every child with magical ability and has a scholarship fund for those who cannot pay. The press is relatively diverse and free, and the most widely read newspaper, *The Daily Prophet*, operates under capitalist principles and is often critical of those in power. Nevertheless, Rowling is not unambiguous in her portrayal of the Ministry, the ostensible "good guys." She sets up a secondary conflict between the bureaucratic Ministry of Magic and the intelligentsia of Dumbledore and Hogwarts. Although both groups share an external opponent, they have different views on the best way to defeat Voldemort's forces. Cornelius Fudge, the Minister of Magic for the first five books, is a largely ineffectual politician who cares more about keeping order and maintaining his own popularity than facing the truth about Voldemort's return. In *Order of the Phoenix*, the practical antagonist is not Voldemort, but the Ministry, specifically in the form of Dolores Umbridge. After Harry sees Voldemort return to corporeal form, he and Dumbledore attempt to spread the news and prepare for war. Fudge appoints Umbridge to Hogwarts, temporarily sacking Dumbledore, to assert the primacy of the Ministry's version of events and state control over public institutions. Rowling writes Umbridge as a child abuser equally evil to Voldemort. In short, the Ministry takes on qualities of the very force they are trying to resist.

Unlike other fairy-tale heroes, Harry more practically has to contend with both his enemy Voldemort and a conservative Ministry of Magic that wants to maintain the status quo at all costs. Rowling thus highlights the cleavages within liberal democracies, which operate through a dialectic of various parties and institutions, as opposed to the totalitarian nature of fascism or feudalism. The Ministry occupies a complicated position—an institution that purports to represent and protect the people but is ultimately concerned with self-preservation.

Although the Ministry is often the antagonist, Rowling is unequivocal in her valorization of the intelligentsia and the academy, particularly its embodiment in Dumbledore. As Harry tells Scrimgeour, he is "Dumbledore's man through and through"[18] and the texts demand the readers to be so as well. Throughout the series, much of the danger in which Harry seemingly randomly finds himself—especially in the first two books—Dumbledore implicitly arranges, as part of his student's schooling in Defence against the Dark Arts. Dumbledore controls the narrative and much that Harry experiences; yet despite his power, he does not act or plan with malevolent intent. Professor McGonagall suggests that Dumbledore's powers and knowledge of the dark arts are equal to Voldemort's, but that he is too "*noble* to use them."[19] Dumbledore's nobility is different from the aristocratic aspirations of Voldemort, however, because he tempers his substantial political and magical power with acquired wisdom and liberal tolerance. Dumbledore is also always in a superior epistemological position, although Harry's unreliable perspective sometimes seemingly disputes this. Indeed, in *Harry Potter and the Deathly Hallows*, Harry questions his devotion to Dumbledore after reading Rita Skeeter's scathing biography. However, by humanizing Dumbledore and demonstrating how his wisdom came through a *process* of rebellion and maturity—just as Harry's does—the texts embrace the bildungsroman narrative of individualism and structural interpellation rather than the static essentialism of Voldemort. Just as the academic middle class appropriates Hogwarts Castle, it redefines the nobility.

The text also privileges the institution Dumbledore represents, Hogwarts School of Witchcraft and Wizardry. Hogwarts Castle is the location of a perfect synthesis of medieval and contemporary—the school embodies the positive aspects of both. In terms of the medieval, Hogwarts retains a legacy of tradition, chivalry, fortress-like security, art and iconography, and a historical awareness. The school contains suits of armor, winding staircases, gothic halls, and secret passageways. Yet Hogwarts is also socialist-democratic, and promotes values such as tolerance and diversity; the main role of the school is not only academic education, but also moral and ideological socialization. In *Half-Blood Prince*, we learn that the academy operates as a meritocracy and offers scholarships to students who cannot pay fees. Rowling represents Hogwarts as a legitimate agent of socialization through its role as reproducer of the intelligentsia, and thus it is representative of cultural—and in this case, also magical—capital. Voldemort wants to take back the Castle—literally—so he can control the reproduction of ideology in the young and impose his particular paradigm onto magical society. After Dumbledore's death, Voldemort takes over Hogwarts and immediately institutes curriculum changes to conform to his pureblood supremacy. When he seizes control of the Ministry, the government employees offer little resistance for fear of retribution. It is the Order of the Phoenix, the underground movement founded by Dumbledore and by extension the intelligentsia, that takes on the responsibility for spreading information and resistance through pirate radio. At Hogwarts, the students enact a more explicit rebellion under the banner of Dumbledore's Army. In the end, the very armor of Hogwarts is mobilized to fight for the status of the place as Academy rather than Castle, and thus naturalizes the claim of the intelligentsia to this all-important ideological state apparatus.

This conflict between Voldemort's extreme conservatism, the bureaucratic democracy of the Ministry of Magic, and the traditional middle-class moderates of Hogwarts forms the political unconscious of the series, the Marxist meta-narrative. The texts articulate History in the Jamesonian sense by drawing parallels between the magical and nonmagic worlds. Rowling privileges the academy over the other two competing institutions, and the intelligentsia is the only group that emerges unscathed. The Battle of Hogwarts concludes with the students scattered among the House tables. The triumph of Dumbledore's ideology dismantles the greatest divisions that previously seemed essentialized by the Sorting Hat and the novel ends with the next generation embracing choice. His son anxious about the sorting, Harry comforts him by articulating the new order: "you'll be able to choose Gryffindor over Slytherin. The Sorting Hat takes your choice into account."[20] The series finishes not with Voldemort's defeat, but rather with a vision of banal middle-class labor and the integration of the next generation into the Academy. In other words, the fulfillment of narrative lack is not the magical and epic vanquishing of evil, but the realization of a quiet life that readers can also achieve.

## REPRESENTATIONS OF CLASS

From the beginning of *Harry Potter and the Philosopher's Stone,* Rowling emphasizes the importance of class and ideology in the series. The novel begins not with the title character, but rather with a description of his nonmagic relatives: "Mr. and Mrs. Dursley . . . were proud to say that they were perfectly normal, thank you very much. They were the last people you'd expect to be involved in anything strange or mysterious, because they just didn't hold with such nonsense. Mr. Dursley was the director of a firm called Grunnings, which made drills."[21] The Dursleys exemplify the aspirations and fears of the newly mobile middle class without the traditional concomitant value placed in deferred gratification. They represent Rowling's strongest indictment of a consumerist Britain she believes to be blindly immersed in the dominant ideology, fearing and consequently loathing any deviations from this norm. In particular, Harry's relatives are emblematic of what Barbara Ehrenreich describes as "the retreat from liberalism and the rise, in the professional middle class, of a meaner, more selfish outlook, hostile to the aspirations of those less fortunate."[22] Indeed, Vernon Dursley goes to great lengths to prevent Harry from attending Hogwarts, as he is opposed not only to the success of his hated nephew, but to any taint of association with a world outside—and naturally inferior, in his view—of the upper and middle classes. Vernon places value on the academy not for the sake of education but rather as a ticket to social mobility through networking—he sends Dudley to Smeltings, a private school similar in form to Hogwarts but whose values are embodied in a uniform that includes a large stick for hitting rival classmates. The individualism and aggression that the Dursleys value is limited to what exists inside their petit bourgeois existence: the domination of others and procurement of commodities rather than self-education or enlightenment, let alone taking on the responsibility to fight evil.

The Dursleys' position within capitalism determines their relationship to the consumer culture. Vernon does not create anything, but rather sells drills—a tool used in the intermittent stages of manufacturing that itself does not produce anything. Rowling associates his business with his economic location, a vague middling position within a larger structure. Julia Park notes, "the Dursleys want for nothing and yet they stingily dole out the things that Harry, their own flesh and blood, needs,"[23] contrasting them with the textually privileged Weasleys. The Dursleys reinvest the fruits of Vernon's middle-class labor in consumer goods for their beloved son Dudley, Harry's nonmagical counterpart. One of the first descriptions of Dudley Dursley portrays him as a caricatured child of late-capitalist permissiveness. Dudley's senseless consumption—inscribed onto his enormous body—is without utility or purpose. Petunia and Vernon indulge Dudley and perpetuate "the permissive, hedonistic message of the consumer culture."[24] Ehrenreich criticizes this permissiveness, arguing that "the child of authoritarian parents can at least withdraw into fantasies of freedom or revenge, but the child of overly permissive parents has little inner space to retreat to."[25] Indeed, Dudley's mindlessness and reliance on manufactured entertainment has its origin in the permissiveness of his class. However, keeping with Rowling's overall message of transcending external conditioning, even Dudley appreciates Harry after their experience with the dementors.

In the wizarding world, the elite consists of old-money aristocracy embodied in the Malfoys. Harry first meets Draco Malfoy in a clothing shop on Diagon Alley, before he has any knowledge of the wizarding world. Draco immediately educates Harry in the class and race structure of the magic world: "I know I'll be in Slytherin, all our family have been—imagine being in Hufflepuff, I think I'd leave, wouldn't you? . . . [T]hey [i.e., Harry's parents] were *our* kind [pureblood] weren't they? . . . I really don't think they should let the other sort in, do you? They're just not the same; they've never been brought up to know our ways. . . . I think they should keep it in the old wizarding families."[26] Draco articulates the sentiment of the majority of the wizard elite, echoing the feudal rhetoric of blood and hierarchy. Significantly, the Heir of Slytherin, Voldemort himself, is a half-blood; he uses his magical skill, which translates into social capital, and his mother's pedigree not only to enter the pureblood aristocracy, but also to become the leader of the pureblood movement. Voldemort believes he can overcome his half-Muggle lineage—the "pure" categories he creates, however, are false. Voldemort's attachment to Hogwarts is evident, not as institution of PMC education but as the location of his integration into wizarding society and the beginnings of his ascension to power. He looks to Hogwarts' past rather than what the Castle has become, appropriating the feudal and rejecting the academic connotations that have been more recently inscribed.

On the other side of the socioeconomic spectrum, the house-elves are the most marginalized group in the wizard world. The elves appear to be almost genetically engineered as slave laborers. They work in the background, magically cooking and cleaning without being seen, much like the invisible servant class of the old British aristocracy. Indeed, Harry only discovers their existence in his second year at Hogwarts. Magic binds them to those whom they serve— they are incapable of disobeying orders and enact their own punishments if they speak ill of their masters. As the dominant ideology interpellates them as subaltern subjects, they completely inhabit their assigned roles. Elves like Winky fear freedom and embrace their subjugation. The elves also use childish language with poor grammar, often referring to themselves in the third person as if they internalize a lack of agency. Reflecting the dominant ideology of the wizarding world and the elves' own acceptance of their subjugation, the text depicts them as inferior creatures, dirty and naked.

As the most conscientious of the three friends, Hermione forms the Society for the Promotion of Elfish Welfare, which Ron pejoratively labels, "the House-Elf Liberation Front." The conflict here is between Hermione's argument that ideology is at work in subjugating the elves, whereas Ron and others claim that the elves's position is merely natural. When Harry, Ron, and Hermione visit the kitchen in *Goblet of Fire*, the elves appear genuine in their desire to serve the students and resistant to Hermione's calls to assert their right to unionize. Hermione believes that culture conditions the house-elves into subservience; her position relies on the charge of false consciousness, that the dominant ideology hails the elves into internalizing a position of servitude despite the often miserable working conditions and verbal and physical abuse. Although Dobby is not completely "free" in Hermione's sense, occasionally still punishing himself for speaking ill of his current employer and not wanting "too much" freedom, he demonstrates the possibility of overcoming the apparent limitations of his species and realizes that he can be a social and economic subject as well—he buys clothing and presents for Harry and takes a dominant role toward Winky, whom he nurses back to health when she overindulges in butterbeer. "The Hogwarts house-elves . . . edg[e] away from Dobby, as though he was carrying something contagious,"[27] but Dobby's love of freedom supports Hermione's claim that the elves live under false consciousness. Although difficult, the possibility exists for them to assert their own agency and break out of the mold created by the dominant ideology. In the end, Dobby makes the most individual choice of all—when to die. He risks his life to save Harry's, not only because the wizard set him free and always treated him well, but also because he understands that Harry's cause benefits all magical and nonmagical creatures. Dobby's trajectory moves from absolute oppression and abjection to being an active subject in his own right.

The house-elf Kreacher offers a more complicated example. Although his beliefs and interactions with wizards prove how deep these interpellations can run, his narrative role also demonstrates the folly of buying into the prevailing view that house-elves are inherently inferior beings. Rowling paints Kreacher as lowly and despicable, mean and filthy—in short, as his name implies, he is subhuman: "Except for the filthy rag tied like a loincloth around its middle, it was completely naked."[28] The choice of pronoun disavows personhood and subjectivity but has concrete consequences in proving fatal to Sirius. Kreacher is always-already a creature rather than a person, named as such from birth. The elf wholeheartedly subscribes to the idea of pureblood supremacy, even though the ideology places him squarely at the bottom of this hierarchy. When Harry discovers that Kreacher was an active agent in orchestrating Sirius's death, Harry rages about the elf's betrayal, disbelieving that "Hermione kept telling us to be nice to him."[29] Harry's shock comes from his previous disregard of Kreacher as a threat; he denied that Kreacher has the ability to act on his own will. After Sirius's death, Harry sees Kreacher as innately evil. Dumbledore, however, refutes this essentialism, arguing, "Kreacher is what he has been made by wizards, Harry. . . . Yes, he is to be pitied. His existence has been as miserable as your friend Dobby's."[30] Once again, Dumbledore is the voice of bourgeois liberal reason, schooling Harry in the tolerant values he spreads through his role at Hogwarts. By placing this incident with Kreacher in a larger context, the headmaster addresses the problems of pureblood and wizard-centric ideology. Indeed, Kreacher's conversion in *Deathly Hallows* supports Hermione's claim that the elves are victims of false consciousness rather than a natural position in the social order. It is unlikely that he, like Dobby, denounces his pureblood ideology, yet his alliance with Harry does point to the possibility for elves of envisioning a different sort of social hierarchy.[31]

Harry realizes that the majority opinion can be wrong and that he must exercise tolerance and use his own judgment rather than conforming to the dominant worldview. Among the values Dumbledore teaches, individualism and acceptance of others are paramount. However, we do see limitations to this liberal bourgeois ideology: Dumbledore does not effect structural change. Rather than educating the Hogwarts elves into rejecting their false consciousness and accepting a wage system, he supports individuals such as Dobby who overcome their interpellations on their own. Additionally, education is not mandatory for all children; all are invited to Hogwarts but must choose to attend. The intelligentsia in Harry Potter favors individual worth and achievement of bourgeois liberalism rather than the socialist view that advocates the more systemic equalization of class and racial hierarchies. Once again, the emphasis is clearly on individual choice rather than imposing equality. When Winky is freed in disgrace, Dumbledore allows her to continue engaging in slave labor in the Hogwarts kitchen. The elves must choose to be free and Dumbledore will not force freedom upon them.

The most sympathetic portrayal of class is that of the Weasleys. A class division exists within the racial category of pureblood: the Weasleys occupy a lower-middle-class rather than an aristocratic position, although their lineage is entirely magical. They have no landed wealth and Arthur Weasley has a civil servant job at the Ministry of Magic; Molly Weasley tends house and takes care of their seven children. Both are accomplished wizards and loyal supporters of Dumbledore and Hogwarts. They live modestly, sharing clothes and school supplies. The Weasleys provide a sharp contrast to the Dursleys: they are proud of what little they have and would never exploit others for gain. Although the Dursleys would appropriate Harry's fortune if they knew of its existence, the Weasleys are too proud to accept any money from Harry. The eventual union of Harry and Ginny Weasley is thus an imaginary resolution that synthesizes traditional middle-class values with the inherited Potter wealth.

The Weasleys also demonstrate an ideological division within purebloods. Instead of hating Muggles, Arthur Weasley studies them. Arthur represents an older generation that prefers employment in his field of interest rather than one with substantial compensation. Percy Weasley provides a contrast to his father—he was Head Boy at Hogwarts and upon graduation takes a job as an assistant to a prominent member of the Ministry. As Ron explains, "He said he's been having to struggle against Dad's lousy reputation ever since he joined the Ministry and that Dad's got no ambition and that's why we've always been— you know—not had a lot of money."[32] Percy's idea of success is quite different from that of the rest of his family. He exhibits a "premature pragmatism" that Barbara Ehrenreich identifies as the yuppie mentality: "They were putting aside, at far too early an age, their idealism and intellectual curiosity in favour of economic security, which was increasingly defined as wealth."[33] Once he begins his job at the Ministry, Percy cuts himself off from his family. Rowling portrays him negatively: he has few friends and adheres too strongly to the rules. He lacks a personality outside of his ambition and the expectations of those in power. Yet by the end, he matures beyond petty concerns and rejoins his family at the Battle of Hogwarts.

In addition to providing an alternative depiction of a pureblood family, the Weasleys also demonstrate a split in the middle class.[34] The text privileges the values of the Weasleys, but repeatedly points to their subordinate position within the economic system. Harry feels guilt at having a fortune that the Weasleys do not accept when he tries to share; always conscious of the disparity in wealth, he attempts to compensate by purchasing gifts and treating Ron and Ginny. Yet in *Goblet of Fire*, when Harry and Ron have a temporary falling-out, Harry takes out his anger at Ron in a classist way: "he hated everything about Ron, right down to the several inches of bare ankle showing beneath his pajama trousers.... [H]e would even have liked Ron to throw a punch at him, but Ron just stood there in his too small pajamas."[35] He is aware that

Ron is self-conscious about his second-hand clothing and Harry latches on to that insecurity as a way to express his own putative superiority. Significantly, the text codes their argument as a part of the turbulence of adolescence; once Harry gets a taste of class-based loathing, he never again criticizes Ron or the Weasleys for their lack of financial resources. Rowling writes this incident as a natural part of Harry's evolution, analogous to rebelling against authority figures or exploring his sexuality.[36]

Whereas the Dursleys' bourgeois labor is about the fruits—moving ahead on the social ladder in order to purchase status and goods—in the end Harry follows a calling as an Auror. The narrative moves from a representation of the newer middle class to the traditional middle class that Ehrenreich describes, thus indulging a nostalgia and suggesting that our socioeconomic cultural trajectory can be reversed: history will repeat itself in a better way. Indeed, the imaginary resolution is that, of course, Harry does not require employment in order to support his family financially, so he is free to choose whatever employment he desires.

## WHY POTTER? WHY MARXIST?

Any Marxist analysis of Harry Potter would be incomplete without an ac-knowledgment of the contradictions between the ideology the original text promotes and the Harry Potter consumerist phenomenon.[37] Instances of the Harry Potter brand occur in cinema, on Internet sites, in video games, and in many other media. One can also purchase nonmagic equivalents of many of the products Harry encounters, such as Bertie Bott's Every Flavor Beans and every sort of costume and wand imaginable. The very culture industry whose ideology the original text opposes appropriates Harry Potter. Readers love the Potter series for a number of different reasons; in late-capitalist society, a prod-uct is successful if its consumers desire more. The ideological message of Harry Potter allows parents to indulge in consumer goods while still schooling their children in traditional values of moderation.

## NOTES

1. Frederic Jameson, *The Political Unconscious: Narrative as Socially Symbolic Act* (Durham: Duke UP, 1981), 79.

2. Ibid.

3. Barbara Ehrenreich, *Fear of Falling: The Inner Life of the Middle Class* (New York: Pantheon Books, 1989), 3.

4. J.K. Rowling, *Harry Potter and the Sorcerer's Stone* (New York: Scholastic, 1997), 101.

5. Ibid., 102.

6. Ehrenreich, *Fear of Falling*, 85.

7. J.K. Rowling, *Harry Potter and the Prisoner of Azkaban* (New York: Scholastic, 1999), 51–52.

8. For a biographical analogy, we may look to Julia Park's comment on the solidly middle-class author's renunciation of material comfort: "[Rowling's] 'descent' into indigence was willful and clearly temporary." Julia Park, "Class and Socioeconomic Identity in Harry Potter's England," *Reading Harry Potter: Critical Essays*, ed. Giselle Liza Anatol (Westport: Praeger, 2003), 182.

9. Louis Althusser, "Ideology and Ideological State Apparatuses" [1969], *The Norton Anthology of Theory and Criticism*, ed. Vincent B. Leitch (New York: WW Norton & Co., 2001): 1483–1508, 1502.

10. Rowling, *Stone*, 13.

11. Althusser, "Ideology and Ideological Apparatuses," 1505.

12. J.K. Rowling, *Harry Potter and the Half-Blood Prince* (New York: Scholastic, 2005), 512.

13. Ibid., 512.

14. Ibid., 644.

15. Karl Marx, "The Eighteenth Brumaire of Louis Napoleon" [1852], Marxists Internet Archive. 14 April 2006. <http://www.marxists.org/archive/marx/works/1852/18th-brumaire/ch01.htm>.

16. J.K. Rowling, *Harry Potter and the Goblet of Fire* (New York: Scholastic, 2000), 119.

17. Ibid., 119.

18. Rowling, *Prince*, 348.

19. Rowling, *Stone*, 11. Italics in original.

20. J.K. Rowling, *Harry Potter and the Deathly Hallows* (New York: Scholastic, 2007), 758.

21. Rowling, *Stone*, 1.

22. Ehrenreich, *Fear of Falling*, 3.

23. Park, "Class and Socioeconomic Identity," 187.

24. Ibid., 175.

25. Ibid., 90.

26. Rowling, *Stone*, 77–78.

27. Rowling, *Goblet*, 378.

28. J.K. Rowling, *Harry Potter and the Order of the Phoenix* (New York: Scholastic, 2003), 107.

29. Ibid., 832.

30. Ibid.

31. The werewolf example, although similar to the case of Kreacher and Dobby, demonstrates that not all negative characters can be redeemed. The issue of choice is emphasized yet again. Fenrir Greyback is the animalistic, lower-class werewolf who chooses not to control his desire for consumption—a yearning coded as libidinal. By contrast, Remus Lupin is a member of the intelligentsia who uses a potion to control—that is, civilize—his werewolf condition.

32. Ibid., 72.

33. Ehrenreich, *Fear of Falling*, 211.

34. In Fred and George, the Weasleys also demonstrate the possibility of upward mobility as a result of merit. In their new dragonskin jackets, the twins embody achievement owing to innovation and hard work. The tainted prize money from the Triwizard

tournament is redeemed in its conversion to a small-business loan, that backbone of the economy.

35. Rowling, *Goblet*, 335–36.

36. Similarly, in *Deathly Hallows*, we learn of Dumbledore's flirtation with Grindelwald and his totalitarian ideology. Their slogan, "for the greater good," undergoes a reappropriation as Dumbledore realizes that the greater good is not a justification for any means, but rather an ethos to which it is vital to adhere at every step. The older and wiser Dumbledore argues that love for wizard and Muggle alike is essential in living a fulfilled life. In this realist series about education and socialization, Rowling emphasizes process—brushes with so-called bad ideologies make the eventual investment in the privileged values seemingly more authentic.

37. A small sampling of further reading: Andrew Blake, *The Irresistible Rise of Harry Potter* (London: Verso, 2002); Rebecca Sutherland Borah, "Apprentice Wizards Welcome: Fan Communities and the Culture of Harry Potter," in *The Ivory Tower and Harry Potter: Perspectives on a Literary Phenomenon*, ed. Lana Whited (Columbia: U of Missouri P, 2002), 343–64; Tammy Turner-Vorbeck, "Pottermania: Good, Clean Fun or Cultural Hegemony?" in *Harry Potter's World: Multidisciplinary Critical Perspectives*, ed. Elizabeth E. Heilman (New York: Routledge, 2003), 13–24.

# 10

# Secret Domination or Civic Duty: The Source and Purpose of Magical Power in Harry Potter

*Margaret J. Oakes*

By chapter 5 of book I in the Harry Potter series, the stage is set for the most violent confrontations that will plague the wizarding world in the subsequent books, culminating in the decisive battles in *Order of the Phoenix*, *Half-Blood Prince*, and *Deathly Hallows*. When Harry is in Madame Malkin's shop in *Sorcerer's Stone* ordering his first set of robes, he meets Draco Malfoy, the boy who is not only Harry's opposite in his pale blond looks but also in his attitudes toward other wizards. Draco's first words describing how he can force his parents to buy him whatever he wants remind Harry of his selfish cousin Dudley, and his second set of comments begins to reveal an attitude of bigotry and self-importance also reminiscent of the Dursleys, although, ironically, its target includes people like the Dursleys. Draco proclaims archly that his entire pureblood family has been in the house of Slytherin at Hogwarts, refers to Hagrid as a servant and a savage, and concludes about the new students at Hogwarts "they [shouldn't] let the other sort in . . . I think they should keep it in the old wizarding families."[1]

These pointed remarks about separation by genetic inheritance hint at the fatal rift in wizard culture. Some whose bloodlines include only wizards, such as the Malfoy family and their relatives the Lestranges and the Blacks, so fervently hate Muggles, the Muggle-born "Mudblood" wizards, and mixed-blood wizards that they band together as "Death Eaters," following Lord Voldemort, with the intent to rule these "inferiors" (and kill as many of them as they can). J.K. Rowling has confirmed in an interview that "[I]f we're talking about prejudiced people within the Wizarding World, what they care most about is your blood status."[2]

But why would those with magical powers that enable them to exercise extensive control over both the natural and human worlds be concerned at all with nonmagical Muggles, or other wizards with Muggle blood? As is often the case in a situation of bigotry, Death Eaters don't hate Muggles or Mudbloods because they truly feel superior to them. They hate them because they believe that these nonwizards and "tainted" wizards threaten the control of magic from outside the wizarding world. Death Eaters fear that they can lose their power to those who do not possess it or those they believe should not possess it, either through the accident of nature that produces a witch from human parents, such as Hermione, or by half-bloods who manage to inherit their powers from the wizard parent (including Lord Voldemort himself, a point to which I return later).

Other wizards, however, do not feel this way. Those such as the members of the Order of the Phoenix and others do not believe that their magical ability is threatened by nonmagical people, or even by the genetics of the lone witch or wizard in a magical family. This divide in attitude is not, as we might assume, a knee-jerk reaction determined by one's family background: the Weasleys are a pureblood wizard family, and Sirius (and even, as we eventually learn, Regulus) Black believes that this bigotry is wrong. However, if it isn't necessarily bloodline that influences one's outlook toward the nonmagical, what in the nature of magical ability could create a schism that causes the magical community worldwide to turn on itself and nearly bring about its own extinction?

The key is in how each group of wizards views its relationship with magical powers. To the Death Eaters, full confidence in their magic is only attainable if it is impossible that that power could be usurped by anyone else. Thus, their attitudes are characterized by a wary secrecy concerning magical expertise, a conviction that magic should be used for control of others, a refusal to acknowledge the need for the training of inborn magical powers, and a rejection of a peaceful if sometimes uneasy parallel existence with the Muggle world. The last, vehemently held opinion triggers the worst violence in the Potter series. As a bookend to Harry's encounter with magic bigotry in the first book, *Deathly Hallows* opens with a scene that shocks even the hardened Death Eaters who witness it. Voldemort is meeting with a group of his most faithful followers in the Malfoy family home, which he has commandeered for his headquarters. A spellbound figure suspended upside down over the meeting table is revealed to be Charity Burbage, the former Hogwarts professor of Muggle Studies. Voldemort announces her "crimes," which involve sympathy toward Muggles and a public plea that, in Voldemort's words, wizards "must accept these thieves of their knowledge and magic."[3] He then sends her body crashing into the table below with the Killing Curse. Despite the horror they show at this scene, these supporters and others increasingly echo these views through the course of the books in both word and deed. Indeed, books IV and V begin with three of the most infamous attacks on Muggles: the death of Riddle house caretaker Frank Bryce by Voldemort's killing curse; the horrible scene later at the

Quidditch World Cup when the innocent Muggle family Roberts, including children, are levitated upside down over the campsite and almost killed when they are allowed to fall;[4] and the nearly successful dementor attack on Dudley Dursley.[5]

Rowling's narrative reveals, however, that this view of Muggle blood and the danger it poses is completely wrong. Magic is an inborn ability. This is the foundational fact of being a wizard; according to Rowling herself, "magic is a dominant and resilient gene."[6] The Death Eaters' error is their interpretation of that genetic passage: the false fear that magic can be somehow stolen or transferred to a nonmagical individual, exemplified in the official statement of the Ministry of Magic after Voldemort and his supporters take it over, that Muggle-born wizards could only practice magic because they have "obtained magical power by theft or force."[7] Thus for them, only the pureblood is reliably a "real" wizard, and their obsession with maintaining their power justifies the extermination of those who are "impure" based on Muggle blood relationships or Muggle sympathizing, as in the case of Professor Burbage, and of Muggles themselves. Throughout the series, Rowling shows that the bigotry of Voldemort and his followers, like most opinions that divide people by race, ethnicity, or aptitude, is nothing more than a way to rationalize violence and domination and to hide self-doubt and shame.

## FEAR AND LOATHING IN THE WIZARDING WORLD: "IT'S IN THE BLOOD"—OR IS IT?

It is a commonplace of the novels that an individual is born magical or not but also that it can occur in different ways: "Rowling's world is more of a continuum than an absolute opposition."[8] There are only seven "pureblood" families identified in the series, including the Longbottoms and Gaunts, as well as those already mentioned. More often than not, wizards are of mixed blood; Ron comments that wizards would have died out if they had not intermarried with Muggles.[9] Being part Muggle seems to have no effect on the degree of one's inborn talent, and in fact the overwhelming evidence in the books argues silently that it is a contributing factor in having great powers: Harry, Voldemort, Dumbledore, and Snape are all the children or grandchildren of Muggles. Even more hated, of course, are the Muggle-born such as Hermione and Lily Potter; Hermione is abused by Malfoy and other Slytherins in every book with taunts of "Mudblood" and she is largely ignored by Snape and Umbridge in their classes. Pureblood wizard families also fear their own lineage being tainted by the birth of a Squib. This is partly why Merope Gaunt Riddle (who is a witch but whose powers are enfeebled due to her fear of her father) is so abused by her family, the debased but ferociously proud last descendents of Salazar Slytherin.[10]

The very unpredictability of inborn magical ability creates the fear that underlies the bigotry and violence of Death Eaters. In book VII the resurfaced

Death Eaters fully articulate and act on the assertion that Muggles and mixed bloods are dangerous because they are capable of "stealing" magical skill: as Catherine and David Deaval have noted, "Much of the series is building up to a war on the Muggle population and those who are not full-blooded magical families."[11] This belief has been the basis of Voldemort's plans for a much longer period, however. When Kreacher the house-elf relates the tragic story of Regulus Black's suicide, he affirms that even at that time Voldemort hungered "to bring the wizards out of hiding to rule the Muggles and the Muggle-borns."[12] Voldemort's part-Muggle background provides the psychological rationale for his bigotry: as Maier argues, "in his hatred of his own partially 'filthy Muggle' heritage (Chamber of Secrets 231) . . . [h]e projects his own failings in purity and ability onto those he deems as his inferiors who surround him, or onto those wizards who feed his insecurity with their evident potential for greatness."[13] Although genetics does not guarantee magical ability in the wizard or Muggle populations, the Death Eaters manipulate this unpredictability to suit their own purposes. When Voldemort takes over the Ministry, government officials promulgate the fiction that "research" has shown that only a wizard can pass on magical abilities to an offspring, and thus Muggle-borns are necessarily suspect. However, as Ron logically points out, if magic can be stolen, there would be no such thing as a Squib.[14]

We also know that Squibs cannot learn magic: Hogwarts's caretaker Argus Filch enrolls in a "Kwikspell" magic correspondence course, and his embarrassment when Harry learns of it and his obvious lack of success attest to that conclusion.[15] An accurate interpretation of the wizarding genetic pattern is that since the ability cannot be transferred by nongenetic means, it is impossible for someone not born with it to "learn" magic entirely through external means. But Voldemort and his followers insist otherwise: they assume that magic must be protected and limited to purebloods because others could learn and steal the secrets that secure their power. On the other hand, the good wizards in Rowling's world do not fear openly sharing magical information within the wizarding world, nor that Muggles might be able to learn or steal anything from them. In fact, aside from Arthur Weasley's fascination with Muggle "artifacts," Muggles are generally regarded as somewhat "slow" and pathetic in their ineptitude, as I discussed in my essay in *Reading Harry Potter*.

An analogy to understand these conflicting views of magic actually exists in the Muggle world—not in Rowling's created world, but our own. Death Eaters see magic in the same way that the ancient tradition of alchemy was viewed, with its success depending on the secrecy of its materials and processes. The earliest Egyptian papyri extant containing information on chemical processes date from c. 300 BCE, and historian of chemistry John Maxon Stillman observes that "these arts in Egypt were originally under control of the priesthood and by them were carefully guarded and surrounded with secrecy and mystery."[16] One of the papyri is even explicit about its intent to conceal: "Interpretation drawn from the sacred names, which the sacred writers employ for the purposes of putting at fault the curiosity of the vulgar. The plants and other things which they make use of ... have been designated by them in such a way that for lack of understanding they [the vulgar] perform a vain labor in following a false path."[17] Stillman adds, however, that the incorporation of astrology and the occult into what were essentially "chemical arts" seems to have increased over later centuries, as well as the "cultish" nature of those who styled themselves alchemists.[18] Beginning in the sixteenth century, when Copernicus, Kepler, and Galileo based their conclusions in astronomy on repeatable and verifiable observations, and later when Bacon, Descartes, and others began to call for a systematic taxonomy of knowledge, we find correspondence to Rowling's "good" wizards' views: "natural philosophy," and a spirit of shared inquiry of substances and processes.

In our current world, we would classify "magic" along with "alchemy" as practices of superstition and self-deception about the human capacity to understand and control nature. But for Rowling's wizards, magic can be seen as the appropriate relationship with their rather daunting and unpredictable environment, in which plants attack people, skeletal horses fly, and buildings move their own parts. Although the success of magic's techniques can depend on the degree of inborn skill and the educational level of the wizard, magic is an open aspect of wizard society not dependent on secrecy. Readers can also observe that magic is a body of knowledge that has been enlarged over time as wizards have built on the work of their predecessors: Knutsen explains that titles used in Hogwarts's classes such as *A Study of Recent Developments in Wizardry* show how "magic changes and evolves." He adds that wizards learn to control their world "in ways that are mechanical rather than occult."[19] Thus, for good wizards, magic is more analogous to the way we think of science: a public body of information that is communally developed and can safely be shared by those who are born with the aptitude to learn and exercise that knowledge. In my previous essay, I argued that wizards use magic the way we use technology. This analogy is also useful here. In our world, patent law makes the use of another's technological invention illegal, but too much confidentiality is seen to inhibit technological advancement rather than benefit it. For good wizards, the potency of magic is not in its mystery, but in a combination of innate talent and training in its use.

Even the most casual reader of the Harry Potter series should at this point be asking, "But what about Nicholas Flamel?" Flamel, the figure behind the secrets of *The Sorcerer's Stone*, was a real fourteenth-century person, a scrivener, who by the seventeenth century was the bearer of a legend about his alchemical success in creating a Philosopher's Stone and thereby obtaining immortality. It is clear in book I that Rowling's version of Flamel does not subscribe to a view of magic that includes principles of mystery and exclusivity in Muggle alchemy; he is merely a wizard who specializes in a particular area of magic, and his friendship with Dumbledore attests to a shared philosophy about the open nature and democratic uses of magic.

In contrast, Voldemort and his supporters operate through secrecy and domination. The disciplines and procedures of science require an openness that could allow anyone to learn and repeat a process, memorize a formula, or understand a theory. Death Eaters fear erroneously that treating magic as we do science would mean that its control would be lost to them. This fear results in a disproportionate backlash in which any perceived incursion into the magical world by anyone with Muggle blood must be despised and obliterated. The vicious principles of power over the nonmagical through magical violence is displayed in the statue erected in the Ministry of Magic after Voldemort's takeover in book VII. Looming above the saying "Magic is Might," huge statues of a witch and wizard sit on elaborate thrones made up of thousands of naked, tortured-looking Muggles, reminiscent of Hieronymus Bosch's depiction of the damned in Hell. Hermione fearfully sums up the new attitude around the Ministry, and the fundamental difference in outlook between the two opposing groups of wizards: "Muggles . . . In their rightful place."[20]

## THE EDUCATION OF A WIZARD

Like musical talent, which can manifest in a wide variety of ways in human beings, the degree and scope of magical talents fluctuate greatly from person to person and are nurtured through years of training and practice. The very existence of the three magical schools mentioned in the books—Hogwarts, Beauxbatons, and Durmstrang—shows that the more widely held belief in the magical world is that magic is a gift insufficient in its raw state, and that mastery "must be acquired through dedication and study in order for any natural 'talent' to flourish."[21] The education received at the wizarding schools is meant to develop whatever degree of genetic magical capabilities the individual possesses through control over internal processes—analysis, concentration, and self-discipline. Knutsen recaps the wizard's recipe for success: "He must be determined, deliberate, and pay great attention to correct diction;"[22] in other words, not only does the wizard have to learn the correct wording of a spell, he or she must learn and practice how to do it correctly.

Both the internal training and the lack of success when the intellectual processes are not fully mastered are seen throughout the years at Hogwarts. In their very early classes, the need for repetition and precision by the students is emphasized as Hermione corrects Ron's attempts to make a feather float. She says pompously, "You're saying it wrong, [i]t's Wing-gar-dium Levi-o-sa."[23] Harry never masters the art of Occlumency in *Order of the Phoenix*, despite Snape's most intense efforts and the fact that he knows the dangers of Voldemort's ability to enter his mind. Even upper-level students have difficulty with the wizarding equivalent of the driver's exam as the sixth-year class practices the concentrated mantra of "Destination, Determination, and Deliberation" needed to master Apparition in *Half-Blood Prince*.[24] Neville Longbottom's skills provide an individual example of this need for education: what appears to be complete ineptitude in the first four books of the series reveals itself to be prodigious talent and bravery that needs to be correctly reined in and managed. His determination and mastery of skills begin to appear in the D.A. meetings in book V, when "only Hermione mastered the [Shield] Charm faster than Neville."[25] Neville proves himself to be a worthy product of magical education at the last stand at Hogwarts. When Voldemort recognizes his abilities (knowing that Neville is the son of two Aurors) and actually asks him to be become a Death Eater, Neville shows his mettle with the retort, "I'll join you when hell freezes over."[26] After Voldemort's defeat, he goes on to become an Auror himself and the Herbology professor at Hogwarts.

Sarah Maier contends that the unfortunate fate of every Defense Against the Dark Arts professor "demonstrates the vulnerability of the students to the Dark Arts if they fail to understand that some knowledge, without rules, is dangerous."[27] Harry, highly gifted but not the most studious of Hogwarts's students, experiences the dire results of the lack of proper training in the use of dark magic: his use of the "Half-Blood Prince's" handwritten "Sectumsempra" curse in his *Advanced Potion Making* book causes grave physical injury to Draco because Harry does not know what the spell is for.[28] This incident actually raises the ire of Professor McGonagall, attesting to the fact that the use of a spell by an untrained wizard who does not know its consequences is considered a serious breach of wizarding rules.

Although Death Eaters and their children attend Hogwarts, they express the belief that the inborn ability in a pureblood makes magical education unnecessary to make one a skilled and powerful wizard. This view increases the mystique about having magical powers as well. Disdain for public promulgation of magical knowledge is longstanding among Voldemort and his followers. In Tom Riddle's early adulthood, he briefly returns to Hogwarts to ask for a professorship, but Dumbledore knows that his goal as the Defense Against the Dark Arts teacher is to train more followers. Voldemort reveals his real opinion about the worthlessness of education early in the conversation, when he wonders aloud why someone with Dumbledore's talents would prefer to stay at Hogwarts in lieu of a potentially powerful position at the Ministry.[29] For him, the purpose of education is to attain personal power and control over others. This viewpoint accounts for Draco Malfoy's lofty statements in book VI about his future plans. As he explains to his sycophantic friends, Voldemort's strategy might require Draco to leave Hogwarts: "I don't see [education] as that important these days. . . . When the Dark Lord takes over, is he going to care how many O.W.L.s or N.E.W.T.s anyone's got? . . . It'll be all about the kind of service he received."[30] Not only is personal devotion—a type of slavery, in reality—more important than a high degree of training, the educational system itself conflicts with the Death Eaters' mind-set about blood status. Magical education includes the training of non-purebloods, a twofold objection for Death Eaters as it not only acknowledges the ability of those who are Muggle-born and of mixed blood, but also makes public the potential avenues of power inherent in magical skill.


## THE PURPOSE OF THE POWER

Two of the most famous magicians in literary history are Prospero and Dr. Faustus, the latter having a long reputation that spreads across the literature of several languages. Both revere education at first, but both suffer the consequences of using their acquired knowledge of magic inappropriately. Starting from the Prologue of Christopher Marlowe's play, Faustus is portrayed as rejecting the proper ends of education for personal misuse: "swoll'n with cunning of a self-conceit, / ... And glutted now with learning's golden gifts, / He surfeits upon cursed necromancy, / Nothing so sweet as magic is to him" (Prologue 20, 24–26). He decries (not altogether unreasonably, especially as one thinks of Professor Umbridge's repeated phrase, "There will be no need to talk" in book V) the emptiness of the scholasticism being taught him in favor of an active, controlling magic for personal gain:

> O what a world of profit and delight,
> Of power, of honor, of omnipotence
> Is promis'd to the studious artisan?
> All things that move between the quiet poles
> Shall be at my command . . . . (I.i.54–58)

Although Prospero neither exhibits Faust's hubris nor suffers his damnation, he neglects his duties as Duke of Milan and does not seem to perceive that his education and talents might be used for the improvement of his State. As he explains to Miranda, "I thus neglecting worldly ends, all dedicated / To closeness and the bettering of my mind" (I.ii.89–90). Prospero does not study magic for wealth or material pleasures, but puts his personal desire for more knowledge ahead of the need to learn how to use it.

The arrogant Faustus and the book-loving Duke misuse their magic in almost completely opposite ways, but they are both at fault—and both suffer—because of the inappropriate purposes to which they put their education and magic. Faustus fails because he never achieves the realization that the enormous talents held by the magical individual require better uses than conjuring up ghosts of beautiful women and taunting the Pope. His selfish insistence that his magic be used only for personal gain causes him to devolve from styling himself "great emperor of the world" (I.iii.104) to engaging in parlor tricks to self-destruction. Faustus rejects the authority of his educational community and resolves to work alone now to attain greater magical knowledge—"Then fear not, Faustus, but be resolute, / And try the uttermost magic can perform" (I.iii.14–15)—that "uttermost magic," of course, being the ultimate Dark Magic of calling up the devil himself. He also denies the duty of the conscientious use of magic—he refuses to take on the roles of scholar, doctor, or lawyer which could benefit many, preferring only to please himself. In contrast, Prospero abrogates both his familial and civic duty by focusing too much on his magic and shutting himself up in his ivory tower: he acknowledges in the same conversation with Miranda: "And to my state grew stranger, being transported / And rapt in secret studies" (I.ii.76–77). He comments ruefully that "my library / Was dukedom large enough" (I.ii.109–110). As Duke, he had inherited the responsibility for the care of Milan. However, he not only neglected using his magic for purposes of bettering the state, he neglected ruling at all.

These famous figures of magic reflect, in different ways, the abuse of magic by Voldemort and his followers. Magical education in Rowling's world implies a responsible use of that powerful gift. There are, of course, limits to the use of magic that prevent exerting power over those aspects of human life that seem "untouchable": the dead cannot be resurrected, and the Principal Exceptions to Gamp's Law of Elemental Transfiguration[31] identify five items that cannot be created by magic: life, love, food, and information are all mentioned explicitly, and Rowling has explained in an interview that wizards cannot materialize money: "There is legislation about what you can conjure and what you can't. Something that you conjure out of thin air will not last."[32] But this idea of "legislation" implies that the rules of magic are extended to self-imposed societal limitations and management of magical power. We see this in small, everyday ways in each book of the series: the use of magic by underage wizards during summers away from Hogwarts is prohibited by the Decree for the Reasonable Restriction of Underage Sorcery; the International Confederation of Warlocks' Statue of Secrecy prevents wizards from interfering with Muggle life or letting Muggles see them performing magic;[33] apparition lessons require training and a test equivalent to obtaining a driver's license.[34] Laws in the wizarding world also control the uses of particular kinds of magic. The Dark Arts are distinguished from "regular" magic and its use strictly forbidden, and there are things—like conjuring money—that wizards are not allowed to do, seemingly for reasons of social justice. Every wizard knows from an early age that magic cannot be used without considering how it will affect the surrounding society, both individual people and the larger population, both magical and Muggle; as Sarah Maier argues, "Self control and respect for the law are vital in the education of young witches and wizards so that they might become good citizens."[35]

In order to understand magic in Rowling's series as a functioning presence in the civic society, we must remember that wizarding culture is an active, if largely invisible, segment of actual British society. Early in *Half-Blood Prince*, we learn about the intersection of the political worlds of Muggles and wizards when the British prime minister recalls Cornelius Fudge's first visit: Fudge explained the existence of the magical populace and assured that the Ministry of Magic had the regulation of that slice of British life entirely under control.[36] It is not clear whether the Ministry of Magic exists as a parallel to the Muggle British government or is actually considered a division under the prime minister, but it clearly operates much the same way as any large bureaucratic entity: many departments with rivalries within and between them, opportunities for political advancement, and regulations concerning every aspect of life, from commerce, to law enforcement, to international relations, to animal control. The existence of this extensive group of laws and regulatory bodies implies that the public effects of the use of magic are a constant concern for the wizarding community. Additionally, because bureaucracies necessarily come with legions of workers to carry out their functions, one can see that the notion of the "public servant" is a greatly valued one in the wizarding culture. And although the particular Ministers of Magic featured in the Harry Potter series—Cornelius Fudge, Rufus Scrimgeour, and Voldemort's puppet Pius Thicknesse—are an unfortunate low in the history of Ministry leadership, participation in the wizarding political arena generally indicates great intelligence and magical skill, as well as expertise in a specific area.

But governmental participation is not the only way in which magic is a civic concern. Although not every wizard will engage in public service in a professional capacity, everyone is required to use their magic with a certain degree of maturity, as the age limitations on magic demonstrate. The two conversations mentioned earlier in which Voldemort and Draco express disdain for their Hogwarts education also reflect this larger gulf between the supporters of Voldemort and the good wizards concerning the purposes of magical knowledge. When Voldemort questions Dumbledore's lack of interest in the position of Minister of Magic, Dumbledore reminds him that the Ministry was never attractive to the newly graduated Tom Riddle, either. The highly awarded Riddle "refused all offers"[37] of promising job prospects, instead taking a position as a buyer ("obtainer" may be a more accurate term) of shady or dangerous items for Borgin and Burkes, the dealer in Dark Magic objects. Draco's boasting to his friends on the train echoes this sentiment, but whereas Voldemort at least knew the value he could gain from working through the system at Hogwarts, Draco believes that his family and connections with Voldemort and the Death Eaters will leapfrog him into that hierarchy of power without even finishing school.

Both attitudes pervert the purposes of education and of magic itself. Like Prospero, the Dark Lord and his followers believe that attaining magical expertise is for personal betterment only, and like Faustus, they turn to the Dark Arts to attain individual glory and power. Bill McCarron describes the difference as "the conflict of power versus authority. Power is usually a negative concept imposed from the top down, whereas authority is a positive undertaking earned by those who hold it and works from the ground up."[38] For Voldemort, education is a means of obtaining power for the oppressive domination of everyone around him, not acquiring the responsible authority that earns respect and can be used for the public good. The good wizards believe that, as McCarron observes,

"Authority, faithfully practiced, generates a shared power, not one that is arbitrarily imposed."[39] As Harry and Dumbledore sit in the netherworld between life and death in *Deathly Hallows*, Dumbledore admits that, like Grindelwald and Voldemort, he was tempted by power and knew that he would succumb to it—thus his persistent refusal to accept the position of Minister of Magic. His conclusion that "those who are best suited to power are those who [like Harry] have never sought it"[40] exemplifies the difference between the right and wrong uses of magic.

Voldemort and his followers go further than Prospero or even Faustus in twisting magic to suit their desires. As Rebecca Stephens notes in her chapter from *Reading Harry Potter*, another major distinction between Voldemort and other powerful wizards such as Dumbledore and Harry is that Voldemort truly operates alone, with only a following of servants, without real friends or anyone for whom he cares. Because he has no conception of love for anyone else, he cannot think of other people in terms of affection, loyalty, or self-sacrifice. That separation from other beings mirrors the dark wizards' view of magic as secretive and for the purposes of control over others by force: "Magic is Might." On the other hand, Harry's relationships with others who are of lower status, have less power, or are quite different from him, including Dobby and Kreacher, Luna Lovegood, and Hagrid, teach him again and again "the importance of relating to others in a just and fair way."[41] This way of thinking, while not usually vocalized, is demonstrated throughout the books by the good wizards. I cited the Muggle attack at the Quidditch World Cup in the introduction of this essay to show the viciousness of the Death Eaters: Catherine and David Deaval draw attention to the reaction of the Weasley family. Both Arthur and his sons earn their belittling title of "blood traitors" as "they do not hesitate to put themselves in danger in order to help the Muggle family."[42]

The sense of community that extends beyond the borders of magical power and the Death Eaters' attempts to eliminate that diversity are repeatedly at war as the complex web of the narrative culminates in book VII. Hermione, fellow Gryffindor Dean Thomas, Ministry employee Dirk Cresswell, and Tonks' father Ted are some of the many Muggle-born and mixed-blood wizards on the run from the Muggle-Born Registry Commission. While sneaking into Dolores Umbridge's office in the Ministry, Harry stumbles upon a roomful of workers putting together a pamphlet entitled "Mudbloods and the Dangers They Pose to a Peaceful Pureblood Society."[43] Other nonhuman magical beings such as goblins and giants are also being hounded by the Ministry, and even those magical beings who are in league with the Dark Lord are "separated" from the purebloods: Fenrir Greyback, a werewolf, is not allowed to bear the Dark Mark, for example.[44] One of the reasons that Griphook the goblin refuses to assist Harry, Ron, and Hermione when they need to get into the Lestranges' vault at Gringotts Bank is the ancient hierarchy historically exploited by wizards and increasingly enforced under Voldemort's rule. Griphook notes that Harry is "odd" because he dug a grave for Dobby and saved Griphook's life: "Goblins and elves are not used to the protection or the respect that you have shown this night." It is only when Hermione chimes in that as a Mudblood, "I've got no higher position under this new order than you have,"[45] that Griphook acknowledges that there can be goodness among the "wand-carriers," as the goblins call them. It becomes clear that the Death Eaters focus on the differences among magical beings and use those differences to divide and conquer, not only through direct persecution but also by setting the various groups against one another.

As demonstrated by the wide variety of combatants on Harry's side during the final Battle of Hogwarts (including centaurs, giants, house-elves, and even Peeves the Poltergeist and Argus Filch), the idea of unity in the magical world is the single concept that wins the day for the good wizards. It is also the thought that keeps Harry going as he struggles to unravel the mysteries presented to him in book VII concerning the Horcruxes, the Deathly Hallows, Snape's involvement with the Death Eaters, and, most significantly to Harry personally, the secrets of Dumbledore's past. Harry faces a serious blow when he begins to doubt Dumbledore's faithful adherence to the principle of universal freedom from fear of magical power misused. Rita Skeeter's "tell-all" biography reveals Dumbledore's youthful friendship with the evil wizard Gellert Grindelwald, but even in the damning letter from Dumbledore to Grindelwald that so shakes Harry is the seed of the right and fair standard by which Dumbledore lived and died. I quote the letter almost in its entirety to show the nuances of his position toward wizard/Muggle relations:

Your point about Wizard dominance being FOR THE MUGGLES' OWN GOOD—this, I think, is the crucial point. Yes, we have been given power and yes, that power gives us the right to rule, but *it also gives us responsibilities over the ruled*. We must stress this point, it will be the foundation stone upon which we build.... We seize control FOR THE GREATER GOOD. And from this it follows that where we meet resistance, we must use only the force that is necessary and no more. [italics added][46]

In these words the widely divergent paths taken by the good and the dark wizards are easily discerned. When Dumbledore ends his friendship with Grindelwald shortly after writing this letter, Grindelwald adopts the slogan "For the Greater Good" and uses that notion to do exactly what Dumbledore warned against—the right to rule becomes domination, the sense of responsible care becomes exploitation and abuse, and necessary force becomes excessive violence. These are the same rationales used by Voldemort to justify his actions: the "Greater Good" becomes "the good for purebloods only," and he carries on the evil created by Grindelwald, even killing Grindelwald when, in remorse, the latter lies to him about the location of the Elder Wand.[47] Dumbledore, however, abandons the dangerous implications of this philosophy and works for the rest of his life to uphold the rightful sense of "For the Greater Good" by supporting the rights of the Muggle-born and dying while fighting Voldemort and all he stands for. The bigotry and desire for supremacy that drives the Dark Lord and Death Eaters will never win the day over the power "of love, loyalty, and innocence," which "have a power beyond the reach of any magic."[48] And even that magic is represented in its best form as being a public and communal matter, to be learned and promulgated for the benefit of every being regardless of their differences. This is a main lesson of the Harry Potter series. The true meaning of the ideology that nearly destroys the wizarding world in its abuse is seen in Elphias Doge's eulogy of his schoolboy friend Albus Dumbledore: "he died as he lived, working always for the greater good:"[49] the good of all.

## NOTES

1. J.K. Rowling, *Harry Potter and the Sorcerer's Stone* (New York: Scholastic, 1997), 78.

2. Melissa Anelli, John Noe, and Sue Upton, "PotterCast Interviews J.K. Rowling, part one," *PotterCast #130*, http://www.accio-quote.org/articles/2007/1217-pottercast-anelli.html. (accessed August 2008).

3. J.K. Rowling, *Harry Potter and the Deathly Hallows* (New York: Scholastic, 2007), 12.

4. J.K. Rowling, *Harry Potter and the Goblet of Fire* (New York: Scholastic, 2000), 15, 120, 142.

5. J.K. Rowling, *Harry Potter and the Order of the Phoenix* (New York: Scholastic, 2003), 18–19.

6. *J.K. Rowling Official Site.* http://www.jkrowling.com (accessed 28 August 2008).

7. Rowling, *Hallows*, 209.

8. Heather Arden and Kathryn Lorenz, "The Ambiguity of the Outsider in the Harry Potter Stories and Beyond," in *The Image of the Outsider in Literature, Media and Society*, ed. Will Wright and Steven Kaplan (Pueblo, CO: Society for the Interdisciplinary Study of Social Imagery, 2002), 431.

9. J.K. Rowling, *Harry Potter and the Chamber of Secrets* (New York: Scholastic, 1999), 116.

10. J.K. Rowling, *Harry Potter and the Half-Blood Prince* (New York: Scholastic, 2005), 210.

11. Catherine Jack Deavel and David Paul Deavel, "Character, Choice, and Harry Potter," *Logos* 5, 4 (2002): 52.

12. Rowling, *Hallows*, 193.

13. Sarah Maier, "Educating Harry Potter: A Muggle's Perspective on Magic and Knowledge in the Wizard world of J.K. Rowling," in *Scholarly Studies in Harry Potter: Applying Academic Methods to a Popular Text*, Studies in British Literature Vol. 99, ed. Cynthia Whitney Hallet (Lewiston, NY: Edwin Mellin Press, 2005), 23.

14. Rowling, *Hallows*, 209.

15. Rowling, *Chamber*, 127–28.

16. John Maxon Stillman, *The Story of Alchemy and Early Chemistry* (New York: Dover, 1960), 137.

17. Ibid., 88.

18. Ibid., 138.

19. Torbjorn Knutsen, "Dumbledore's Pedagogy: Knowledge and Virtue at Hogwarts," in *Harry Potter and International Relations*, ed. Daniel H. Nexon and Iver B. Neumann (Lanham, MD: Rowman & Littlefield, 2006), 200, 201.

20. Rowling, *Hallows*, 242.

21. Maier, "Educating," 16.

22. Knutsen, "Dumbledore's Pedagogy," 202.

23. Rowling, *Stone*, 171.

24. Rowling, *Prince*, 384.

25. Rowling, *Phoenix*, 553.

26. Rowling, *Hallows*, 731.

27. Maier, "Educating," 18.

28. Rowling, *Prince*, 522.

29. Ibid., 442.

30. Ibid., 151. In contrast, the Weasley twins, despite their spectacular method of demonstrating in book V that they will not continue their education, do not intend to use their considerable talents for political or violent ends.

31. Rowling, *Hallows*, 292.

32. "World Exclusive Interview with J.K. Rowling," *South West News Service*, 8 July 2000.

33. Rowling, *Chamber*, 21.

34. Rowling, *Prince*, 354–55.

35. Maier, "Educating," 19.

36. Rowling, *Prince*, ch. 1.

37. Ibid., 433.

38. Bill McCarron."Power vs. Authority in *Harry Potter and the Order of the Phoenix*," *Notes on Contemporary Literature* 34, 5 (2004): 8.

39. McCarron, "Power," 9.

40. Rowling, *Hallows*, 718.

41. Janice C. Prewitt, "Heroic Matriculation: The Academies of Spenser, Lewis, and Rowling," *Philological Papers* 53 (2006): 31.

42. Deavel, "Character," 60.

43. Ibid., 209, 296–97, 249.

44. Rowling, *Hallows*, 453.

45. Ibid., 488–89.

46. Ibid., 357.

47. Ibid., 719.

48. Ibid., 710.

49. Ibid., 20.

**III**

# The Socio-Cultural Impact of the
# Harry Potter Series

# 11

# Hermione and the House-Elves Revisited: J.K. Rowling, Antislavery Campaigning, and the Politics of Potter

*Brycchan Carey*

In an essay published toward the end of the long gap between the publication of *Harry Potter and the Goblet of Fire* in 2000 and the appearance of *Harry Potter and the Order of the Phoenix* in 2003, I argued that "the Harry Potter novels are among the most politically engaged novels to have been written for children in recent years" and that "the central concept of the novels, Harry's personal struggle with the dark lord Voldemort, provides a site for discussion of a democratic society's response to elitism, totalitarianism, and racism."[1] With hindsight, I concede that the first of those two statements may have been overassertive. Children's literature has, from the start, been didactic, reformative, morally instructive, character building, socially aware, and—from a variety of standpoints from furthest right to deepest left—politically engaged. Much recent children's literature has been entirely consistent with that tradition. The Harry Potter novels certainly are politically engaged, but they are not unique in being so.

My second statement not only stands but has become an even more accurate description of the series. Harry's personal struggle with Voldemort does indeed provide a site for discussion of a democratic society's response to elitism, totalitarianism, and racism and, as the series progresses, we see the central figures less as school children and more as combatants in a cataclysmic war between the upholders of the ideals of freedom, equality, and brotherhood, and the advocates of an arbitrary and repressive government founded on principles of racial segregation and depending on indiscriminate terror to cow its subjects into submission. The French Revolution; the Second World War; the War on Terror: all these and more are being fought again and again in Rowling's books. And at the heart of the books, as I argued in 2003, there is one message in particular: the promotion of political participation for young people. J.K. Rowling's young characters, whether as Death Eaters, members of the Order of the Phoenix, or founders of the Society for the Promotion of Elfish Welfare, are all involved in the political process in one way or another. Even those paragons of individualist free enterprise, Fred and George Weasley, are socially active in that they work together, both as twins and together with "Dumbledore's Army," to harness the resources of the commercial world for the forces of good. Few wizards in Rowling's universe are socially and politically inactive and fewer still are politically unaligned. That disinterest in political affairs and seclusion from the wider concerns of society that often characterizes the sort of suburban estate where the Dursleys live is simply not to be found in the wizarding world.

In my 2003 essay, I took as my test case Hermione Granger's campaign on behalf of a group of enslaved magical creatures—the house-elves—and I demonstrated how her Society for the Promotion of Elfish Welfare (S.P.E.W.) reflected historical pressure campaigns, particularly the antislavery campaigns of the eighteenth and nineteenth centuries. At the same time, I showed the ways in which Rowling's inclusion of the enslaved house-elves arose from a long tradition of depicting slaves, and enslaved magical creatures, in children's literature. By the end of *Goblet of Fire*, I argued, Rowling had asserted three important positions with implications for the way the reader conducts him or herself in the world beyond the text: first, that discrimination based on race is evil; second, that even superficially egalitarian societies conceal deep inequalities and injustices; and, third, that it is the duty of the individual to confront those injustices. In *Goblet of Fire*, young readers are invited to follow in Hermione's footsteps—even if her path initially seems unpopular—and take political action against bigotry. In this chapter, I am going to pick up where I left off in *Reading Harry Potter*, and complete the assessment of the house-elves issues that I began then. I will continue to show that the house-elves subplot provides an opportunity for Rowling to present a model of political participation that young people can engage with and emulate in their own lives. However, my sense now is that Rowling's treatment of house-elf enslavement in the final three novels becomes less radical than the earlier novels seemed to promise. After a brief move to direct action, Hermione's campaign peters out and by the end of the series the house-elves remain in bondage. Nevertheless, in the later novels Rowling continues to tap into literary and historical prototypes and archetypes, which suggest, first, that she sees political issues in the novels as reflections of real-world political and historical dilemmas and, second, that she sees the house-elf problem—indeed, the problem of slavery itself—as inseparable from wider political questions.

At the end of book IV, Hermione's campaign remains politically marginalized and the house-elves remain in servitude. Worse still, the elves appear to be their own worst enemies, refusing in most cases to accept that freedom is a right that can—and should—be grasped immediately. This problem is dramatized in the differing ways in which Dobby and Winky react to their emancipation. Dobby embraces his rise in status from slave to proletarian by a brave attempt to embrace the realities of the free market economy. He finds, however, that the market does not necessarily work in his favor: "Dobby has travelled the country for two whole years, sir, trying to find work!" he "squeaks," speaking of himself, as house-elves do, in the third person, "but Dobby hasn't found work, sir, because Dobby wants paying now!" With a glut of cost-free slave labor on the market, it is not surprising that most potential employers "slammed the door in Dobby's face." More surprising is the attitude of the other Hogwarts house-elves who, in response to his account of himself, "started edging away from Dobby, as though he was carrying something contagious." Perhaps he is. The freedom that he proudly embraces has made a wreck of Winky, who regularly bursts into convulsive sobs and whose appearance is frightful mess, not least because since emancipation she has started to hit the butterbeer. Dobby's two years searching for work and Winky's descent into alcoholism are hardly promising advertisements for freedom. Nevertheless, Hermione remains optimistic. "The other elves will see how happy [Dobby] is, being free," she argues, "and slowly it will dawn on them that they want that too." Harry's mordant reply is: "Let's hope they don't look too closely at Winky."[2]

As with the off-putting acronym S.P.E.W., this exchange initially suggests some authorial ambivalence toward Hermione's campaign. Again, however, I think this would be a misreading. Rowling alerts us both to Hermione's idealism and to her naiveté, and reminds us that these are not contradictory characteristics, particularly in a fourteen-year-old. Hermione's antislavery campaign is based in a passionate belief in justice, equality, and freedom, not in a carefully reasoned set of economic calculations. Hermione's campaign offers young readers a model of how (and in some cases how not) to run a political pressure group aimed at alerting the world to the existence of an injustice. It does not offer suggestions on managing the labor supply in a deregulated free-wage economy. Yet, although Hermione has no economic solution, that does not mean that Rowling does not have views on the matter. Dobby reveals that after unsuccessfully searching for work he has been employed at Hogwarts by Professor Dumbledore at a mutually agreed wage. The comic irony is that Dobby has successfully persuaded Dumbledore to pay him substantially lower wages than were originally offered (a Galleon a week instead of the proffered ten).[3] Nevertheless, by negotiating a mutually acceptable wage, by offering a contract that promotes Dobby's welfare, and by offering Dobby work in the hope of undermining a socially damaging labor practice, Dumbledore emerges not as a *free* trade employer but as a *fair* trade employer. Rowling seems to be suggesting that the problem of house-elf enslavement in the wizarding world, like the problems of poverty and exploitative labor practices in our own world, can be solved only by energetic idealism combined with practical efforts by enlightened employers to secure fair deals for exploited workers. That is to say, emancipating elves or outlawing house-elf enslavement is not by itself enough; there needs also to be a wholesale change in political and economic organization that offers work on equitable terms to those emerging from slavery—just as in the real world, the Fair Trade movement was created in the hopes of mitigating the historical legacies of slavery and colonialism.

It is not spurious to make such connections because Rowling herself continuously invites the reader to draw parallels with the world beyond her text. For example, although house-elves are the most significant enslaved figures in the novels, they are not the only characters to put us in mind of the historical realities of slavery. It cannot be a coincidence that Rowling names one of the few major Black figures in the series, Kingsley Shacklebolt, in terms familiar to all historians of slavery. Clearly, the name "Shacklebolt" is designed to put us in mind of shackled slaves, whereas the name "Kingsley" might remind some readers of the trope of "Guinea's Captive Kings," to use a well-known phrase from Joseph Warton's poem "To Liberty" (1744).[4] But Shacklebolt's connection with historical slavery in the Potter novels is implied only and not developed. The only explicit slavery issue in the series concerns house-elves and Hermione's campaign on their behalf. Yet, despite the best efforts of Hermione and Dumbledore, at the end of *Goblet of Fire*, the house-elves remain in bondage.

In 2003, my assumption was that their story would be elaborated upon in future installments and would most likely reach a resolution. This did not precisely turn out to be the case. Although individual house-elves continue to play important roles in the later novels, with Dobby and Kreacher's interventions proving pivotal at times, the wider question of house-elf enslavement receives less attention. Despite having invested a great deal of energy in the campaign, Hermione seems almost to forget about S.P.E.W. after *Goblet of Fire*, and both the organization and Hermione's views on house-elves receive only the briefest attention. The few references that do occur do not suggest that either Rowling or Hermione have changed their position regarding house-elves; merely that Rowling was more interested in exploring other plot developments. Thus, the few mentions of S.P.E.W., or of Hermione's views on house-elves, come as passing comments. For example, in *Order of the Phoenix*, we learn that Hermione harbors ambitions to pursue house-elf welfare as a career. Ron and Harry are discussing their plans to become Aurors. When asked about her career plans, Hermione responds, rather snootily, by saying, "I think I'd like to do something really worthwhile." To the boys' outraged response that being an Auror is certainly worthwhile, Hermione "thoughtfully" counters, "yes it is, but it's not the only worthwhile thing . . . I mean, if I could take SPEW [*sic*] further . . ."[5]

Although S.P.E.W. is barely mentioned again throughout the series, Hermione does indeed take things further, by shifting her focus from pressure politics to direct action. Ron is shocked by Hermione's tactic of leaving knitted woolen hats out for the elves, hidden under the piles of rubbish that they have to clear away. "It's not on," he says, understanding perfectly well that a house-elf who is given clothes becomes free: "You're trying to trick them into picking up the hats. You're setting them free when they might not want to be free."[6] Dobby later confides to Harry that this is the view of the Hogwarts house-elves: "None of them will clean Gryffindor Tower any more, not with the hats and socks hidden everywhere, they finds them insulting, sir."[7] Dobby confirms that he has been cleaning Gryffindor Tower himself, a deeply ironic outcome for Hermione who, by seeking to promote elfish welfare and by attempting to emancipate the suspicious elves, has both alienated herself from the creatures she is hoping to help while at the same time inadvertently increasing the workload of one of the few free elves. Hermione's foray into direct action is thus no more successful than her attempt at pressure politics. She means well but has failed to think through the consequences of her actions.

In *Half-Blood Prince*, other than for one brief reference, S.P.E.W. vanishes entirely. The single memory of its existence comes from Harry's perspective, not Hermione's. When learning in Dumbledore's Pensieve of the framing of the house-elf Hokey for the murder of her mistress Hepzibah Smith, we learn that an outraged Harry "had rarely felt more in sympathy with the society Hermione had set up, S.P.E.W."[8] Hermione is not present to witness this, and Harry does not communicate his sympathies to her. Shortly after, when it is revealed to Hermione that Harry has been ordering house-elves to follow and report back on Draco Malfoy, Hermione says nothing but merely "looked indignant." After all, Harry recalls, "House-elves were always such a touchy subject with her."[9] Hermione's indignant appearance illustrates that her position has not fundamentally changed, but her silence on the matter, combined with the use of the adjective "touchy," would seem to indicate that Rowling has lost interest in the question of house-elf enslavement as a significant plot element. Calling Hermione "touchy" suggests that her previously heated responses to hearing about house-elf enslavement were out of proportion, and this diminishes the seriousness both of Hermione's beliefs and the problem of elfish enslavement. Likewise, Hermione's failure to speak out at this point seems somewhat at odds with her previously forthright pronouncements on this "rotten and unjust system."[10] It also seems at variance with the outspoken and morally certain Hermione who, shortly before, excoriated Harry for adding the luck potion Felix Felicis to Ron's breakfast drink in order to improve his chances of winning at Quidditch. In fact, Harry had not cheated but had merely pretended to spike Ron's drink in order to provoke a placebo effect in Ron.[11] Nevertheless, the episode shows that Rowling clearly does not want us to think that either Hermione's moral compass or her readiness to speak out has disappeared. Hermione's indignant silence on the house-elf issue suggests that for Rowling the house-elves are no longer a priority.

It is impossible, of course, to fully understand an author's intentions with her work. Indeed, a writer's full and complex set of intentions may not even be clear to herself. It is nevertheless puzzling that such a major plot element in book IV should be submerged in the later volumes. One obvious explanation is the Hollywood factor. Hermione's campaign—and the characters of Dobby and Winky—were omitted from the screen version of *Goblet of Fire*, probably more because of the enormous cost of computer-generated imagery, or the need to condense a long novel into a short movie, than any sinister intention to stifle the political element of the novel. Following the release of the film version of *Philosopher's Stone* in November 2001, Rowling was no doubt working with the film industry at least half in mind as she completed *Order of the Phoenix*— which went on sale just a few months before the release of the film version of *Chamber of Secrets* in November 2003. Aware of the cost of animation, Rowling may have curtailed the house-elf subplots accordingly. And yet, this is not an entirely convincing explanation for the omission of S.P.E.W. House-elves do appear in the later novels, and there are crucial roles for both Kreacher and Dobby in all of the last three books of the series. Moreover, it has been reported that Rowling went ahead with her development of Kreacher in *Deathly Hallows* in the face of Hollywood attempts to excise him from the series. According to the MTV Movie Blog in June 2007, Rowling intervened in the attempt to remove Kreacher: "'Jo reads each draft,' producer David Heyman had said on Saturday, 'she reads each screenplay, and she said, 'You know, I wouldn't do that if I were you. Or you can, but if you get to make a seventh film, you'll be tied in knots'."[12]

This intervention suggests that Rowling is quite prepared to continue with her authorial vision for the series, even where it inconveniences the film industry. Her decision to subordinate the role of S.P.E.W. in the later novels cannot, therefore, be seen as a simplistic response to the pressures of Hollywood accountants. Instead, we must consider the role that S.P.E.W. plays in the narrative if we are to explain its demise. Hermione's campaign serves important functions in *Goblet of Fire*: it develops Hermione's character as a political campaigner and organizer; it highlights the deep inequities that lurk in the basements of Hogwarts and, by extension, the wider wizarding world; and it exposes the collusion between a corrupt government and a subservient press, typified in Hermione's exchanges with Rita Skeeter, the tabloid hack. Nevertheless, pressure politics remains a characteristic of a healthy democracy; S.P.E.W. is only a viable organization while the political process remains more-or-less intact. It becomes untenable once Voldemort returns, Death Eaters infiltrate key posts at the Ministry of Magic, and basic democratic rights such as due process of law and the freedom of speech are suspended. Hermione remains committed to house-elf welfare in the final three books of the series—that much is clear—but the developing political landscape requires that she change her tactics. This explains why, in *Order of the Phoenix*, S.P.E.W. moves from being a pressure group to being a direct action organization, a movement mirrored by the rise of those other direct action organizations: Dumbledore's Army and, of course, the Order of the Phoenix itself. Rowling's point seems to be that in an unfree society, the right to peaceful protest is lost. Accordingly, the story of S.P.E.W. reaches its zenith in Chapter 21 of *Goblet of Fire*, "The House-Elf Liberation Front," in which Harry, Ron, and Hermione visit Dobby and Winky in the Hogwarts basement kitchens and discover the extent to which house-elf labor underpins, literally in this case, the wizarding world. After this revelation, which one would imagine would only harden Hermione's resolve, S.P.E.W. becomes increasingly untenable as a democratic pressure group. Hermione's shift to direct action in *Order of the Phoenix* occurs at the same time that Dolores Umbridge is taking over Hogwarts: a move that presages the collapse of the wizarding world as a stable and free society. Although individual house-elves remain an important part of the story thereafter, Hermione's campaign effectively ends at the point that the normal political processes of the wizarding world are curtailed.

Although S.P.E.W. may have vanished, in the later books of the series the house-elves themselves remain hard at work in the stately homes and school kitchens of the wizarding world. Two elves in particular have important roles. Rowling introduces the malevolent and mentally disturbed Kreacher and, while it is difficult to say that she develops the character of Dobby, it is certainly true to say that she extends his story. In *Order of the Phoenix*, Dobby's role is primarily advisory, alerting Harry to various useful bits of house-elf knowledge such as the location of the Room of Requirement—the hidden room which becomes the training ground for Dumbledore's Army. In *Half-Blood Prince*, Dobby becomes a more active participant in Harry's resistance movement, spying both on Kreacher and Draco Malfoy and reporting back to Harry. Dobby is a free agent who in several places proclaims his pride in his freedom, and yet he seems voluntarily to submit to a kind of servitude to Harry, his emancipator. In Rowling's universe, this makes perfect sense because Harry represents all that is good in the wizarding world. Dobby's choice is thus both logical and enlightened. The same cannot be said of his manner, however, which continues to be unnecessarily obsequious. Assuming that Rowling has indeed thought through the implications of this, which in this case should not be taken for granted, one forms the impression that Rowling intends us to understand that servitude is the natural and inescapable condition of house-elves. This reading is not contradicted by events in the remainder of the series, as we shall see, but one also suspects that it is an unintended effect rather than a conscious intention. Either way, Dobby's loyalty is tested, as is Kreacher's obedience, when Harry summons Kreacher from the Hogwarts kitchens. Dobby arrives too, since the two are locked in combat. Harry takes command, which leads to a revealing exchange. "Twisting Kreacher's wizened arm into a half-nelson," Harry shouts "Right—I'm forbidding you to fight each other! Well, Kreacher, you're forbidden to fight Dobby. Dobby, I know I'm not allowed to give you orders—." Before the "but" can be uttered, Dobby interrupts to assure Harry that "Dobby is a free house-elf and he can obey anyone he likes and Dobby will do whatever Harry Potter wants him to do!"[13] Thus, although Harry quickly checks his initial assumption that he can order Dobby around, it does not prove to be wrong. While recognizing Dobby's status as a free elf in form, Harry is nevertheless assured of Dobby's compliance since at this stage Dobby interprets freedom to mean only the freedom to "obey anyone he likes" rather than the freedom to take direct control of his own actions.

Here and elsewhere, Harry's relationship with house-elves shows how even the best of us can become complicit in morally objectionable practices. When, in *Goblet of Fire*, Ron claims that the house-elves are "happy" and Hermione retorts "it's people like *you* . . . who prop up rotten and unjust systems," Rowling is highlighting the sort of casual misunderstanding of complex moral problems that allows ordinary and otherwise decent people to overlook great evils.[14] Likewise, Harry's instinctive sense of command demonstrates Rowling's view that even morally impeccable figures such as Harry can unconsciously "prop up rotten and unjust systems." This is borne out by Harry's relationship with Kreacher who, at the start of *Half-Blood Prince*, reluctantly becomes the property of an equally reluctant Harry—who felt that "the idea of owning him, of having responsibility for the creature that had betrayed Sirius, was repugnant."[15] Harry's sense of repugnance is based not on a moral objection to the institution of house-elf slavery itself, we should note, but rather (and perhaps understandably) on Kreacher's role in the death of his godfather. Indeed, Harry's instinctive sense of the duties of a slave owner is unerring. His first words to Kreacher on hearing that the elf is now his property are "Kreacher, shut up!" The elf complies, thus confirming that he is Harry's slave, and Harry accordingly banishes him to the Hogwarts kitchens where "the other house-elves could keep an eye on him."[16] In books V and VI, Kreacher is of course a thoroughly unpleasant individual, and an active agent of the Death Eaters, for whom little sympathy is due. Nevertheless, as a free agent in free society in the real world, he would be arrested, charged, tried, and sentenced before being condemned to forced labor. As a slave in Rowling's wizarding world, however, he is subject only to the arbitrary authority of his present owner.

Although house-elves play relatively minor roles in *Order of the Phoenix* and *Half-Blood Prince*, this trend is reversed in *Deathly Hallows* where both Dobby and Kreacher emerge to intervene at key moments. Although Dobby continues to act very much in character, Kreacher undergoes an astonishing reversal of personality. Both elves, however, continue to display patterns of behavior that accord with the ways some enslaved people responded to, or were portrayed as responding to, actual historical events in the world beyond the Potter novels.

For most readers, Dobby's death comes as one of the most shocking moments in the final installment. Nevertheless, it is well within the traditions of literature about slavery. The event occurs after Harry and the gang are imprisoned in the cellar of Malfoy Manor. Bellatrix Lestrange takes Hermione away for questioning under torture. Meanwhile, Harry, Ron, and the other prisoners manage to break free of the ropes with which they have been bound, but are unable to leave the cellar until Dobby appears, seemingly summoned by the spirit of Dumbledore. Dobby magically removes the other prisoners to safety, while Harry and Ron ascend to save Hermione. In the fight that ensues, Lestrange holds Hermione hostage, a dagger at her throat, when Dobby reappears to save the day by dropping a heavy chandelier on Lestrange's head. Harry, Ron, and

Hermione escape, but Lestrange lands the dagger in Dobby's chest. He dies immediately afterward.[17]

Although Dobby saves the life of Harry and the others, he pays with his own life. The rather heavy irony is that that Dobby, born a slave, dies defending and proclaiming liberty: "how dare you defy your masters," shrieks Lestrange, to which Dobby responds "Dobby has no master! . . . Dobby is a free elf."[18] There seems little doubt that the reading Rowling consciously intended is that Dobby is a heroic free agent, a martyr for the cause, who willingly lays his life down in the service of larger goal. But other readings are possible. For instance, Dobby can be seen merely as a commodity whose life is expendable, a statistic in a wider struggle, whose mind-forged manacles prevent him from truly acting as a free agent. In other words, despite his formal manumission, Dobby, whose dying words are "Harry . . . Potter . . . ," chooses merely to swear allegiance to a new master rather than to embrace true self-determination. Ultimately, Dobby sacrifices himself in the service of his new master rather than living as a fully realized individual.

This latter reading is unlikely to reflect Rowling's conscious intentions, but it is supported by a long history of representations of slaves and former slaves in British and American literature, most of whom die violently, many by suicide, and many by self-sacrificing acts in defense of their masters or former masters. One can go back as far as the seventeenth century, with its representations of Othello and Oroonoko, to see how, respectively, freedom, or the attempt to seize freedom, leads violently to the grave. In the eighteenth century, many, perhaps most, of the literary representations of the enslaved concluded with their death either by suicide or a broken heart. It was not until the rapid growth of the slave narrative as a form in the nineteenth century that the emancipated, such as Olaudah Equiano, Mary Prince, and Frederick Douglass, were able to conclude their stories—stories significantly written or told by *themselves*—triumphantly alive. Even so, abolitionist accounts of the enslaved routinely concluded with their violent deaths. Consider, for example, Harriet Beecher Stowe's *Uncle Tom's Cabin* (1852) in which Uncle Tom is beaten to death for refusing to reveal the location of the escaped slaves Cassy and Emmeline.

Indeed, there are parallels between Dobby's story and Uncle Tom's that bear further investigation.[19] Dobby appears to turn away from other house-elves and to focus more on the affairs of humans, his former enslavers; indeed, Dobby willingly spies on Kreacher, which, regardless of Kreacher's political sympathies, suggests that Dobby places loyalty to humans above loyalty to other house-elves. In this sense he might be described as an "Uncle Tom" figure in the modern, American, pejorative sense. But at the same time we should remember that is it far from clear whether Stowe's character—who dies as a martyr, defending other slaves, not Whites—can himself be described in these pejorative terms. Dobby more closely resembles the Uncle Tom of Stowe's novel than the Uncle Tom of popular idiom in that he dies at the hands of those who regard him as property and in the act of defending escaping captives.

More generally, Dobby's role in the Harry Potter series is analogous to Tom's because he becomes the *cause célèbre* who makes visible the suffering of the elves and who alerts the world, through Hermione's abolitionist (or at least ameliorationist) activities to the "rotten and unjust systems" lying at the core of the wizarding world. Indeed, Dobby's death seems at last to have converted the skeptical Ron to the cause of house-elf welfare, and in that conversion he, in turn, converts Hermione's affection for him into open love. In the calm before the storm of the Battle of Hogwarts, Ron interjects with the following:

"Hang on a moment!" said Ron sharply. "We've forgotten someone!"
"Who?" asked Hermione.
"The house-elves, they'll all be down in the kitchen won't they?"
"You mean we ought to get them fighting?" asked Harry.
"No," said Ron seriously, "I mean we should tell them to get out. We don't
   want any more Dobbys, do we? We can't order them to die for us—"

As a result of this thoughtful intervention, Hermione drops the Basilisk fangs she is holding, flings her arms around Ron, "and kissed him full on the mouth."[20] This is an important stage in their realization of their love for one another, but it also marks a key moment in the divergence between Hermione's philosophy, here echoed by Ron, and Harry's. Although Ron and Hermione seek to protect Hogwarts's house elves, Harry wants to enlist them into his army. At this point, Rowling appears to endorse Ron and Hermione's position rather than Harry's although, as we shall see, ultimately the Hogwarts house-elves do choose to enter the battle on Harry's side.

   If Dobby's closest parallel in Anglo-American literary culture is Uncle Tom, we might also ask if Kreacher has any literary or historical antecedents. Indeed he does, although I speculate that Rowling is less familiar with his eighteenth- and nineteenth-century literary prototypes than she is with Stowe's celebrated novel. Like Dobby, Kreacher becomes a "grateful slave" who repays the kind treatment he receives from Hermione with political loyalty.[21] Hermione's approach to Kreacher represents the third phase of her involvement with house-elves. In *Goblet of Fire*, she formed the pressure group S.P.E.W. In *Order of the Phoenix*, she embarked on a program of direct action. In *Deathly Hallows*, her attempt at Elfish Welfare is more personal and more narrowly ameliorative than emancipatory. In a scene that consciously or otherwise echoes much abolitionist literature, we see an emotional connection form between Harry, Hermione, and Kreacher in which it is established that they are equal at the emotional level. This scene, in which Kreacher reveals his mistreatment at the hands of Voldemort, uses language almost identical to much abolitionist writing, which was frequently grounded in the eighteenth-century literature of sensibility, and which foregrounded the tears of suffering slaves as well as the tears of those who sympathized with them. Even Ron is affected:

Kreacher began to sob so hard that there were no more coherent words. Tears flowed down Hermione's cheeks as she watched Kreacher, but she did not dare touch him again. Even Ron, who was no fan of Kreacher's, looked troubled. Harry sat back on his heels and shook his head, trying to clear it.[22]

Establishing the equality of feeling was a central argument of abolitionist poets and novelists, and Rowling's deployment of the technique is almost indistinguishable from earlier writing. "Nothing is more frequent," argued Hannah More in 1788, "than this cruel and stupid argument that [Africans] do not *feel* the miseries inflicted on them as Europeans would do." After all, she thought, in her patrician manner, "Tho' few can reason, all mankind can feel."[23] Harry comes to similar conclusions about house-elves: "as he watched Kreacher sobbing on the floor, he remembered what Dumbledore had said to him, mere hours after Sirius's death: *I do not think Sirius ever saw Kreacher as a being with feelings as acute as a human's . . .*"[24] At Hermione's prompt, and in much the same way as some eighteenth-century slave owners, Harry decides to treat Kreacher with more respect, although he falls short of the final act of emancipation. Unlike Dobby, Kreacher is his own property. Harry seems more willing to emancipate other people's slaves than his own.

Hermione and Harry's improvement of Kreacher's working conditions produces a profound alteration in his attitude toward them. Rather than continuously cursing at them and performing any task with reluctance at best, he starts to bow politely, serve soup with a comically obsequious tone, apologize for the time taken to complete difficult tasks such as locating the larcenous Mundungus Fletcher, and he even whistles while he works.[25] Harry's attempt to mitigate Kreacher's daily grind is reminiscent of similar ameliorative schemes that were suggested during the era of Atlantic slavery. A fictional slave owner in Henry Mackenzie's 1777 novel *Julia de Roubigné*, for example, writes to a friend about the benefits of a "humane" plantation in which the enslaved are spared physical violence and allowed some freedom of movement:

I have had the satisfaction of observing those men, under the feeling of good treatment, and the idea of liberty, do more than almost double their number subject to the whip of an overseer. I am under no apprehension of desertion or mutiny; they work with the willingness of freedom, yet are mine with more than the obligation of slavery.[26]

Of course, such supposedly humane arrangements relied on there being an unpalatable alternative. Ameliorative slaveholders in the eighteenth and nineteenth centuries held as a final sanction the threat of selling their slaves to less "enlightened" slaveholders should they fail to perform as required. Whether Kreacher is under this threat is not revealed in *Deathly Hallows*, but it is made clear that he understands very well where his immediate best interests lie. At the end of the novel, Kreacher, the elf who had betrayed Sirius

Black, leads his fellow house-elves into the Battle of Hogwarts on the side of Harry and the Order of the Phoenix:

The house-elves of Hogwarts swarmed into the Entrance Hall, screaming and waving carving knives and cleavers, and at their head, the locket of Regulus Black bouncing on his chest, was Kreacher, his bullfrog's voice audible even above this din: "Fight! Fight! Fight for my master, defender of house-elves! Fight the Dark Lord, in the name of brave Regulus! Fight![27]

If Kreacher is rewarded for this conspicuous act of loyalty to his owner and his cause, Rowling does not reveal it. Indeed, the final sentence of the final formal chapter (not counting the epilogue "Nineteen Years Later") concludes with Harry "wondering whether Kreacher might bring him a sandwich."[28] It seems somewhat surprising, given all that has gone before, that Rowling would conclude the story with such a moment of stasis: indeed, with such a regressive moment. Perhaps S.P.E.W. and its aims have been only temporarily forgotten at this moment of calm and, with the sandwich over, Harry will set about emancipating his battle-weary slave rather than making further demands of him. If this is case, Rowling does not advertise it. The novel thus concludes with Harry as a relatively humane but otherwise unrepentant slaveholder.

Again, there is historical precedent. Arguably, the house-elves' position at the end of the series is very similar to that of the enslaved and formally enslaved people who fought for the British in the American Revolution. Promised freedom and wages—without which freedom means little—thousands of eighteenth-century African Americans fought for the British and against the colonists who held them in bondage. Many were indeed emancipated. Few, however, ever received their wages. By the mid-1780s, a large number of emancipated American slaves were being shunted around the British Empire: some to Nova Scotia, some to London, and some to the newly created African colony of Sierra Leone, where most died quickly and horribly.[29] The British in the 1770s were happy to accept the slaves' help on the battlefield, but less happy to offer them a fair reward. In Rowling's world, Harry Potter too benefits from the entry of the house-elves into the war, but he likewise neglects to repay the debt. One is left wondering whether Rowling is making a specific point about the ways in which marginalized groups, co-opted and feted in wartime, are abandoned once they are no longer useful, or whether she has merely failed to think through the implications of this plot element. With this, we run up against the problem of the boundaries of the text. Rowling has shown signs in public of wanting to add further narrative strands to her creation and in various interviews has expanded on the fate of several of her characters beyond their appearances in the novels. In one online interview, she answered a question on Hermione's later career:

KATIELEIGH: Does Hermione still continue to do work with SPEW and is life any better for house elves!

J.K. ROWLING: Hermione began her post-Hogwarts career at the Department for the Regulation and Control of Magical Creatures where she was instrumental in greatly improving life for house-elves and their ilk. She then moved (despite her jibe to Scrimgeour) to the Dept. of Magical Law Enforcement where she was a progressive voice who ensured the eradication of oppressive, pro-pureblood laws.[30]

Significantly, the words "abolition" or "emancipation" do not appear in this interview, which thus, even with its "progressive" language of "improvement," accords with the status quo that is maintained at the end of the final Potter novel. Whether we can count such interviews as part of the series is debatable, of course, but what seems clear throughout is that Rowling sees house-elf enslavement as an institution that is capable of much improvement but which cannot be eradicated. This is troubling since it militates strongly against the general message of the series, which is that great evils can be overcome, and should be overcome. The laudable actions of Hermione in pursuit of house-elf welfare lead to the equally laudable concerns of Ron at the Battle of Hogwarts. Yet, in both cases, slavery is not overthrown.

The ultimate message of the Potter books seems to be that commitment to action is just as important as the completion of that action. An uncharitable reading of the series would be to say that Rowling's position is that it does not matter whether slavery is overthrown, just as long as the erstwhile emancipators do their bit. A more generous reading would be that Rowling recognizes that not all evils can be done away with in a day. By defeating Voldemort, Potter and his allies pave the way for future improvements to the working conditions of house-elves and, perhaps, to their eventual emancipation. Just as William Wordsworth thought slavery would be swept away by the new Rights of Man espoused by the French revolutionaries of 1789, so Rowling reveals that house-elf enslavement is merely one facet of a greater evil. If Voldemort is defeated, "this most rotten branch of human shame / Would fall together with its parent tree."[31]

In 2003 I wrote: "for young people in the real world, denied the opportunity to do head-to-head battle with evil, the model of the political pressure group exemplified by S.P.E.W. is the most promising route for an apprenticeship in politics."[32] This remains a valid reading of *Goblet of Fire*, I believe, but is less convincing when applied to later novels in the series. But my more general thesis that "a significant aspect of Rowling's project is the promotion of political participation for young people" continues to be more generally true.[33] Indeed, the importance of participation becomes more urgent as the normal political structures of the wizarding world become increasingly threatened toward the end of the series. As Rowling's narrative concludes, we see Harry, Ron, and

Hermione engaged in "total war" against the forces of evil. In that conflict, the immediate needs of the house-elves seem to be overlooked. Nevertheless, Rowling provides plenty of clues to suggest that ultimately their welfare, as well as the welfare of all oppressed groups in the wizarding world, is of central concern to a free and equitable society. This message, and the message that political freedoms must be fought for and stoutly defended, is at the heart of Rowling's project.

## NOTES

1. Brycchan Carey, "Hermione and the House-elves: the Literary and Historical Context of J.K. Rowling's Anti-slavery Campaign," in *Reading Harry Potter: Critical Essays*, ed. Giselle Liza Anatol (Westport, CT: Praeger, 2003), 103–45, 105.

2. J.K. Rowling, *Harry Potter and the Goblet of Fire* (New York: Scholastic, 2000), 378–83.

3. Rowling, *Goblet*, 379.

4. Joseph Warton, "To Liberty" (1744), *Odes on Various Subjects* (London: R. Dodsley, 1746), 13. At the end of *Hallows*, Shacklebolt defeats Pius Thicknesse, the puppet Minister for Magic. I wonder if Rowling had in mind the eighteenth-century figure Phillip Thicknesse, the arch defender of slavery and early theorist of racism? It is just barely possible, but it does seem odd that two P. Thicknesseses should occupy such similar roles just by coincidence. For discussion, and an example of Thicknesse's writing, See Peter Fryer, *Staying Power: The History of Black People in Britain* (London: Pluto Press, 1984), 162–63. This history was popular with liberal and left-leaning British readers in the 1980s and 1990s, and there is every chance that Rowling would have come across it.

5. J.K. Rowling, *Harry Potter and the Order of the Phoenix* (New York: Scholastic, 2003), 228.

6. Rowling, *Phoenix*, 255.

7. Ibid., 385.

8. J.K. Rowling, *Harry Potter and the Half-Blood Prince* (New York: Scholastic, 2005), 439. A few pages earlier, when the grotesque Hepzibah asks Hokey "How do I look?" and Hokey replies "Lovely," Rowling writes "Harry could only assume that it was down in Hokey's contract that she must lie through her teeth when asked this question" (433–34). Although this appears to open up the possibility that house-elves negotiate terms with their owners, more likely this is just a flippant comment and by "contract" we should understand "orders."

9. Rowling, *Prince*, 451.

10. Rowling, *Goblet*, 125.

11. Rowling, *Prince*, 293, 299.

12. Jennifer Vineyard, "Kreacher Comfort: MTV Solves A 'Harry Potter' Mystery," *MTV Movie Blog*, posted 25 June 2007, http://moviesblog.mtv.com/2007/06/25/kreacher-comforts-mtv-solves-a-harry-potter-mystery/ (accessed 21 May 2008).

13. Rowling, *Prince*, 420–21.

14. Rowling, *Goblet*, 125. Rowling's emphasis.

15. Rowling, *Prince*, 52.

16. Ibid., 52–53.

17. J.K. Rowling, *Harry Potter and the Deathly Hallows* (New York: Scholastic, 2007), 457–76.

18. Rowling, *Hallows*, 474.

19. Simplistically describing Dobby as an "Uncle Tom" is not helpful, because since 1852 the name has acquired a pejorative sense in the United States that is not entirely derived from the character in Stowe's novel and which in any case, although not entirely unknown, is rarely heard in the United Kingdom.

20. Rowling, *Hallows*, 525.

21. George Boulukos has recently explored the long literary history of "the trope of the grateful slave." See *The Grateful Slave: The Emergence of Race in Eighteenth-century British and American Culture* (Cambridge: Cambridge University Press, 2008).

22. Rowling, *Hallows*, 197–98.

23. Hannah More, *Slavery, A Poem* (London, 1788), 11. For discussion of More's poem and the equality of feeling trope in abolitionist rhetoric, see Brycchan Carey, *British Abolitionism and the Rhetoric of Sensibility: Writing, Sentiment, and Slavery, 1760–1807* (Basingstoke: Palgrave Macmillan, 2005), 37–38, 84–88.

24. Rowling, *Hallows*, 199.

25. Ibid., 220, 227.

26. Henry Mackenzie, *Julia de Roubigné, A Tale, in a Series of Letters*, 2 vols. (London: W. Strahan and T. Cadell, 1777), II, 40. For discussion, see Carey, *British Abolitionism*, 63–67.

27. Rowling, *Hallows*, 734.

28. Ibid., 749.

29. For an extended discussion of the episode, see Fryer, 191–202.

30. "Webchat with J.K. Rowling, 30 July 2007," http://www.bloomsbury.com/ harrypotter/default.aspx?sec=3&sec2=1 (accessed 22 January 2009.)

31. William Wordsworth, *The Prelude* [1805], in *William Wordsworth*, ed. Stephen Gill (Oxford: Oxford UP, 1984), X, 224, 226.

32. Carey, "Hermione," 106.

33. Ibid.

# 12

# (Dis)Order and the Phoenix: Love and Political Resistance in Harry Potter

*Tracy L. Bealer*

Late in the penultimate volume of J.K. Rowling's Harry Potter series, Albus Dumbledore, Hogwarts headmaster and mentor to the eponymous hero, reiterates his contention that love is the one magical power that Harry's nemesis Lord Voldemort cannot master or combat, and therefore love is the only practical way to defeat him.[1] Despite Harry's skepticism that love is the best weapon to wield against the powerful Dark wizard who murdered his parents and whom Harry is destined to challenge in a duel only one of them can survive, Dumbledore insists that Harry is profoundly empowered by his capacity to trust and care for other human beings, and that Voldemort will be undone because of his inability to do the same. Other fantasy series generally recognized as influences on Rowling, such as *The Lord of the Rings* and *The Chronicles of Narnia*, rehearse a similar structure: those who love, survive. However, what sets Rowling's recapitulation of this paradigm apart is that she articulates both Voldemort's emotional disability and Harry's affective strength through the political machinations of the wizarding world they inhabit.

Many scholars addressing the interplay between Harry and his enemies in the first four books of the series tend to marginalize the political maneuverings described in the novels in favor of explicating the more supernatural aspects of Voldemort's villainy. As Richard Garfinkle notes in his analysis of Voldemort, the Dark wizard seems uninterested in confining his dominion to the political realm: "In personality [Voldemort] is a petty tyrant, interested in flashy exercise and the showing off of power, not in the systematic repression of a truly dangerous dictator."[2] Although it is true that Voldemort is not interested in limiting his considerable power within the confines of government—indeed, he seeks nothing short of immortality—books VI and VII of Rowling's series detail Voldemort's absorption of the legislative, judicial, and educational institutions of the wizarding world into his realm of influence. This campaign culminates in the opening chapters of *Harry Potter and the Deathly Hallows* (2007) with Voldemort's installation of his followers in the chief executive offices of the Ministry of Magic, the Wizengamot Court, the *Daily Prophet*, Gringotts Bank, and (he believes) Hogwarts School of Witchcraft and Wizardry. The process begins, however, in book V. *Harry Potter and the Order of the Phoenix* (2003) depicts an unstable and struggling Ministry of Magic that simultaneously conceals and denies Lord Voldemort's return. There is, therefore, an undeniably political element to Voldemort's supernatural evil in the series, which implies that at least part of the task set before Harry and his friends and family who oppose Voldemort involves explicit political resistance. As Adam-Troy Castro notes in his essay, "From Azkaban to Abu Ghraib: Fear and Fascism in *Harry Potter and the Order of the Phoenix*, "In year 5, politics enters the world of Harry Potter";[3] I suggest that political resistance in the fight against evil never again exits Rowling's magical world.

The intensified focus Rowling places on wizarding political institutions as the series develops requires a critical engagement with when, how, and why the magical world's civic institutions become instrumentalized by proponents of Dark magic, and concurrently, how Harry's and his friends' resistance to the misuse of political power corresponds with fighting Voldemort. Castro's essay, along with Susan Hall's "Harry Potter and the Rule of Law: The Central Weakness of Legal Concepts in the Wizard World" from *Reading Harry Potter* offer astute descriptions of the civic organizations in Rowling's fictional world. However, whereas Castro and Hall are primarily interested in analyzing the internal logic of, respectively, the wizarding penal and judiciary systems, in this chapter I explore how and why Harry's interactions with these compromised institutions inform and influence his existential conflict with Voldemort. Although the Ministry of Magic's capacity for corruption is demonstrated most centrally in *Order of the Phoenix* by newly installed Defense Against the Dark Arts professor Dolores Umbridge's Ministry-sponsored misinformation campaign against Harry and Dumbledore, the ominous implications of Minister of Magic Cornelius Fudge's incompetent waffling are hinted at as early as *Chamber of Secrets*.[4] Voldemort remains his principal enemy in *Order of the Phoenix*, but Harry must also engage in civil disobedience in order to combat the oppressive and dangerous political regime that has infiltrated his school. By closely examining the strategies Harry and his friends use to resist the despotic rule of Umbridge, this essay proposes to answer how Dumbledore's conviction that love is paramount in defeating Voldemort corresponds with the mode of political resistance Rowling privileges in *Order of the Phoenix*.

## THE TYRANNICAL PEDAGOGY OF DOLORES UMBRIDGE

*Order of the Phoenix* argues that the abilities both to love and to resist evil require individuals to negotiate a balance between order and disorder,

structure and chaos. Fawkes—the phoenix alluded to through both the title of book V and the eponymous anti-Voldemort resistance group described
in its pages—is itself an allusion to Guy Fawkes, the infamous seventeenth-
century British political radical.[5] When book V opens, the Order of the Phoenix,
comprising Hogwarts professors, Ministry of Magic employees, and many
of Harry's adult friends, including his godfather Sirius Black, has been, appropriately, reborn to combat a Lord Voldemort returned to full power and
joined by his reenergized minions. Although Harry witnessed Voldemort's
full-bodied return firsthand at the conclusion of book IV and is eager to help
destroy the wizard who killed his parents, the Order restricts membership to
of-age wizards who are out of school. So, for the bulk of the book, Harry
and his friends must confine their resistance activities to Hogwarts. However, as *Order of the Phoenix* reveals, the school proves to be an important
front in the fight against Voldemort and his followers. Because the Ministry of Magic's academic policies—rules that, in fact, have little to do with
education—seek to discredit Harry's account of Voldemort's return, Hogwarts
serves as a parallel sphere for the battle between the forces of good and those of
tyranny.

Minister of Magic Cornelius Fudge's use of the magical community's mainstream press (a flurry of stories in the *Daily Prophet* branding Harry a delusional
liar and Dumbledore a senile relic), judiciary (seating the full Wizengamot to
try Harry for a minor offense in an attempt both to discredit and to expel him),
and educational system creates the political equivalent of images in the Mirror
of Erised—a carefully manufactured reality in which the Minister's deepest
desire, that Lord Voldemort has not come back, looks true. Disturbingly, these
attempts at mass manipulation strongly resemble the casting of the Unforgive-
able Imperius Curse, in which a wizard or witch controls the thought, action,
and memory of a victim for his or her own ends. The etymological allusion to
"imperialism" suggests a fundamental similarity between magical and munic-
ipal attempts to occupy and control the mental space of other human beings,
and implies that both are deeply morally suspect. The tyrannical pedagogy of
Umbridge reveals how deeply important the school is to Fudge's misinformation initiative. Indeed, the powers Umbridge methodically accumulates during
her tenure suggest a totalitarian regime's commitment to singular control of
speech, action, and even thought in the name of perpetuating Fudge's willfully
ignorant version of reality.

Book V details the strategies Harry and his classmates employ to resist and
undo Umbridge's repressive decrees. In analyzing these strategies, I rely on
Kristina Thalhammer et al.'s *Courageous Resistance: The Power of Ordinary
People*.[6] This sociohistorical study describes different resistance movements
and methods of opposition to tyranny and genocide in the twentieth century.
Although I acknowledge the significant and undeniable distinction between
historical crimes against humanity and a fantasy series, I maintain that Thalhammer's vocabulary provides a useful avenue to explicating the novel's claims
about communal resistance and the political power of love.

The significance of *Order of the Phoenix*'s story arc is to suggest that in learning to resist Umbridge, the students, and in particular Harry himself, are also learning how to successfully fight Voldemort. Their opposition to Umbridge's "invasion" of Hogwarts, encapuslated in their formation of a shadow Defense Against the Dark Arts class nicknamed Dumbledore's Army (D.A.), negotiates a balance between order and disorder, loyalty and dissent, that Harry will need to recapitulate physically and emotionally in order to resist and overthrow a far more dangerous invasion: that of Voldemort into his mind. Throughout the course of book V, Rowling parallels Umbridge's increasing influence at Hogwarts with Voldemort's manipulative intrusions into Harry's dreams. Not only does this device imply that fear-mongering reactionary politics can end up reflecting and reinforcing tyranny in disturbing ways, but it also introduces the argument that Harry's willingness to engage in collective resistance—bolstered by his love for and reliance on his friends—will prove more vital in direct conflict with Voldemort than the Occlumency lessons designed to help him close his mind.

In many ways, Harry conforms to Thalhammer et al.'s definition of a courageous resister before the events of *Order of the Phoenix*. The first four books each include a central conflict with Voldemort or one of his followers in which Harry "voluntarily engage[s] in other-oriented, largely selfless behavior with a significantly high risk or cost to [himself]."[7] However, book V shows that Harry's willingness to risk his life is not the only character trait necessary for defeating evil. The novel consistently emphasizes the profound efficacy and functional value of the "social capital" produced by and through communal resistance. According to *Courageous Resistance*, social capital does practical work by "enhanc[ing] [the group's] ability to stay together for the 'long haul' to accumulate the necessary evidence and expertise to win public support in order to press their case." More importantly for Rowling, it creates relationships that nurture the resisters: "Many resisters depend on the trust and comradeship that develops in their local networks to sustain their motivation and commitment in the face of fear, frustration, and setbacks."[8] Rowling takes this latter benefit of social capital and suggests that "trust and comradeship"—what Dumbledore calls love—will not only assist in Voldemort's defeat, but in fact will enable it.

Before linking Harry's participation in communal resistance with his crucial capacity to love, it is necessary to clarify the nature of what he's resisting: Umbridge's dictatorial tenure at Hogwarts. Adam-Troy Castro, who is also interested in explicating the wizarding government using conceptual language from Muggle political science, identifies Umbridge's legislative style as "fascist," arguing that "her measures make Hogwarts increasingly less a school dedicated to education than a virtual penal institution more interested in keeping its students under strict control at all times."[9] Castro's argument corresponds with the speculation articulated by Arthur Weasley in the novel, that Fudge fears Dumbledore wants to be Minister of Magic;[10] this supposition leads Castro to claim that Fudge "suspects Harry, and his mentors at Hogwarts, of using rumors to prepare their own power grab" and "he therefore institutes a series of draconian measures designed to control what he sees as the subversive elements at the wizarding school."[11] I categorize Umbridge's reign as totalitarian, not fascist, based on Sirius's retort to Mr. Weasley that Fudge's insinuations of a possible coup mask an epistemological crisis for the Minister: "Fudge just can't bring himself to face [Voldemort's return]. It's so much more comfortable to convince himself Dumbledore's lying to destabilize him."[12] Fudge's inability to accept the reality of Voldemort's re-emergence leads him and Umbridge, his undersecretary at Hogwarts, to use their political power to produce and perpetuate restrictions on the citizens' and students' capacity for independent and critical *thought*—a move that distinguishes totalitarian regimes from fascist ones.

David Halberstam, in *Totalitarianism and the Modern Conception of Politics*,[13] further distinguishes totalitarianism from autocracy by the former system's obsession with manufacturing one truth: "Totalitarianism is . . . not satisfied with consolidating its power over the state in order to rule by decree for the benefit of those in power. . . . [T]otalitarianism goes so far as to abolish the most basic human freedom, the freedom of thought. . . . [T]he very nature of the totalitarian project is to establish total control over every individual, in order to impose its single-minded truth on the world."[14] As Hogwarts High Inquisitor[15] and interim headmistress, Professor Umbridge institutionalizes restrictions on the right to free association (Educational Decree Number Twenty-four); she consolidates the power to punish solely within her authority (Educational Decree Number Twenty-five); she censors the alternative press on school grounds (Educational Decree Number Twenty-seven), all in the name of preventing Harry and Dumbledore from communicating and substantiating their account of Voldemort's return to other students. In short, she must, as Harry perceives, "bring every aspect of life at Hogwarts under her personal control"[16] in order to prevent the truth about Voldemort from being accepted by the student population. Because Castro and I emphasize different aspects of Umbridge's reign—Castro, the punitive suppression of revolt, and I, the willful production of a distorted version of reality—we arrive at different political categorizations. However, our analysis of the effect is the same: Umbridge oppresses the student body for the sole purpose of quashing subversive thought and action.

Professor Umbridge also politicizes her Defense Against the Dark Arts classroom to promote the Ministry's version of the current wizarding sociopolitical atmosphere. Because, according to the Ministry, the world outside Hogwarts is utterly benign, there is no reason to teach the students practical defenses against the Dark Arts. Consequently, Umbridge's students follow a syllabus vetted by the Ministry, and "wands away" becomes her pedagogical mantra. Harry's criticism that the theory around which she plans to structure her Defense Against the Dark Arts class is no use in the current fraught environment provokes a condescending and duplicitous response from Umbridge, "This is school . . . not the real world."[17] However, Umbridge's position is designed to, as Hermione Granger incisively remarks, "interfere"[18] at the school by strictly policing Harry's and Dumbledore's articulation and dissemination of information about Voldemort's return in order to manage and legislate the vital connection between Hogwarts and the "real world."

This commitment to domination, coupled with the inherent power dynamics of any classroom in which teachers assume authority over students, forecloses Harry's and his friends' first attempt at resisting Umbridge's control. Umbridge establishes a strict hierarchy in her classroom, designed to situate herself as unquestioned and unquestionable leader and her students as passive receivers of the "knowledge" her chosen textbook provides. On the first day of class, Hermione tries to destabilize Umbridge's authority, and she does so by operating within an acceptable pedagogical matrix: she asks a question.[19] Hermione raises her hand, does not speak until called on, and asks Umbridge to clarify her course aims—all well within her rights as a student. Umbridge, because her authoritarianism forbids any questioning, counters Hermione and the students who follow her lead by creating a power structure that forecloses the possibility of dissent in her class. When the discussion becomes heated, Umbridge insists that students must raise their hands before speaking, and then simply refuses to look at Ron Weasley when he complies.[20] Through exhibiting the authority vested in her as a professor, Umbridge constructs a system of order that thwarts the students' right to speak.

Umbridge reinforces this system through detention and the sadistic physical punishment of those who fail to conform. In his multiple detentions with Umbridge, Harry must literally inscribe the Ministry's insulting indictment of his character on his body—copying the line *I must not tell lies*"[21] with Umbridge's magical quill causes the directive to be painfully etched into the skin of his right hand, leaving him with another scar he will carry for the rest of the series.[22] This particular punishment also betrays Umbridge's totalitarian leanings, literalizing Halberstam's observation that such regimes "view the individual as a subject fully inscribable by the ideas and practices that reflect the particular social organization."[23]

As Professor McGonagall explains to Harry, both pedagogical and political realities preclude opposing Umbridge in the classroom. Not only does she have "every right" to punish her students as she sees fit, but antagonizing Umbridge has consequences that transcend detention and the docking of House points: "You know where she comes from, you must know to whom she is reporting."[24] Any attempts Harry and his friends make to destabilize Umbridge's control in her classroom will be frustrated by her inherent authority as a teacher, as well as further endangering Hogwarts's autonomy. Therefore, Harry, Hermione, Ron, and other like-minded students must find a way to operate outside the sanctioned space of Umbridge's classroom and her rules for the school if they wish to evade her decrees and learn to protect themselves in the real world they know to be dangerous.

## "FEELING A BIT . . . *REBELLIOUS*"

Again led by Hermione, students frustrated by Umbridge's refusal to teach them practical magic and bristling at her oppressive decrees form a shadow Defense Against the Dark Arts class. This group, which christens itself Dumbledore's Army, combats the monolithic control Umbridge attempts to instantiate at Hogwarts. The existence of the group flouts Educational Decree Number Twenty-four, which prohibits the formation of unauthorized student groups. More importantly, the D.A. also resists the Ministry's manufactured version of reality. The purpose of the group, as articulated by Hermione, is "preparing ourselves . . . for what's waiting out there."[25] The students who join the D.A. believe that there is something outside Hogwarts far more dangerous than Umbridge admits, and therefore implicitly endorse Harry's account of Voldemort's return and reject the Ministry's misinformation campaign. The class, led by Harry due to his unusual and advanced experience confronting Dark magic, is practical in all senses of the word—the students practice countercharms, jinxes, and defensive spells in order to arm themselves against a world that they accept now includes a resurrected Dark Lord and his reinvigorated followers.

The structure of the D.A. embodies the novel's argument that successful resistance will negotiate a balance between order and disorder, compliance and dissent. In a particularly sophisticated touch, the room in which the D.A. meets is a cartographical metaphor for precisely this negotiation between order and disorder. The Room of Requirement, which appears at the will of the castle's inhabitants and conforms precisely to the desires of its summoner, escapes representation on maps of the Hogwarts castle, but is perfectly in line with the needs of the D.A. Additionally, the group's power dynamics confirm that the students are not proponents of anarchy. The members vote on D.A. policy, and implicitly endorse a democratic power structure. They believe that there should be a central figure of authority at Hogwarts, but that the leader should be Dumbledore, a just and superior wizard who cares for and about his students. As Torbjørn Knutsen observes in an essay considering Dumbledore's pedagogical style, the headmaster is "a liberal realist—a teacher who entertains a deep conviction about the value of traditional liberal virtues but who recognizes that some conflicts are irreconcilable and that power—and alliances of power— are important when push comes to shove. Dumbledore apparently assumes that Harry Potter and his fellow students are endowed with the qualities of reason and freedom."[26] It is almost superfluous to note that according to Knutsen's analysis, Dumbledore's pedagogy is an absolute inversion of Umbridge's. Whereas she discourages critical thought and suppresses intellectual expression in her students, Dumbledore appreciates and encourages "the qualities of reason and freedom" in his charges.

As Rebecca Stephens points out in "Harry and Hierarchy: Book Banning as a Reaction to the Subversion of Authority" from *Reading Harry Potter*, Dumbledore models a brand of authority that is benevolent but circumscribed.[27]

The headmaster's recognition that "alliances of power" are particularly efficacious in "irreconcilable" conflicts is another lesson manifested through the D.A. Hermione's insistence that the members sign a ledger and elect Harry as leader[28] imposes a cohesion and organization on the students that is democratic in spirit. However, although Harry leads the exercises, the group's modus operandi and raison d'être confirm what the alliance's name suggests: these students are "Dumbledore's." In a narrative reinforcement of this conceptual point, because the students name their organization after him, Dumbledore is able to continue to protect them from the Ministry's punishment by taking the blame for the illegal group after one of the members informs Umbridge of its existence.[29]

One of the interesting elements of Rowling's depiction of the students' acts is that their rebellion consists of enacting an adequate education. The students' campaign, although operating outside Umbridge's pedagogical authority, is committed to replicating the logical and just organizing principles of an ideal classroom. Because Umbridge has so perverted the purpose of magical training by and through her commitment to totalitarian domination at Hogwarts, opposition logically takes the form of re-imposing sound academic instruction: the D.A. has a classroom, a professor, and an official roll.

Even the infamously ill-behaved Weasley twins' spectacular exhibitions of dissent in the novel conform to the balance between order and disorder that Rowling establishes through the structure of the D.A. Although Hermione initially dismisses the twins' brand of magical mischief, even she is left "feeling a bit... *rebellious*"[30] after their carefully orchestrated campaign of subversive upheaval, because, as Castro rightly points out, "[t]hey're the ones who demonstrate, by vivid example, that Umbridge cannot remain in power as long as those she seeks to terrorize simply refuse to cooperate with her."[31] Although Fred and George themselves term their magically wrought chaotic displays "mayhem,"[32] the pandemonium is always carefully planned and executed to achieve maximum benefit for the students loyal to Dumbledore and the greatest consternation for Umbridge. The first phase of systematic mischief produced by the Weasley twins is a plague of fireworks set loose in Hogwarts's halls.[33] In addition to drumming up business for their nascent joke shop, the number and variety of bewitched fireworks both result in chaos and, more importantly, undermine Umbridge on her first day as Hogwarts Head. The twins' fireworks provoke a disaster that requires Umbridge to "run... all over the school answering the summonses of the other teachers, not one of whom seemed to be able to rid their rooms of the fireworks without her."[34] As this passage reveals, Fred and George's mischief also creates a subversive space for the other professors, to a witch and wizard all disgusted with Umbridge. The twins *and* the teachers in effect use her own insistence on supreme authority to undercut her. By pretending to require her assistance in disposing of the fireworks, the professors extend to its most absurd implications Umbridge's power to oversee the other teachers (Educational Decree Twenty-two).[35]

Fred and George's second outburst is similarly designed to strengthen anti-Umbridge resistance. They coordinate their transformation of a Hogwarts corridor into a swamp with Harry's clandestine use of Umbridge's fireplace to communicate with Sirius at Order of the Phoenix headquarters.[36] Shortly before dropping out of Hogwarts for good and opening their magical joke shop, Fred and George explicitly align their innovative merchandise with anti-Umbridge resistance, offering markdowns to those who promise to use the products to further enrage and destabilize Umbridge.[37] The remaining students follow Fred and George's directive enthusiastically, using their Skiving Snackboxes to upset the order of Umbridge's classroom by vomiting, fainting, and developing spontaneous nosebleeds.[38] Fred and George's resistance by chaotic spectacle conforms to an ordered method for creating disorder, even within the previously sacrosanct space of the classroom. The Weasley twins' campaign is the novel's most concise rehearsal of the type of resistance defined by *Courageous Resistance* because its public nature yields visible results: "The more public the resistance is, the more likely it is to yield change in repressors' behaviors and policies."[39] The spectacular nature of the Weasley twins' second and final subversive prank provokes a reaction from Peeves the Poltergeist that further solidifies Rowling's establishment of the interplay between order and disorder. Throughout the earlier books in the series, the mischievous spirit is a constant source of inappropriate and unruly disruptions for students and faculty alike. In striking contrast, his jaunty salute in response to Fred's valedictory directive to "Give her hell from us, Peeves"[40] establishes the trickster as an active collaborator in, rather than antagonist to, an organized campaign of chaos to unseat Umbridge.

However, this victory is not the climax of the novel because Rowling, as well as her characters, realize that the wizarding world's most dangerous enemy is not Umbridge. Her reign at Hogwarts eventually ends quite ignominiously with an abduction by a furious clan of centaurs,[41] but the closing chapters of the novel and the series as a whole are more concerned with how to resist an even more dangerous tyrannical figure: Lord Voldemort. As Harry and his friends have been combating Umbridge's tenure at Hogwarts, Harry has been increasingly disturbed by vivid dreams and visions that reveal his intimate connection with the thoughts, feelings, and even sensory apprehensions of Voldemort. The Dark wizard eventually lures Harry and his friends to the Ministry for the purpose of retrieving a prophecy by projecting a false vision of torturing Sirius into Harry's consciousness. These two plots and two enemies initially seem disparate. The defensive spells Harry teaches his friends through the D.A. are useful against school adversaries like Malfoy, Crabbe, and Goyle, but the battle between D.A. members and Voldemort's Death Eaters reveal how ill-matched underage and outnumbered wizards can be against adult enemies. However, Harry's final possession by Voldemort suggests that it is the willingness to join such an egalitarian collective, not superior magical powers, which will lead to Voldemort's ultimate defeat. Harry's relationships, both with members of the

D.A. and the Order of the Phoenix who come to rescue him from Voldemort's trap, protect his mind more reliably than the individual defense of Occlumency ever could.

## THE DEPARTMENT OF MYSTERIES

Harry spends a large part of *Order of the Phoenix* feeling isolated from his friends and abandoned by Dumbledore. He initially refuses to tell anyone about the abusive detentions with Umbridge because he understands the conflict to be "a *private* battle of wills [italics added]."[42] Similarly, he wants to go after Sirius by himself when he experiences the falsified vision;[43] D.A. members Neville Longbottom and Luna Lovegood must insist, along with Ron and Hermione, on being included. Harry's tendency to cast himself as the only courageous resister, what Hermione calls his "*saving-people-thing*,"[44] is significantly trumped by the part of him that seeks out and nurtures relationships in his direct encounter with Voldemort in the closing chapters of book V.

In addition to opposing Umbridge and endorsing Dumbledore, the D.A. introduces Harry and the reader to what will turn out to be his most crucial method of resisting Voldemort: forging and maintaining emotional connections to other people. At the feast welcoming the students back to school, the Sorting Hat issues a directive through its song that intimates the most efficacious way to resist evil. The students must resist internal squabbling and unite in order to avoid weakening the school to the point of its destruction.[45] Although the Sorting Hat worries that the process of Sorting the students into different Houses might contribute to institutionalizing the very divisions it warns against, the D.A. models a way to maintain both unity and difference within Hogwarts without hierarchy.[46] Students from all houses are welcome in the D.A.—one of its founding principles is that "anyone who wants to learn" should be allowed membership in the group.[47]

In the Ministry, after the Death Eaters have disabled all Harry's friends and killed Sirius, he is left alone to witness Dumbledore's duel with Voldemort. In an attempt to force Dumbledore's hand, Voldemort fully possesses Harry's mind and body and dares the stronger wizard to defeat him by killing the boy he loves, causing Harry immense pain in the process. Crucially, when Harry's anguished thoughts turn to Sirius, Voldemort is forced from his mind. Thinking that at least death will allow him to reunite with his recently murdered godfather, "Harry's heart filled with emotion, the creature's coils loosened, the pain was gone."[48] This episode literalizes the novel's contention that love, a necessarily interpersonal "emotion," not only opposes but actually disables evil. Therefore, the D.A. and the Order of the Phoenix itself are important not just because they make their members better wizards, or because they are engaged in the fight against evil, but because they institutionalize and strengthen interpersonal bonds, loyalty, trust, and love.

Dumbledore's and Harry's revealing and fraught reckoning at the close of book V commences a corrective to a generalized lack of disclosure on the parts of Harry's adult caretakers throughout the first five novels of the series—a silence that often results in the very kind of isolation for Harry and his friends that *Order of the Phoenix* critiques.[49] Lisa Hopkins, in her essay "Harry Potter and the Acquisition of Knowledge" in *Reading Harry Potter*, describes Harry's "defining condition" as "ignorance."[50] As Dumbledore admits in this book V conversation, it is a condition that Harry's teachers and adult friends have, at times, abetted. Dumbledore's decision not to tell Harry about the prophecy that dooms him to a final battle with Voldemort stems from a loving impulse, but it also alienates Harry and his friends from the Order, and unfortunately, aligns the well-meaning witches and wizards with agents of, if not misinformation, then the suppression of information. Dumbledore's apology to Harry for keeping this knowledge from him indicates that parental love must also negotiate a balance, one between protection and trust, especially when it comes to Harry's destined battle with Lord Voldemort.[51] *Half-Blood Prince* confirms Dumbledore's commitment to including Harry more fully in undermining Voldemort, both through informing him of the Dark wizard's past through trips in the Penseive, and inviting him on a harrowing trip to retrieve a Horcrux hidden in a seaside cave. This final collaboration between the two particularly reinforces the necessity of collective action to defeat evil. The defenses Voldemort designed assumed a single wizard would be pursing the Horcrux (another indication of his inability to understand the appeal of interpersonal emotional bonds). Because of Harry's assistance, the two are able to escape the cave relatively unscathed.

The novel argues that the personal and the political are identical. The existence of affective bonds between Harry and his friends, between Harry and Sirius, and between Harry and Dumbledore are a way to defeat Voldemort not only ideologically but also *practically*. According to Dumbledore's explanation for how Harry has successfully repelled the Dark Lord from his mind and body, love is the ultimate human expression of the balance between order and disorder that Rowling has been describing and that the D.A. has been enacting throughout the novel. The headmaster tells Harry of a room in the Department of Mysteries that is never left unlocked, and that harbors the "most mysterious" of magical powers, which Dumbledore defines as "at once more wonderful and more terrible than death, than human intelligence, than forces of nature." He explains that precisely because Harry has access to this power, which drove him to rescue Sirius, and because Voldemort lacks it completely, the force in fact literally rescued Harry because Voldemort "could not bear to reside in a body so full of the force he detests. In the end, it mattered not that you could not close your mind. It was your heart that saved you."[52] Harry's thoughts of Sirius, which Voldemort could not tolerate, were an expression of love: a power so disordered that it eludes analysis and resists definition. Rowling conveys that love is a mystery that destabilizes categorization by being both wonderful and terrible, but it nonetheless orders Harry's behavior and priorities to protect those he cares about. Because his heart is open to loving and being loved, his mind and body will be safe. *Order of the Phoenix*, then, demonstrates through political resistance and emotional resilience that love, the only magical power also accessible to Muggles, is the ultimate personal and political weapon against the evil of Lord Voldemort.

## EPILOGUE: HEROES AND HORCRUXES

In *Harry Potter and the Deathly Hallows*, the punitive suppression of dissent that Castro assigns to Umbridge is fully realized through the political minions of Lord Voldemort, demonstrating the importance of the political resistance mastered by the young wizards in book V. The Dark wizard institutionalizes his psychological weapons of fear, suspicion, and paranoia by remaining largely invisible to the wizarding citizenry, but enacting policies through the Ministry, such as the Muggle-Born Registration Commission, and through Hogwarts, such as mandating compulsory attendance and forcing all students to declare their Blood Status. These moves legislate unjust hierarchies between wizards and humans. The "Taboo" associated with speaking the Dark wizard's name aloud is a particularly elegant encapsulation of this dynamic. Harkening back to Dumbledore's warning to Harry in book I, that "[f]ear of a name increases fear of the thing itself,"[53] Rowling's choice in book VII allows Voldemort to *literalize* that fear; he imbues the word itself with magical properties that summon either Death Eaters or rogue gangs of wizard enforcers called Snatchers.[54]

In the last three installments of the series, the D.A. and the Order of the Phoenix continue their work of resistance and rebellion to this more visible and pervasive totalitarian regime. During the largely unnarrated but undoubtedly harrowing seventh year, Harry's friends endure at Hogwarts while he, Ron, and Hermione take their anti-Voldemort activities outside school walls and into the wizarding world at large. Neville Longbottom assumes leadership of the D.A. According to Neville's admirably humble and casually cavalier account, D.A. members underwent brutal beatings and threats against their families while trying to destabilize a Hogwarts curriculum shaped by Snape. Similarly, former D.A. members join with Order witches and wizards to form an alternative news source on the Wizarding Wireless Network.[55] Eventually, those wizards and witches take refuge in the Room of Requirement, this time outfitted as an underground headquarters, and actively and heroically participate in the "Battle of Hogwarts," prompted by Voldemort's invasion of the school. These developments in the series's last book confirm and extend the crucial role of communal resistance to political oppression in Rowling's wizarding world, and, as Carey argues in his chapter, how child readers might absorb this message to fight injustice in their own world.

However, the relationship between communal resistance and love modeled through the D.A. and the Order has even more interesting implications for the mystical evil that Harry must combat in order to defeat Voldemort's political, psychological, and physical domination. During the course of *The Deathly Hallows*, Harry and Dumbledore discover that Voldemort has split his soul and installed the amputated bits of his self into objects called Horcruxes. As Dumbledore realizes, Voldemort has performed this magic at great cost—he must murder someone to create each Horcrux—and at great detriment to his power. His social isolation and physical and emotional fragmentation are such that Voldemort cannot perceive that two parts of his self have already been destroyed.[56] Knowing his own death is imminent, Dumbledore sets Harry the task of annihilating the remaining Horcruxes and thereby defeating Voldemort conclusively; both the literal and conceptual "will" of Dumbledore stipulate that Harry complete this task by and through the relationships he has fostered throughout the series, particularly with his two best friends. In the end, each of them, as well as Neville, destroys a part of Voldemort's soul and thereby materially contributes to his downfall: Hermione does away with Helga Hufflepuff's cup using a basilisk fang; Ron stabs Salazar Slytherin's locket with the sword of Gryffindor; Neville also uses the sword to kill Nagini. Tellingly, Dumbledore loses his right hand—and eventually his life—by succumbing to the solitary temptation of one of the Horcruxes. Thus, the final two books of Rowling's *Harry Potter* series argue that by engaging in communal resistance and being receptive to the love and trust it fosters, Harry's companions will not only protect his mind, his body, and his heart, but will also ensure the destruction of his enemy.

## NOTES

A shorter version of this paper was presented at the Pop Culture Association/American Culture Association 2008 National Conference, San Francisco, CA, March 19–22. Thanks to Nicole and Scott Fisk whose suggestions improved my essay.

1. J.K. Rowling, *Harry Potter and the Half-Blood Prince* (New York: Scholastic, 2005), 510–11.

2. Richard Garfinkle, "Why Killing Harry Is the Worst Outcome for Voldemort," *Mapping the World of Harry Potter*, ed. Mercedes Lackey and Leah Wilson (Dallas: Benbella Books, Inc., 2005): 179–94. 183.

3. Adam-Troy Castro, "From Azkaban to Abu Gharib: Fear and Fascism in *Harry Potter and the Order of the Phoenix*," *Mapping the World of Harry Potter*, ed. Mercedes Lackey and Leah Wilson (Dallas: Benbella Books, Inc., 2005): 119–32. 119.

4. Fudge unjustly imprisons Hagrid as a reactionary response to the re-opening of the Chamber in the second book, and in *Goblet of Fire*, he allows the dementors to incapacitate Barty Crouch Jr. before he can give his testimony confirming Voldemort's return.

5. The allusion also operates as a witty conceptual link between Fawkes's ability to initiate rebirth through fire and Guy Fawkes's "Gunpowder Plot" to blow up Parliament. Fawkes, though later proven to be a relatively minor player in the anarchic conspiracy

to blow up the houses of Parliament on November 5, 1605, remains the metonym for the plot. He lends his name to the day of commemoration in Britain during which it is customary to set off fireworks and burn "guys"—effigies of Fawkes ("The Gunpowder Plot." *About Parliament.* 11 September 2007. United Kingdom Parliament. Accessed 25 August 2008 <http://www.parliament.uk/faq/gunpowderplot.cfm#gun7>.).

6. Kristina E. Thalhammer et al. *Courageous Resistance: The Power of Ordinary People* (New York: Palgrave, 2007).

7. Ibid., 5.

8. Ibid., 29.

9. Castro 2005, 124.

10. J.K. Rowling, *Harry Potter and the Order of the Phoenix* (New York: Scholastic, 2003), 93.

11. Castro, 123.

12. Rowling, *Phoenix*, 94.

13. Michael Halberstam, *Totalitarianism and the Modern Conception of Politics* (New Haven: Yale UP, 1999).

14. Ibid., 39–40.

15. In addition to referencing the leaders of any number of historical religious and political inquisitions, Umbridge's self-designation can also be productively read as an allusion to Dostoevsky's "Grand Inquisitor" who takes it upon himself to "protect" human beings from existential freedom.

16. Rowling, *Phoenix*, 551.

17. Ibid., 244.

18. Ibid., 214.

19. Ibid., 241.

20. Ibid., 242.

21. Ibid., 266.

22. However, whereas Harry's first scar is a lightning-shaped metonym for an attack he did nothing to provoke or survive, what Elaine Ostry terms the "automatic and indelible" marker of his status, *this* wound becomes unmoored from its disciplinary purpose and signifies when and how Harry learned to actively resist. Elaine Ostry, "Accepting Mudbloods: The Ambivalent Social Vision of J.K. Rowling's Fairy Tales," *Reading Harry Potter: Critical Essays*, ed. Giselle Liza Anatol (Westport: Praeger, 2003), 98. In *Prince*, newly installed Minister of Magic Rufus Scrimgeour attempts to convince Harry to serve as a public relations agent for the floundering Ministry. Harry refuses by and through referring to these marks: "'I haven't forgotten, Minister....' He raised his right fist. There...were the scars which Dolores Umbridge had forced him to carve into his own flesh" (347). He again uses his scar as an embodied metaphor for his antagonism towards a compromised Ministry in book VII, J.K. Rowling, *Harry Potter and the Deathly Hallows* (New York: Scholastic, 2007), 131.

23. Halberstam, 22.

24. Rowling, *Phoenix*, 248–49.

25. Ibid., 325.

26. Torbjørn L. Knutsen, "Dumbledore's Pedagogy: Knowledge and Virtue and Hogwarts," *Harry Potter and International Relations*, ed. Daniel H. Nexon and Iver B. Neumann (Lanham, MD: Rowman & Littlefield, 2006): 197–212. 204.

27. Rebecca Stephens, "Harry and Hierarchy: Book Banning as a Reaction to the Subversion of Authority," in *Reading Harry Potter*, ed. Giselle Liza Anatol (Westport: Praeger, 2003): 51–65, 57.

28. Rowling, *Phoenix*, 391.

29. Ibid., 618.

30. Ibid., 634.

31. Castro, 129–30.

32. Rowling, *Phoenix*, 627.

33. Ibid., 632–34.

34. Ibid., 634.

35. The film version of *Phoenix* does a particularly good job of visually portraying the efficacy of the Weasley twins' resistance through a scene of the fireworks smashing into and destroying the numerous framed Educational Decrees hanging in the castle's entryway (*Harry Potter and the Order of the Phoenix*, Dir. David Yates, Perf. Daniel Radcliffe, Rupert Grint, and Emma Watson, Warner Brothers, 2007).

36. Although Harry does not want to consult Sirius about any political matters, but rather to ask a deeply personal question about his father (*Phoenix*, 671), the communication in and of itself is subversive and forbidden, and the twins are unaware that Harry wants to speak with Sirius as a godson, not as a junior resistance operative.

37. Rowling, *Phoenix*, 675. As *Prince* confirms, the twins continue to marry their entrepreneurism with anti-Ministry resistance. In addition to the playful subversion that Castro applauds (i.e., the Constipation Sensation: U-No-Poo), Fred and George sell a line of Defense Against the Dark Arts products (119). Harry uses one of their Decoy Deontators to gain access to Umbridge's new office in book VII (Rowling, *Hallows*, 250).

38. Rowling, *Phoenix*, 677–78.

39. Thalhammer, 117.

40. Rowling, *Phoenix*, 675.

41. She resurfaces, her latent bigotry now explicit, as Head of the Muggle-born Registration Commission in *Hallows*, distributing anti–Muggle and Muggle-born propaganda (250) and chairing Blood Status interrogations of wizards and witches (chapter 13).

42. Rowling, *Phoenix*, 269.

43. Ibid., 761.

44. Ibid., 733.

45. Ibid., 207.

46. The D.A.'s insistence on institutionalizing unity *and* difference is endorsed most emphatically by Voldemort's threat to end Sorting at Hogwarts, leaving Slytherin as the only House. Rowling, *Hallows*, 732.

47. Rowling, *Phoenix*, 332.

48. Ibid., 816.

49. Thanks to Emily Honey who prompted me to think about both this persistent withholding on the part of adult witches and wizards who care for Harry, and the dangerous situations into which Harry's resulting ignorance often places him.

50. Lisa Hopkins, "Harry Potter and the Acquisition of Knowledge," in *Reading Harry Potter*, ed. Giselle Liza Anatol (Westport, CT: Praeger, 2003): 25–34, 25.

51. The argument that some information *should* be kept from children and young adults is articulated must fully through Lucius Malfoy's relationship with his son Draco.

Throughout the series, Draco's father tells him everything (the story of Slytherin's heir, the logistics of the Triwizard tournament, the return of Lord Voldemort). Rather than preparing Draco to engage productively with the world, this knowledge leads the young wizard to thrust himself into situations well over his head, promising Voldemort to kill Dumbledore in book VI, and having to be rescued from his vow (we find out in *Hallows*) by Snape.

52. Rowling, *Hallows*, 844.

53. J.K. Rowling, *Harry Potter and the Sorcerer's Stone* (New York: Scholastic, 1997), 298.

54. Rowling, *Hallows*, 381–82, 389.

55. Ibid., 441–43.

56. Rowling, *Phoenix*, 507.

# 13

# Militant Literacy: Hermione Granger, Rita Skeeter, Dolores Umbridge, and the (Mis)use of Text

*Leslee Friedman*

Conventional wisdom among feminist scholars over the past thirty years or so dictates that acts of subjective creation rather than objective passivity are what define a female character who truly breaks the mold of traditional patriarchal constructions. Perhaps most fundamental to this theoretical understanding of female characters is Sandra Gilbert and Susan Gubar's essay, "The Queen's Looking Glass: Female Creativity, Male Images of Women, and the Metaphor of Literary Paternity." Although Gilbert and Gubar's essay deals specifically with male authorship of women, their interpretation of the traditional Snow White fairy tale is a nearly archetypal feminist reading at this point, and feeds into current notions of who the heroine is or is not in any given text.

Gilbert and Gubar position the witch in Snow White as the most desirable female role model in the fairy tale. They point out that it is she who is "a plotter, a *plot-maker*, a schemer, a witch, an *artist*, an impersonator, a woman of almost infinite creative energy. . . . " [italics added][1] According to Gilbert and Gubar, the Queen *creates* plans in order to escape the confines inherent to the female state of existence; she spins tales of herself as a peddler, an old woman, and a farmer's wife.[2] Although the witch does not succeed in accomplishing her aims, the scholars see Snow White as being even less successful in her strategies of survival, plying the traditionally passive arts of the female sphere as a way to taste "the only measure of power available to a woman in a patriarchal culture."[3] This power proves to be illusory at best and only allows her to trade the queen's literal coffin for the metaphorical coffin of objective docility in her future role as queen.[4]

Roberta Seelinger Trites follows up on this line of thinking in her aptly named book, *Waking Sleeping Beauty: Feminist Voices in Children's Novels.* Trites's focus in this book is the way in which female characters in more contemporary young adult novels establish their own subjectivity, specifically through language and invention. She argues that disenfranchised characters, particularly female ones, learn to "recognize [their] subjectivity through the art of writing... to assume agency in [their] life by means of [their] chosen art."[5]

Although their readings of various characters are compelling, neither Gilbert and Gubar nor Trites deal specifically with the female *reader* in these essays. The lack of attention paid to her, however, is significant. The writer/artist figure is clearly agentive, clearly rebellious, and clearly subjective. Established binaries, then, and the fact that these scholars offer them no challenge, tacitly position the female reader as opposite all these things: thus passive, accepting, objective.

To complicate these theory-based approaches to the issue of gender and reading, I incorporate Meredith Rogers Cherland's *Private Practices: Girls Reading Fiction and Constructing Identity*, an ethnographic work on the reading practices of sixth-grade girls in suburban Canada, a place she calls Oak Town. The insights Cherland presents about girls' reading and the ways it intersects with the dual and essentialist nature that Oak Town residents assume gender to have are worth considering for the purposes of this chapter. Cherland found that, similarly to the "rules... identified in other studies of contemporary Western cultures" the inhabitants of Oak Town "behaved according to North American culture's tacit 'rules' for constructing gender: 'male' and 'female' were seen in terms of binary categories, defined in contrasting relation to each other; men were *seen as more physically assertive than women*." [italics added][6] Thus it does not seem surprising that one man was quoted as saying that reading is "kind of like sleeping. It's a waste of time. Doesn't seem productive for me."[7] The men in Cherland's study "read for utilitarian purposes" and rarely admitted to reading fiction, or anything that could not be seen as having some sort of direct impact on their careers or physically performed hobbies.[8] In contrast, the reading of fiction was not just seen acceptable for girls; rather, the community of Oak Town *expected* girls to participate in the pastime. Cherland observes: "the reading of fiction is a pastime that women friends *share* with each other... something a girl can be proud of—an appropriate time-filler for girls."[9] Phrased differently, reading is something that keeps girls in their "appropriate" social positioning and teaches them early on how to fulfill the communal obligations that are a woman's "appropriate" domain.

The ways in which female characters in J.K. Rowling's Harry Potter series engage in the activities of reading and writing work to undermine the idea that such signatory binaries exist. In this chapter I focus on *Harry Potter and the Goblet of Fire* and *Harry Potter and The Order of the Phoenix*. I will concentrate largely on the characters Hermione Granger, Rita Skeeter and Dolores Umbridge. Through these three characters Rowling makes a clear point that the female hero is someone who engages in dialogue and action with her text, someone who balances passivity with aggression and objectivity with subjectivity. Hermione eventually triumphs over both women who write in these novels not because Rowling has an antifeminist vision whereby women who create are evil but rather because Hermione understands that all creativity exists within community: a community of people *and* a community of words. Hermione acts and/or creates intertextually, something that neither Skeeter nor Umbridge ever bothers to do. Finally, I will comment on two significant events in *Harry Potter and the Deathly Hallows* to argue that in the final book Rowling expands her views on the subjects of literacy, community, and the way those elements interact with the idea of a passive–aggressive binary.

Rowling has always very clearly aligned Hermione's powers with her relationship to text. Although Hermione accomplishes a series of impressive feats in the first book, the most noteworthy is when she solves Professor Snape's puzzle. Significantly, this puzzle is not like the verbal riddle Harry has to solve to pass the Sphinx in *Goblet of Fire*. This puzzle appears in written/textual form, and Hermione tells Harry that they will not be stuck at this obstacle to the Sorcerer's Stone, that "Everything we need is here *on this paper*" [italics added].[10] Despite Hermione's reassurance to Harry, not everything they need is on the paper. Were Harry left by himself to read and solve the puzzle it is not clear that he would be able to pass this particular barrier. Although Hermione soon after minimizes her powers of engaging with text as relatively unimportant in her infamous statement, "Books! And cleverness! There are more important things—friendship and bravery and—"[11] it instead comes across that Hermione's "more important things" are equally important, but in different ways. Hermione has shown no lack of friendship and bravery in accompanying Harry and Ron down the trapdoor. However, her contributions once inside have depended on the knowledge she acquired through her unfairly maligned "books and cleverness." Hermione essentially makes magic happen when reading, whether by the literal act of magic as instructed by text or—as in the case of the puzzle—by entering into a relationship with the text where she not only receives information but finds ways of engendering action with that information.

In the first volume of *Reading Harry Potter*, Veronica L. Schanoes echoes this sentiment in her essay, "Cruel Heroes and Treacherous Texts: Educating the Reader in Moral Complexity and Critical Reading in J.K. Rowling's Harry Potter Books," by looking at one of the moments in which Hermione does not interact with text, but rather contents herself with merely reading and passively trusting it. Schanoes points out that Hermione's uncharacteristic and disempowering crush on Lockhart springs from her unwillingness to question Lockhart's written chronicles of himself: "While books are the source and medium of [Hermione's] intellectual strength, they also form the bedrock of her knowledge, with the result that she has an extremely difficult time questioning the validity of the books themselves."[12] It is a mark of the fact that Hermione learns from her mistakes regarding reading that by the fourth book she has learned to doubt text, to question it and adapt it to her own means. Hermione's power is not her intelligence alone but rather the ways in which she exists within a community of intelligence recorded and shared through words.

This aspect of Hermione's self-growth as well as the development of her critical intellect appears in the way she chooses to attack the problem of house-elves.[13] Rowling frames the storyline of the house-elves as a metaphor for slavery and how the ideology of false consciousness can become presumptive. Hermione interprets the elves' willingness to serve as the result of deep social conditioning, and determines to work for their "rights." Although Rowling uses this situation to showcase ideas of cultural difference—not only between house-elves and humans but between magically raised and Muggle-born wizards—she also manipulates Hermione's position to illustrate the interconnectedness between text and lived-life.

Hermione's first, ill-fated attempt to stand against wizards' traditional treatment of house-elves involves a series of actions, but culminates in her creation of the Society for Promotion of Elfish Welfare (S.P.E.W.).[14] However, not only are the students and adults whom she approaches about joining largely apathetic or hostile to the idea, but the elves themselves are alarmed by her words and ideals. Rowling works with all these aspects of Hermione's frustrated attempts at social reform to examine the ways that critical reading can be at once crucial and also misleading. At one point, Hermione reveals her frustration with one of her most often quoted texts: "It's all in *Hogwarts, A History*. Though, of course, that book's not *entirely* reliable. A Revised *History of Hogwarts* would be a more accurate title."[15] Hermione is referring to the fact that the history tome never once recognizes the presence of house-elves despite their actual omnipresence. The way that Hermione reads through to the missing information in this book is vital to her talent at understanding what is actually happening when a supposedly objective text conspires to perpetuate the invisible status of the nondominant. Only through her ability to critically find these sites of absence and reconstruct what is not immediately evident—in other words, to engage the mental dialogue of the text—is Hermione able to help Harry and herself throughout the series.[16]

However, Rowling uses this moment in Hermione's critical reading trajectory to complicate things a bit further. In the quotation, Hermione reveals her detection of cultural bias and the imposition of invisibility on one type of being by another. The problem is that Hermione refuses to examine the cultural biases she herself brings to the project. In this, Rowling makes her point about the extent of text's usefulness: Hermione is most successful in her analytical engagements with written materials when she can unpack the assumptions she builds into the questions she wants answered. As her reading of the house-elf situation has been less than entirely dialogic—Hermione only pays attention to those facts which give fuel to her sentiments—it is unsurprising that she lacks the ability to make things happen with S.P.E.W. when she embarks on a largely text-based *written* campaign.[17] To begin with, Hermione's acronym is problematic: a point made time and again by Ron, who is not an interactive reader. Hermione's unwillingness to consider the elves' position as anything other than the long-term effects of wizarding brainwashing and exploitation is also apparent in her decision to push Ron's criticisms entirely aside.

Undoubtedly, Ron is opposed to the idea on several levels and thereby more likely to find problems with it. However, for Hermione's plans to have any real impetus, she must be able to communicate them to people who are not inherently like herself: to both speak to and listen to those who see things differently. In her essay, "Rhetorical Traditions and the Reform Writing of Mary Ann Shadd Cary," Anne Marie Mann Simpkins performs a rhetorical analysis of Shadd's successful abolitionist writings to prove that Shadd implemented deep knowledge of her audience and canny intertextuality in order to make her ideas heard: "[the] flexibility of rhetorical structures employed by Shadd . . . lies in her ability to embed rhetorical intertextual strategies that [are] necessary for her to address varied audiences within her abolitionist forum."[18] Specifically, Shadd had a gift for speaking to multiple audiences at once, and infixing information that each separate audience would find appealing or convincing.[19] Hermione's implementation of rhetoric is unsuccessful because she uses it in nearly the opposite manner of Shadd: she does not read with an eye toward multiple perspectives. Not only does Hermione fail to imagine an audience with different textual needs from herself, she is so blind to the concept of intertextual necessity in rhetoric that she chooses—and defends—an acronym that forms a word with negative associations and that actually urges people to eschew her ideas. Although Hermione's concept of audience and the structuring of rhetoric becomes stronger throughout the books, the initial mistakes surrounding her efforts with S.P.E.W. are highly indicative of the ways in which Harry Potter characters must treat reading and writing carefully for it to prove effective as an aid to their efforts. Hermione must learn to extend her literacy habits to people—to "read" them—if she is ever going to utilize her more traditional literacies to their utmost potential.

Another substantial shift in Hermione's relationship to reading comes in book IV as well. This shift reveals that reading is not merely something she can use to teach or spur herself into action. It occurs when Hermione is time and again failed by both library and the printed word. Hermione is not self-reflexive enough to recognize her own interpretive failures in the case of S.P.E.W.; however, elsewhere in *Goblet of Fire*, the library lets her down in a way she cannot fail to notice: it refuses to provide an answer in her search for a way to help Harry in the second task of the Triwizard Tournament. Notably, Rowling words Hermione's struggle to find such a spell/charm/item and so forth, in anthropomorphic terms, stating that "[Hermione] seemed to be taking the library's lack of useful information on the subject as a personal insult; it had never failed her before."[20] Hermione's struggle to coax information out of the books is thereby made dialogic, with the library performing metonymically for the books, throwing back insults to Hermione's questions.

The most significant part of Hermione's seeming failure here is that the book with the answer does exist. It has been in Neville's hands since the beginning of the school year. Later the faux-Moody vents his frustration that Harry never managed to come in contact with his planted clue: "I expected you to ask everyone and anyone you could for help."[21] After all, Neville, Moody explains, would have been able to tell him the answer instantly. In contrast to Hermione, while Neville may have accrued a certain type of his own power by reading the book and affecting its wisdom in areas of herbology, he does not read dialogically in these books. In general, the men of this series neither engage the actual texts, nor do they spread their knowledge of text to each other.

It is worthwhile to elaborate here on the different relationship men bear to text in the books IV and V. Where Hermione embraces text and often trusts it to act in the capacity of a friendly mentor, Harry and the other men in these books regularly find text to be a source of potential abuse and danger. The danger factor of written text becomes more pronounced and more complicated in other books throughout the series: the most obvious example being Riddle's diary in *Chamber of Secrets*. Nonetheless, Harry's interaction with text in books IV and V is plentiful, and repeatedly either useless or threatening.[22] Part of this comes from Harry's inability to trust text to help him. Harry's thought, during the opening of *Goblet of Fire*, upon experiencing pain in his scar, is: "He doubted very much whether a book could help him now."[23] In the end it is unclear whether a book could or not, as Harry is unwilling to take the chance.

The reader actually learns as much about Harry's—and the general male—relationship to text in this series by the *exception* to Harry's reluctance to trust books: Harry's potions book in *Half-Blood Prince*. For a change, Hermione does not trust the book at all, whereas Ron and Harry are amused and pleased by the help its notes offer.[24] Although much of Hermione's mistrust comes off as—and *is*—academic pride, it is important to note that it is not the book itself Hermione does not trust so much as the handwritten notes. Given that handwritten communication is normative in the wizarding world, Harry and Ron have been socialized to understand handwriting as having a tangible author—in this case, they are insistent, a male author.[25] Hermione, however, clearly sees handwriting as problematic, aware that for all that it is represented in personal communication, it is also perilously close to the kind of writing Ginny was engaging in with Riddle. For Hermione, it is less the written words than the fact that they have no clear *author* that presents the problem. Lockhart has taught her that an author's intent can be central to the trustworthiness of a text, and being without a name or any kind of context to put to the author, Hermione is unwilling to simply put her faith in his or her words. A community, textual or otherwise, consists of identifiable *bodies*—of work or of flesh.

Altered Potions' text aside, Harry's mistrust of text is hardly foolish. He has excellent reason to be cautious around the medium. Even outside of the events in *Chamber of Secrets*, Harry's relationship to text is a troubled and often violent one.[26] Text regularly proves itself to be not just less-than-useful, but actively menacing. In *Goblet of Fire*, the goblet releases a long flame that carries on it a "piece of parchment," on which someone has written Harry's name.[27] That tiny scrap of text lands Harry in a competition wherein he is three years younger than any of the other contestants and expected to perform a series of tasks that are literally life threatening. Later in the book, two words engraved on a headstone—"Tom Riddle"—could prove vital to Harry and Cedric Diggory's continued survival. Unfortunately, the words remain hidden from Harry's view until they are of no use to him.[28] Unlike in the case of Hermione, text is rarely obliging or even friendly toward Harry.

Events in *Order of the Phoenix* lead the reader to believe that this is probably the case for many of the other men in the series as well. During Harry's Occlumency lessons, when Snape is trying to explain what Occlumency is, he tells Harry: "The mind is not a book, to be opened at will and examined at leisure."[29] At the same time, Rowling finishes off Snape's diatribe about how Occlumency actually works by having Harry think: "Whatever Snape said, [it] sounded like mind reading to Harry."[30] This entire passage throws into question what denotes reading in these texts. Snape scorns the idea of Occlumency being considered in conjunction with reading in a way that Hermione would not. Harry's cynical reception of Snape's attitude opens up space for men to have the interactive relationship with text that women often do, should he so choose.

Rowling brings this issue of failed literary transmission between males full circle at the end of the book. Voldemort has been so intent on getting the one existing copy of the prophecy concerning him and Harry that he communicates its location to his opponent through a sort of mental telepathy. If one follows Harry's earlier analogy about Occlumency being a way of "reading" the mind, Voldemort's use of Legilimency is an example of him "writing" on the protagonist's mind. Notably, Rowling's foremost villain is the character to use writing in its traditionally "active" and "male" role in this instance. The reader of the series is not supposed to condone Voldemort's actions in general, and as such, must question the use of "writing" as an act of aggression. Akin to other conventional exercises of power through text, however, Voldemort's attempt brings Harry to the Ministry but does not garner the Dark Lord his desired goal—possession of the prophecy. Neville drops and destroys the one extant recording—the one physical, "textual" version of the information—revealing the trouble that the men in Rowling's novels have interacting with each other through written documents. Thus, the singular "print" of the prophecy left existing is in Dumbledore's head, now only available to Harry in spoken format. Overwhelmingly in these texts, for communication between men to be safe, it must occur through oral rather than written means. In contrast, Hermione is at her most helpful and effective when communicating to Ron and Harry through the locus of text. She consistently talks them through her notes, helps with papers, explains parts of books she has read, and conversationally picks apart the *The Daily Prophet*'s rhetoric for the two boys.

Rowling realizes *The Daily Prophet* as Hermione's archenemy in book IV.
As the books do for the library, the *Prophet* exists metonymically in the place
of journalist Rita Skeeter. Because Hermione can only help Harry from the
sidelines of the actual tournament, she instead sets her sights on the woman who
has engaged in a threatening and lie-filled rhetorical campaign aimed against
Harry. Hermione is affronted by Rita Skeeter on two levels: 1) the woman
uses text to manipulate, something Hermione has seen twice over through
Tom Riddle's use of the diary and Lockhart's false accounts in his textbooks
in *Chamber of Secrets,* and 2) Skeeter has absolutely no respect for the text
itself. Skeeter does not bother to so much as even take her own notes, instead
using a charmed pen to do it for her. Later in *Order of the Phoenix,* Skeeter
admits what Hermione and Harry have acknowledged throughout all of *Goblet
of Fire*—that she only writes for the money it brings. She tells Hermione,
"The Prophet exists to sell itself,"[31] not to instruct or to inform; this serves as
the reason for denying Hermione's request to write the story of Voldemort's
re-rising through Harry's point of view. The *Prophet*'s introductory moment
in book IV is through a Skeeter article, and her articles continue to be the
singular ones that *Goblet of Fire* readers view, knitting Skeeter's identification
with the periodical so tightly that Skeeter might as well say *she* exists to sell
*herself.*

Hermione manages to defeat Skeeter because, whereas Skeeter's interaction
with text involves aggressive manipulation and exploitation, Hermione's model
incorporates receptiveness and constructive creativity. Modeling her reading
habits after a conversation with people, Hermione first "listens"[32] to what books
have to tell her and then creates her response or her solutions to problems by
using that knowledge as a foundation. Her solution to the problem of Skeeter's
invasiveness is the perfect example of this technique. The idea starts with a
conversation in which Harry brings up the Muggle act of "bugging." Hermione,
who has previously discounted bugging as a possibility due to facts she learned
in *Hogwarts, A History,* starts to think more freely about what the term
means before, naturally, running to the library. At this point Skeeter has spent
nearly all of book IV with what seems to be power over Hermione, particularly
when the journalist successfully sways Molly Weasley's feelings toward the
young protagonist. In the end, however, Hermione exerts actual power over
Skeeter by way of puzzling things out. As in book I, Hermione reads her
way through the clues and then engages with the texts that give her those
clues in order to overcome a barrier, physical or otherwise. With this dynamic,
Rowling suggests that writing, traditionally understood by feminist critics to
be a locus of reclaimed female power, gives the author a certain type of control
but it can also dissociate her from her surrounding community. Even as Skeeter
writes what she believes people will want to hear,[33] she writes about it without
incorporating input, not even that of the people whom she interviews. Whether
Rowling is buying into traditional notions of what strengthens women here or
not, Hermione triumphs because she exists within a community, albeit one of

textual exchange. Hermione consistently listens to others' voices and then adds her own by way of interaction with the text, which corresponds to action in the physical world.

The relationship between Hermione and Dolores Umbridge frames the uses and misuses of text to gain power even more clearly than Hermione's to Skeeter. Rowling sets this confrontation up from the point where Hermione listens to Umbridge's speech at the welcoming feast.[34] Hermione listens to the actual words of the speech, but the layers of meaning she uncovers with each phrase offer a radically different interpretation than the superficial collection of words would suggest. Krista Ratcliffe argues that popular understandings relate listening even more closely to passivity than reading. She theorizes on what she calls "rhetorical listening," or listening that includes hybridization and analysis of the received information as "a trope for interpretive invention, one on equal footing with the tropes of . . . writing and speaking."[35] Following up on her act of active/rhetorical listening, Hermione sets to questioning Umbridge's Defense Against the Dark Arts curriculum. This class syllabus consists of merely reading Umbridge's selected source text. Hermione has no problem reading but she is well aware that reading must be more than an action in a vacuum. Reading must work in the same way as Ratcliffe's "rhetorical listening"; the reader must engage in the action digestively, discursively, dialogically. So when Umbridge asks her what Slinkhard writes about counterjinxes Hermione answers, "He says 'counterjinx' is just a name people give their jinxes when they want to make them sound more acceptable." However, she continues to opine, "Mr. Slinkhard doesn't like jinxes, does he? But I think they can be very useful when they're used defensively."[36] In this simple analysis of the author's views, Hermione metaphorically makes her point about Umbridge's failings in the area of curriculum: counter to her teacher, she asserts that everything, even things that aren't particularly pleasant, must take place interactively. Even if the text that Umbridge has chosen is a quality one, its use to the class, without practical engagement of its ideas, is completely invalid.

This point is further proven later, when, upon entering the Room of Requirement for the first Dumbledore's Army (D.A.) meeting, Hermione immediately notices the endless supply of tomes on defense. Harry observes that it is these texts that seem to cement Hermione's belief in the rightness of their actions.[37] The presence of these books literally convinces Hermione, as one person would another in an argument or a discussion. Unlike Slinkhard's book, which Umbridge gives them without any type of mechanism for learning from it, these books have the promise of aiding and abetting; if used correctly they can encourage and assist the members of the D.A. to further their skills with more advanced lessons.

Hermione's confrontation with Umbridge in class is far from the last conflict between the two. Umbridge effects a suppression of students' freedom through a series of written decrees. The decrees become an ongoing example of how Umbridge's reliance on writing as a tool of control leads her to believe she has more power over others than she realistically maintains. The first decree Umbridge reveals to the Hogwarts populace tells the students that "Organizations, Societies, Teams, Groups and Clubs are henceforth disbanded."[38] The two major effects of this decree upon which Rowling focuses are the necessity of the Gryffindor Quidditch team to apply for the right to re-form, and the blocking of an underground Defense Against the Dark Arts learning society. Umbridge's exercising of words as power through writing changes very little, however. The head of the Quidditch team (notably a girl, Angelina) goes to her Head of House (also notably female) in order to receive permission to reinstate the team.[39] This solution exemplifies the concept that working within a community (albeit, in this case not a textual one) likely enhances one's chances of succeeding in a task.

While failing in the ability to actually back up the words of her decree in the case of the Quidditch team, a more complete lack of success in her arms occurs in Umbridge's inability to halt the progress of Harry's secret defense skills club. Her inability to shut down the illicit organization is partly due to Harry's willingness to ask for help from the house-elf Dobby. Harry, like Angelina, garners success by making his actions communal. This becomes doubly true when Harry depends on Hermione for help, as she manages two feats essential to the club's ongoing existence. First, she finds a way to protect the club. Significantly, Hermione does this through writing, having all the members sign their name onto an attendance-type list.[40] As each member writes his or her name onto the paper, they unknowingly enter into a bond of trust. When that trust is broken, Hermione uses a type of writing for the breaking-party's punishment as well. As it turns out, when one of the girls does betray the club, she is "horribly disfigured by a series of close-set purple pustules that ... form the word 'SNEAK.'"[41] Hermione consciously uses the written word—and the act of others' reading—to punish, and to make an example of what comes of betrayal.

If Hermione uses writing for what she feels is a necessary evil, she also calls on her incredible book-acquired knowledge to allow the group a way of communication about its arranged meeting times. Hermione alters one of the most frightening aspects of Voldemort's communication with his followers. He imprints a mark on the arms of his followers, which burns to alert them when the next meeting will be held; correspondingly, Hermione gives each of the D.A. members a fake coin wherein the serial numbers change to reveal the date and time of the next gathering. Here she relies on the importance of people reading the coins in order to communicate with the group and assemble them in a collective entity. These coins appear again in *Harry Potter and the Deathly Hallows*. Neville uses them to communicate with those members of the D.A. left in Hogwarts after it has been taken over by Death Eaters.[42] Neville's thought to reuse the coins for this purpose—to rely on written and read communication— indicates the shift that occurs in *Deathly Hallows* regarding issues of literacy. Rather than have Neville act as sole leader, expecting everyone else to read his orders and react to them, Neville only ever says that the group communicates with the coins. The implicit meaning behind his words is that any of the members of the co-ed group might be the one to "write" on the coins, and any of them might be the ones to read. Hermione might have created the device, but Neville is able to adapt what she has given them to reinvigorate and preserve that community.[43]

The decree regarding student organizations is wildly successful compared to one Umbridge later posts. Her latter decree states: "Any student found in possession of the magazine *The Quibbler* will be expelled."[44] The magazine in question is running an interview with Harry that Umbridge believes to be lie-filled. This decree again brings to the forefront Umbridge's fear of what reading can accomplish. As with the Slinkhard book, wherein she limits reading and its practical applications, here she attempts to completely shut down reading as a path to uncontrolled knowledge. Similar to the earlier decree, this one forces the student body to find ways around the new ruling or to simply hide its actions. Where the club banning might have resulted in people being more reluctant to involve themselves, but doing so anyway, banning *The Quibbler* does nothing but issue a challenge to the students to be certain to read the paper:[45] each and every single one finds a way to read the interview without being caught and expelled.

The published interview provides a "turning point" moment in the action of the novel, allowing for several people who had doubted Harry's honesty to see his side of events and to give his version some thought. Rowling specifically makes Umbridge's exercise of ruling through writing not only powerless but detrimental to her own goals. It is not coincidental that Hermione is the one to understand the correlation between all of these events. From the moment Hermione explicates the opening speech for Harry and Ron, Rowling sets Umbridge up less as Harry's nemesis and more so as Hermione's. Tellingly, it is Hermione who is able to free herself and Harry from Umbridge's clutches near the end of *Order of the Phoenix*. Umbridge's defeat at the hands of the centaurs is brought about by her own lack of rhetorical listening skills, her ambition, and her intolerance for others, all serious faults within Rowling's world. However, given that the rivalry between Hermione and Umbridge is based almost entirely in text, that element is conspicuously absent from the final scene between the two women. What is present is Hermione's willingness to utilize her community while in Umbridge's office, starkly in contrast to Umbridge's mistrust of her Inquisitorial Squad and her greed for power.[46]

Hermione's defeat of Skeeter and Umbridge in books IV and V are both examples of how she removes obstacles from Harry's path to destroying Voldemort. Because Rowling constructs Voldemort as either not understanding or purposely destroying morals and emotions, which are used to create community (i.e., tolerance for others, love), neutralizing him is necessary to the maintenance and further development of a healthy wizarding community. Hermione's role in this final, most central defeat within the scope of *Deathly Hallows* is a bit more subtle than it has been in previous books. It is also bound up directly with Dumbledore and a legacy of literacy that he leaves to her—one of the most direct examples of a man communicating through text in the series.

Dumbledore bequeaths his copy of *The Tales of Beadle the Bard* to Hermione.[47] Given that he communicates to her through a text that was written by a character who is also gendered male, one could argue that this is more of the same male writing–female binary reading relationship. However, for Dumbledore to be privy to the information he is attempting to impart to Hermione, he had to have read the text, and interacted with it in his own way at one time; and indeed, Dumbledore later tells Harry of his very active relationship with the text. Additionally, by leaving her the book as a clue, Dumbledore interacts with her through its words, and trusts that she will inquire deeply enough to find his message, to have the conversation in which he cannot directly engage. Dumbledore substitutes text for spoken word, acknowledging its power to open and sustain lines of communication.

If there is a change in Dumbledore's and Neville's relation to text in *Deathly Hallows*, there is a paradigm shift of Harry's relation toward the road of the aggressive/offensive/creator of text versus the passive/defensive/communicator with text. In other words, Harry learns what Hermione has known all along: just because an action—such as reading—seems like a passive reception of knowledge does not mean that the action is not necessary to the accomplishment of a goal. Harry finally realizes this upon the death of Dobby, when he takes into consideration his choices and decides that he must go after the Horcruxes. Or, as Harry thinks of it: "The enormity of the decision not to race Voldemort to the wand still scared Harry. He could not remember, ever before, choosing *not* to act."[48] However, Harry is, in fact, acting: he is about to break into Gringotts. However, he sees his decision in the light of passivity, of not taking an active role. Additionally, there is a shift in Harry's acceptance of authority/acquired wisdom in this moment. To return to a moment wherein Harry accepts what a book tells him as true, Harry trusts the half-blood prince's instructions specifically because his writing occurs "in the margins."[49] The prince is an expert at potions, but outside the traditional hierarchy of the school and its published text. Harry spends most of *Deathly Hallows* mad at Dumbledore for not having left him explicit directions.[50] In choosing to listen to the implicit messages Dumbledore has directed at him through the *Tales* and Hermione, Harry acknowledges that those who operate within the rules and lines of society—granted, the marginalized society of the wizarding world, but a society with a hierarchy all the same—are not necessarily always to be distrusted. What Hermione has always been able to do in working actively outside the traditionally active sphere, Harry has finally learned to try.

Rowling uses Hermione's struggles to explore the accepted notions of the ways female creativity and subjectivity work within tropes of literacy. She posits that by entering into an interactive relationship with text, one can build oneself as subject, potentially overpowering the ideal of artist/writer as subject.

Hermione becomes an Ideal Reader: one who enlivens written texts, freeing them from the static realm, and operating as co-creator to the text through her dialogic reading.[51] In essence, Rowling asserts that positionality within the structures of reading and writing—"active" and "passive"—must be complex and relative, communicative and communal. The subjective possibilities found in the absorption of text only become apparent in Hermione because she opens her mind to different ideas of how to create herself as subject and is willing to do so in conjunction with others. She combines listening with speaking and reading with writing to mold herself as something both individual and collective, harnessing the strengths of each.

## NOTES

1. Sandra Gilbert and Susan Gubar, *Madwoman in the Attic: The Woman Writer and the Nineteenth-Century Literary Imagination* [1979], 2nd ed. (New Haven: Yale UP, 2000), 38–39.

2. Wikipedia, "Snow White," http://en.wikipedia.org/wiki/Snow_White.

3. Gilbert and Gubar, 40.

4. Ibid., 42.

5. Roberta Seelinger Trites, *Waking Sleeping Beauty: Feminist Voices in Children's Novels* (Iowa City: U of Iowa P, 1997), 36. Trites is referencing Patricia MacLachlan's *Journey* specifically, but she also works with Virginia Hamilton's *A White Romance*, Angela Johnson's *Toning the Sweep*, and Francesca Lia Block's *Witch Baby*.

6. Meredith Rogers Cherland, *Private Practices: Girls Reading Fiction and Constructing Identity* (London: Taylor & Francis, 1994), 83–84.

7. Ibid., 84.

8. Ibid., 84.

9. Ibid., 87.

10. J.K. Rowling, *Harry Potter and the Sorcerer's Stone* (New York: Scholastic, 1999), 286.

11. Ibid., 287. Hermione tells this to Harry to encourage him to continue on by himself in order to save the Sorcerer's Stone and put an end to Voldemort's plans for immortality. The line is among the most readily associated with her character.

12. Veronica L. Schanoes, "Cruel Heroes and Treacherous Texts: Educating the Reader in Moral Complexity and Critical Reading in J.K. Rowling's Harry Potter Books," in *Reading Harry Potter: Critical Essays*, ed. Giselle Liza Anatol (Westport: Praeger, 2003), 141.

13. The debate as to whether Hermione's actions toward the house elves are correct or presumptuous is ultimately unimportant to this paper. What is important is her choice to act in the way she believes to be right despite the mockery of others.

14. J.K. Rowling, *Harry Potter and the Goblet of Fire* (New York: Scholastic, 2000), 224.

15. Ibid., 238.

16. Significant examples of this include Hermione figuring out the riddle in book I, as I already discussed in this chapter; putting together the clues Harry has given her

about the voice he is hearing to realize there is a basilisk in the school, *Chamber*, 290; puzzling out Lupin's werewolf nature—although she keeps this from Harry, correctly believing Lupin is no threat to him, *Azkaban*, 345; the way she overcomes Rita Skeeter, as well as in her struggles against Umbridge and in her use of Dumbledore's final gift to her, a book of magical children's tales, all three of which I discuss in this chapter.

17. Hermione goes to the library to research the history of house-elves's enslavement, but it is clear from the reactions of those around her that she is not taking into account aspects of that history that might affect the way house elves feel about their current situation.

18. Ann Marie Mann Simpkins, "Rhetorical Tradition(s) and the Reform Writing of Mary Ann Shadd Cary," in *Calling Cards: Theory and Practice in the Study of Race, Gender and Culture*, ed. Jacqueline Jones Royster and Ann Marie Mann Simpkins (Albany: SUNY P, 2005), 239.

19. Ibid., 232.

20. Rowling, *Goblet*, 486.

21. Ibid., 677.

22. To provide two examples, the piece of paper on which someone else writes Harry's name and places in the *Goblet*, and the note that comes to warn Harry of his impending trial and expulsion from Hogwarts. Rowling, *Goblet*, 271; Rowling, *Phoenix*, 26–27.

23. Rowling, *Goblet*, 21.

24. J.K. Rowling, *Harry Potter and the Half-Blood Prince* (New York: Scholastic, 2005), 240–41.

25. Ibid., 195.

26. Voldemort represents himself metonymically through a journal for the entirety of the second book. Harry manages to stop Voldemort from killing someone only by driving the poisoned fang of a basilisk through the journal, ending its powers. Rowling, *Chamber*, 322.

27. Rowling, *Goblet*, 270–71.

28. Ibid., 638.

29. J.K. Rowling, *Harry Potter and the Order of the Phoenix* (New York: Scholastic, 2003), 530.

30. Ibid., 531.

31. Ibid., 567.

32. I use the word "listen" here in the Ratcliffian sense (see next page), as a site of "interpretive invention" (195).

33. Rowling challenges this assumption when Skeeter publishes an article under duress in the fifth book, one she thinks nobody will want to read. The paper she publishes in sells out more quickly than ever before and has to reprint nearly immediately. Rowling, *Phoenix*, 583.

34. Umbridge gives a very politic speech wherein she announces the Ministry's intervention in Hogwarts policy without ever mentioning either institution directly.

35. Ratcliffe, "Rhetorical Listening," 196. Ratcliffe includes reading in this quote as one of the tropes to which she hopes listening can gain equal status. She actually sees reading as one of "the dominant tropes for interpretive intervention" along with writing (194). However, I think her argument about listening still helps shape how the general public conceives of receptive forms of learning, reading being one.

36. Rowling, *Phoenix*, 316–17.

37. Ibid., 390.

38. Ibid., 351.

39. Ibid., 376.

40. Ibid., 346, 392.

41. Ibid., 612.

42. J.K. Rowling, *Harry Potter and the Deathly Hallows* (New York: Scholastic, 2007), 575.

43. Draco Malfoy is also able to successfully adapt the use of the coins to communicate with Rosamerta, while keeping her under an Imperius spell so as to do his bidding (Rowling, *Prince*, 580–90). Although both Draco's methods and his aims—Dumbledore's death—seem to be in direct contrast with the idea of community, Draco's *motivations*—that is, to keep his family safe—are entirely communally driven, the community is simply a different one than Harry's point-of-view telling allows much sympathy for.

44. Rowling, *Phoenix*, 581.

45. Ibid., 582.

46. Hermione takes Umbridge into the Forbidden Forest, hoping that the centaurs will help rid them of her. The centaurs do help, but they also turn on Hermione. However, the brother of a longtime friend helps them out of the situation, as, despite themselves, they have been kind to him in the past (Ibid. 755).

47. Rowling, *Hallows*, 125–26.

48. Ibid., 502.

49. Rowling, *Prince*, 195.

50. One example of this is Rowling, *Hallows*, 208–09.

51. The concept of Ideal Reader comes from the mind of Jessica Lewis-Turner, who took the time to read this paper and aided greatly in my conceptualization of the way things come together.

# 14

# Doubling, Transfiguration, and Haunting:
# The Art of Adapting Harry Potter for Film

*Michael K. Johnson*

> When we say an adaptation has been "unfaithful" to the original, the very violence of the term gives expression to the intense sense of betrayal we feel when a film adaptation fails to capture what we see as the fundamental narrative, thematic, or aesthetic features of its literary source.
> —Robert Stam, *The Theory and Practice of Adaptation*[1]

> People would have crucified me if I hadn't been faithful to the books.
> —Christopher Columbus, director, *Harry Potter and the Philosopher's Stone* (2001), *Harry Potter and the Chamber of Secrets* (2002)[2]

Few film adaptations of beloved novels appear without an accompanying chorus of complaints about the film's differences and departures from the source text, often expressed, as Robert Stam has pointed out, in terms that connote moral violations (unfaithfulness, lack of fidelity).[3] In both popular and academic circles, the yardstick of fidelity as a means of measuring and evaluating has dominated the discourse on filmed adaptations for almost as long as books have been made into films. That the adaptations of J.K. Rowling's novels have been no different is somewhat surprising given the importance of magical transformation to the wizarding world that Rowling creates, one that celebrates a variety of creative processes that we might consider as metaphors for the art of adaptation. The very ability to adapt, to transform from one thing into another, or to transfigure one thing into another, is essential to Harry's success in each of the novels.

In one of the key scenes in *Harry Potter and the Prisoner of Azkaban*, new Defense Against the Dark Arts professor R. J. Lupin teaches the students how to protect themselves against a boggart through the power of creative adaptation: they learn to transfigure their fears into something else.[4] In a celebration of defying fidelity, the students are taught to alter the boggart's authorial intent (to cause terror) by transforming the creature's text/body into something that causes the exact opposite reaction (laughter). Recent work in adaptation studies, from Stam's *The Theory and Practice of Adaptation*, to Kamilla Elliott's *Rethinking the Novel/Film Debate* (2003), to Linda Hutcheon's *A Theory of Adaptation* (2006), suggests that the time has come to move beyond obsessions with fidelity and seek out new tropes for understanding and analyzing filmed adaptations.[5] An interdisciplinary analysis of the Harry Potter novels and films will benefit from drawing on these new theoretical studies in Adaptation Studies, and I would also suggest that Adaptation Studies itself might benefit from an engagement with this group of novels and films that so effectively illustrate and enact some of those theoretical ideas.

As Linda Hutcheon observes, "Perhaps one way to think about unsuccessful adaptations is not in terms of infidelity to a prior text, but in terms of a lack of the creativity and skill to make the text one's own and thus autonomous."[6] We might take the wizard as our figure for the skilled and creative artist, one whose artistry (like that of an adapter) turns on his or her ability to transform the world/text that he or she encounters. Hutcheon states that "Like classical imitation, adaptation also is not slavish copying; it is a process of making the adapted material one's own. In both, the novelty is in what one *does with* the other text."[7] Transfiguration, the course taught by Professor McGonagall, might serve as an effective metaphor for adaptation as Hutcheon describes it here. A successful transfiguration is one that is neither a mimetic recreation of the original (where the pin cushion remains a pin cushion) nor only a partial transformation (where a cushion runs away from the pins) but one that both retains some identifiable element of the original *and* enjoys its own independent identity (a pin cushion transfigured into a hedgehog).

From the first chapters set at the Dursleys' home, *Azkaban* is concerned with both the ethics and pleasures of adaptation. Harry uses the annoying and obnoxious Aunt Marge as a text through which he expresses his own emotions, adapting and changing Marge's physical being as a means of externalizing and objectifying those emotions. Marge "seemed to be swelling with inexpressible anger," and indeed she is, but it is Harry's anger that inflates her and sends her sailing into the sky above Privet Drive.[8] Marge is both herself and Harry's double, a hybrid construction in which the original text—her body—is both clearly recognizable and clearly altered to express something new. That the adaptive impulse that results in Harry's creation is both unconscious and uncontrolled suggests that inflated Marge is not the novel's central model for a successful adaptation but an early step on Harry's path to becoming an accomplished wizard/adapter.

Focusing on director Alfonso Cuarón's *Prisoner of Azkaban*, and using "transfiguration" as the central metaphor for adaptation, this chapter examines how the film creates specifically cinematic transfigurations not only of the novel's central themes but also of one of the distinctive elements of Rowling's style—multiple intertextual references to other literary texts, forms, and genres.[9] Cuarón places *Azkaban* in multiple cinematic traditions, quoting from and alluding to the classic Universal horror films of the 1930s and French New Wave films of the late 1950s and early 1960s, and even transfiguring the novel's time travel motif by taking us into the clockworks of film history through the use of "old-fashioned" techniques, such as the silent-film era "iris-in" transitional device.[10] If, as Karen Manners Smith argues, the Harry Potter books are part of a long tradition of British boarding school novels "that stretches back to *Tom Brown's Schooldays* (1857)," Cuarón correspondingly alludes to cinematic stories of education, replacing *Tom Brown's Schooldays* with François Truffaut's *The 400 Blows* (1959) as the central point of reference.[11] We might interpret *Azkaban* as much as a transfiguration of *The 400 Blows* as of Rowling's novel, with Harry's filmic narrative doubling his literary one as well as that of young Antoine Doinel, another imaginative misfit adolescent boy whose story provides an ironic counterpoint to Harry's magical and triumphant adventure.

As a cinematic version of the Potter world, *Azkaban* represents a departure from the earlier films of the series, in part because of a greater willingness on the part of the director to risk being the recipient of a Cruciatus Curse from outraged Rowling fans for being unfaithful to the novel. He adds, for example, a clock tower to Hogwarts, and dresses students in jeans rather than wizard robes. *Azkaban* sharpens the narrative focus by emphasizing thematic adaptation over summarizing the novel (a practice followed as well by later films in the series), and Cuarón makes the film his own by emphasizing themes that appeal to his particular filmmaking sensibilities—a mischievous sense of humor, and interests in the experiences of adolescence and in coming-of-age stories—and to his strengths as a visual stylist, such as the ability to create active, image-filled, sometimes chaotic, wide-screen compositions, where an energized *mise-en-scène* is achieved through both character action and camera movement. Successful adaptation, Hutcheon argues, involves "a double process of interpreting and then creating something new."[12] As an interpretation, *Azkaban* provides us with a new way of looking at the novel, not only by bringing certain themes to the forefront, but also by foregrounding intertexts like *The 400 Blows* that most readers of the novel would not have noticed. By being "unfaithful," by taking creative risks in order to make something new, *Azkaban* is, ironically, faithful to the novel's own philosophy of celebrating innovative transfiguration.

## HARRY POTTER AND THE HISTORY OF TIME

Early in the film of *Azkaban*, shortly after Harry has arrived at the Leaky Cauldron, the camera pans past a wizard at a table stirring his cup of tea while he reads. His right index finger twirls above the cup, the upright moving spoon synchronized with the motion of his finger. This is a brief moment in the film, one having little to do with advancing the action of the story, but it is particularly revealing of Cuarón's approach to adaptation. The widescreen framing of the *mise-en-scène* provides ample opportunity for marginal additions such as this one, sometimes in the form of visual gags that take place as the camera pans from one area to another (ghostly horses and riders crashing through windows, chambermaids followed by walking brooms), all contributing to a detailed and textured portrayal of Rowling's wizarding world. Distracted by the magical stirring of the tea, we might not notice that the wizard is reading Stephen Hawking's *A Brief History of Time*. Although the story's time travel sequence doesn't occur until later, both the book and the film foreshadow that forthcoming plot event in multiple ways, and the visual nod to Hawking's book is just one of the playful devices that Cuarón uses to evoke the theme of time and of time travel. That the wizard absently stirs his tea in a counterclockwise direction likewise foreshadows Hermione and Harry's own counterclockwise adventure back in time.

Both versions of *Prisoner of Azkaban* reward re-reading and rewatching by seeding the texts from the very beginning with references to future events, the meaning of which can only be recognized through later readings. When Harry is hit by a stone thrown from nowhere, we may not recognize what the sign means, but we note its existence. As the events of the time travel sequence do not change from one experience of those events to another (the only alteration is in Hermione and Harry's perspective on those events, viewed from a different point in space and through the lens of additional knowledge as to what those events mean), the story's events do not vary when we replay that sequence of time on our DVD player or by sequentially turning the pages of our books. Time travel narratives are often self-reflexively "about" the practice of reading—or, more precisely, re-reading—for much of the pleasure of such narratives comes from recognizing the interplay between the original and the adaptation, the story of the past as it is originally told and the retelling of that story from a different perspective during the time-travel sequence. When we re-read the book or review the film, we newly understand how these moments refer to future events, recognizing in them a new significance. We may have a similar experience when watching a filmed adaptation of a book. Any adaptation asks us take up a position in regard to the text that is tantamount to being in two places at once: in the past (the time of the original text), and in the present (the time of the adaptation). Like the time traveler, our perspective is doubled, as we see both original and adaptation simultaneously.

Magical time travel is just one of the ways the book explores the concept of time. Rowling evokes that theme stylistically in multiple ways: repetitions of the word "time" itself and references to the multitude of mechanical, natural, and linguistic ways we measure and mark the passing of time. Although magical time travel is still in the novel's future, chapter 1 prophecies that later event through examples of less exotic types of time travel: Harry travels back into the past by means of his *A History of Magic* textbook, via a clipping from a back issue of the *Daily Prophet*, featuring a photo of the Weasley family in Egypt, which preserves in the present a moment that occurred in the past, and via a series of letters, all of which were written in the past but are experienced by Harry in his present.

As a concept, we understand time as both an objective measure (the duration between two events) and as something we experience subjectively (time flies, time drags). In the opening chapter of *Prisoner of Azkaban*, I counted well over 100 references to time, some of which are direct, such as the use of the word time itself, references to clocks, to crossing off days on a calendar, and some of which involve Rowling's playful evocation of the many words we use to measure time and of the multiple ways we have developed to describe our subjective experience of time. We measure time by the period (e.g., medieval), by the century, by the year, by the season, by the month, the week, the day, the part of the day (night, evening, etc.), by the clock, by the hour, the minute, the second; we measure time according to social organization, like "summer holiday," and "the school year" to establish our progress in a course of study (as well as using markers like first-year, second-year, etc.); we measure our individual experience of time—our birthdays, for example; we also divide time into past, present, and future (yesterday, now, tomorrow). We also have multiple ways of describing our subjective experience of time; we may wait for a long time or a short time; we might be late or early; time might pass so quickly that we are unaware of its passing, or so slowly that we are aware of every tick of the clock. Each one of these ways of measuring, describing, or experiencing the passage of time is evoked in the opening chapter.

References to time and timekeeping continue to occur throughout the novel. During a Quidditch game, Harry "lost track of time," the darkness of the storm making it seem as if "night had decided to come early."[13] Professor Trelawney teaches students to see the future. Professor Lupin, who has his own reasons for being attentive to time, finds a boggart in a grandfather clock. Harry's surreptitious journey to Honeydukes "took ages," but his return trip seemed "to take no time at all."[14] In Azkaban, where Sirius Black has been "doing time" for crimes he didn't commit, "time travel" is part of the punishment, as prisoners are forced to travel back in the past through their own memories. As Hagrid reveals: "Kep' goin' over horrible stuff in me mind . . . the day I got expelled from Hogwarts . . . day me dad died."[15] When confronted by dementors, Harry experiences the same loop of time, the death of his parents, over and over again, a kind of time travel that is remarkable for the intensity and clarity of the memory, as if he was indeed journeying back to that past moment rather than remembering it.

In adapting a novel to film, as Hutcheon observes, "'equivalences' are sought in different sign systems for the various elements of the story: its themes, events, world, characters, motivations, points of view, consequences, contexts, symbols, imagery, and so on."[16] Cuarón uses the multiple tracks available to film to provide cinematic "equivalences" to Rowling's linguistic practice of seeding her story with time-related words. In particular, the film contains multiple aural and visual references to time and timekeeping: the cuckoo clock at the Dursleys, long shots of magically hidden Diagon Alley that clearly show the clock tower of Big Ben in the background, the grandfather clock in the Minister of Magic's room at the Leaky Cauldron, a choir singing "Ding Dong," the impressively large clock tower at Hogwarts with its massive swinging pendulum. We frequently hear clocks ticking, bells tolling. Timekeeping devices, from the ancient to the modern—sundials, standing stone calendars, and so forth—are ubiquitous at Hogwarts. When Harry meets Lupin to learn the Patronus spell, they are surrounded by candle clocks in the shape of spines, with each vertebrae marked in a Roman numeral to mark the hour. Floating throughout this scene are multiple clockwork miniatures, from orreries to trains circling the tracks, all devices for measuring time. The passage of time is also observed through natural occurrences, particularly seasonal transition as revealed by changes in the Whomping Willow, animal behaviors, such as the migration of birds, and events that signal different parts of the day: bats leaving the forest at night, the moon rising.

In a magical world the subjective experience of time can be realized in objective reality—time can be experienced in ways other than as a sequence of past, present, and future. As Rowling's narration conveys the subjective experience of time ("took ages"), subjective time can likewise be represented cinematically through technical means that alter how viewers experience the filmed event: pixilation to speed up time, slow motion, freeze frames. The sequence involving the Knight Bus alternates between pixilated fast motion and extreme slow motion, as the bus moves via alterations in both time and space to get from one point to another and to avoid Muggle detection. Various editing techniques also alter the way we experience the duration of an event. In the film's opening sequence, the camera moves in from a long shot toward the Dursley house, and as we near Harry's bedroom window, there's a sudden jump cut to a closer view of the window as the camera continues to track toward and through the window into the bedroom. The jump cut, a device frequently employed by French New Wave filmmakers (most famously by Jean-Luc Godard in *Breathless*), does not conceal the edit but makes us aware of it and of the manipulation of time involved as we suddenly "jump" several seconds forward in time and space.

The action in this opening sequence quite cleverly foreshadows the theme of time by having the actors perform as if they were automatons in a clockwork device, mechanically replaying the same sequence of events. Harry, beneath his bed sheets, practices a spell, the sheets light up from within, flicker and fade, and Harry drops the sheets and pretends to be asleep. Mr. Dursley opens the door, turns on the overhead light, looks at Harry, looks at Hedwig in her cage, looks at Harry, looks back at Hedwig, looks at Harry, back at Hedwig, turns off the light, closes the door, and Harry pops back up in the bed. After the first repetition of this sequence, the camera quickly pulls back out of the room to reveal the title, *Harry Potter and the Prisoner of Azkaban*. The camera then zooms back into the room and replays the previous sequence almost exactly, with the exception being that at the end a smiling Harry seems to be truly settling down for sleep. Like the cuckoo in the clock that we see in a later scene, Uncle Vernon pops open the door, pops into the room, and moves his head back and forth first in one direction and then the other—an imitation of the mechanical bird's actions while "cuckooing" the hour.

That the scene's action recurs twice also introduces us to another of the novel's themes: an interest in doubles and doubling. Duality is essential to the horror genre, which the book, with its werewolf and haunted "shrieking shack," draws on. It may come in the classic Ego–Id dichotomy of Dr. Jekyll and Mr. Hyde, or in the similarly split human–beast identities of the werewolf. Many of the characters in the novel have double identities, double lives, or are divided in other ways: Animages, "Mudbloods," half-giants/half-humans. As the first Defense Against the Dark Arts lesson suggests, all the characters have some primal fear hidden in the unconscious—we all have a boggart in the wardrobe. Likewise, we must all sometimes struggle with conflicting social identities, as in Harry's attempts to negotiate between the Muggle and wizarding worlds, a conflict that is realized visually by the image of Harry beneath the sheets reading. Harry's identity as a wizard, a category of being regarded as entirely other by his Muggle relatives, must be hidden from the nonmagical world around him, a world visually split in this opening filmic scene into light and darkness, corresponding to the illumination of wizardly knowledge and the darkness of Muggle prejudice that seeks to suppress his wizardly identity. The scene also foreshadows the later moments in the film when Harry is hidden, not by his sheets, but by an Invisibility Cloak—under which he also achieves a moment of illumination, an overheard conversation that sheds light on Black's relation to his own past. As Harry will discover, Black's doubling similarly involves a sociological split between the public perception of his identity (betrayer of Harry's parents, mad killer) and who he really is beneath his prisoner's uniform (someone whose true loyalty is exemplified by his "other"—canine—form).

The opening sequence also demonstrates director Cuarón's adaptation of *noveau vague* experimental techniques to mainstream filmmaking: the jump cut, as noted earlier, but also its opposite, the extended unedited sequence, the long take.[17] We might contrast the opening sequence of *Azkaban* to that of the previous film in the series, *Harry Potter and the Chamber of Secrets*, to show how Cuarón's visual style differs from the more conventional approach of director Christopher Columbus. *Azkaban* doubles *Chamber*'s opening sequence, which similarly begins with the camera tracking from a long shot to a closer shot of Harry's window. As we move nearer to the window in *Chamber*, we see Harry sitting in front of it, writing, and we cut to an interior shot of Harry continuing to write (a particular type of edit called a match cut or match on action). Cuarón, however, cuts too soon, before the camera reaches the logical point for transition, and, then, where we would expect a cut, the shot continues as the camera glides through the window. The rest of the scene, with the exception of a couple of intercut shots of Harry beneath the sheets, plays out as a single take, the camera pausing to record Uncle Vernon entering and exiting the room, sweeping back out for the title, and then sweeping back in to record another entrance by Uncle Vernon. Then, to highlight Harry's pleasure at fooling his uncle, which would be accomplished conventionally by a close-up of his smiling face, Cuarón uses a technique from the silent-film era, an "iris-in," in which the screen darkens around a smaller circle that remains lit. In this case, the darkening circle is used to outline Harry's face, highlighting his expression without resorting to an edit.

Cinema seems particularly well equipped to realize time-related themes through film form. The cinematic apparatus is in itself already concerned with manipulating space, through framing and camera movement, and time, through the duration of individual shots and editing that shortens or lengthens our experience of an event's duration. A mobile camera provides a measure of the space it moves through just as the length of the shot measures the amount time it takes to move through that space. Notable in *Azkaban* is Cuarón's use of a moving camera to evoke visually the concept of time passing. He does so in two ways. The first is through circling in clockwise and counter clockwise motions. Even when stationary, the camera often observes spiraling movements (the dementors descending from the sky, e.g., or Quidditch players on brooms) or spiral objects like stairways, the snail shell that Hermione throws, the path down to Hagrid's, and the form of the spine-shaped candle clocks. The second is through expansive to-and-fro movements. Even before we see the swinging pendulum of Hogwarts's tower clock, the camera sweeps in and out of places, such as Harry's bedroom at the Dursleys' house, and echoes the motion of a clock's pendulum. When Lupin sees the moon appearing from behind a cloud, the camera similarly swoops in to an extreme close-up of the reflection in his eye, and then swings back out to reveal that the process of transformation has begun. In the earlier scene with the boggart, the camera moves in toward the wardrobe's mirror, in which we see the students reflected, and then reverses itself, moving, as it were, out of the mirror and toward the class. As the scene plays out, we have several such reversals, as the camera rhythmically alternates between moving toward the class and toward the wardrobe. Throughout the film, camera setups are seldom static, and we often move toward or away from characters. Like time itself, the camera is always moving, and that movement often imitates the mechanical actions of timekeeping devices, circling like the hands of a clock, swinging back and forth like a pendulum. The frequent use of these unusual camera movements is a particularly clever example of the director finding a specifically cinematic "equivalent" for a distinctive element of the adapted text's literary style, where word choices constantly evoke the theme of time.

## HARRY POTTER AND *LA NOUVELLE VAGUE*

Filled with allusions to other films, with homages to beloved directors, with shots and techniques that kept audiences aware that they were watching a film, their films embodied the self-reflexivity that is often placed at the core of cinematic modernism.... [I]t is above all this self-reflexivity ... that gives the New Wave its decidedly modern dimension.

—Naomi Greene, *The French New Wave*[18]

As an adaptation, *Prisoner of Azkaban* creates "something new" by transfiguring the novel into a filmic text that is heavy with specifically cinematic allusions and quotations, playfully evoking French New Wave films throughout, both in terms of references to specific films—especially *The 400 Blows*—and in adapting the techniques, such as modernist self-reflexivity and long takes, generally associated with the New Wave. To return to the opening sequence, already discussed in terms of editing, we might consider how the scene is also self-consciously cinematic. As noted, *Azkaban* alludes to the previous film in the series by doubling its opening shot. The light from Harry's wand beneath his bed sheet flickers in a way that is reminiscent of the flickering light of a projector as a leader threads through—an appropriate image for the start of a film. *Lumos*, Harry's spell for light, evokes the essential component of film (photography is "light writing"), and his insistent incantation, uttered at the very beginning of the film, echoes the classic signal for the start of filming ("lights! ... camera! ... action!"), just as the "mischief managed" stated in voiceover after the closing credits substitutes for "cut!"

The repetition of the scene's action creates the first of many moments in the film that involve a repeated loop of time. The omnipresent posters of Sirius Black continually play and replay the same few seconds of his moving image.[19] Lucius Malfoy's animated drawing shows Harry repeatedly crashing on a broom (and introduces into the *mise-en-scène* yet another reference to a particular film technology—animation). These moving picture loops recall an early filmmaking and projection device, the Kinetoscope, thus taking us once more into the clockworks of film history.[20] With this machine, as a clip came to an end, it simply cut back, without transition, to the beginning: a startling jump that is replicated in the *Azkaban* loops. François Truffaut's *Les Quatre cents coups* (*The 400 Blows*) similarly refers to an earlier film technology in one of its most famous scenes, of Antoine Doinel enjoying a carnival ride called The Rotor that spins like a centrifuge, pasting the riders to its walls.[21] As we watch images spin past a stationary camera, the effect is like watching a zoetrope, an early motion picture device involving a revolving cylinder (much like The Rotor) with still images pasted on its interior surface. Viewed through slits cut in the side, the spinning motion creates the illusion of moving pictures.[22]

If Cuarón borrows techniques from Truffaut, he does so in part to point us toward thematic connections between two stories that center on thirteen-year-old protagonists, each in his own way "striking his 400 blows," going through a period of adolescent rebellion, or "youthful delinquency" as Greene translates the phrase, or more colloquially, sewing wild oats, and raising hell—an idea exemplified in the Potter world by the oath that activates the Marauder's Map: "I solemnly swear that I am up to no good."[23]

Each film is concerned in its own way with the theme of time and with the question of identity. Both features begin in a troubled home from which the protagonist runs away to a "magical" place—Hogwarts for Harry, the streets of Paris for Antoine. Both pictures celebrate the special nature of childhood friendships. Both protagonists are rule breakers—Antoine skipping school entirely, Harry sneaking away from Hogwarts to join his friends in Hogsmeade. While doing so, each one discovers a "secret" about his mother: Antoine that his mother is having an affair, Harry that Sirius Black betrayed his mother. Both films, of course, are stories of education, with a significant portion of the action taking place in the setting of a school. *The 400 Blows* alternates between scenes set inside and outside the classroom, with the classroom serving to exemplify an educational system that stifles creativity, institutes uniformity, and that substitutes petty authoritarianism for pedagogy. One can readily imagine a Hogwarts where all classes are taught by Professor Snape, or, worse yet, Dolores Umbridge.

Greene observes a "fundamental contrast between freedom and imprisonment that pervades" *The 400 Blows*, revealed most clearly by contrasting spaces: the closed-in spaces of the schoolroom and of the Doinels' cramped apartment, the open streets of the Paris, which are energetic and full of life and motion, and where the "camera seems to swoop and fly" as if "exulting in the freedom of the streets."[24] The dialectic of freedom and imprisonment in *The 400 Blows* plays out in the story's action as well. As Antoine's tale unfolds, we see him punished for being in possession of a pin-up girl calendar, for writing a rude poem on the classroom wall, for playing hooky, for lying, for stealing a typewriter. Between these periods of punishment and confinement, Antoine enjoys the companionship of his friend Rene, with whom he roams the Paris streets, goes to movies, drinks wine, smokes cigars, and who aids him when he runs away from home. However, as punishment for the typewriter theft, he is separated from Rene, handed over to the police by his father, put into a series of jail cells, each one isolating him more completely than the previous one, and finally sent to an "Observation Center for Delinquent Youth."

Although intertextual readings can be tricky in terms of assigning "intent," *The 400 Blows* is one of the films that Cuarón gave Daniel Radcliffe to watch as preparation for filming *Azkaban*, and there seem to be enough direct allusions to the earlier film to encourage us to look for more indirect or subtextual connections between the two.[25] In *The Chamber of Secrets*, Harry's unruly hair is realized as a kind of disheveled moptop, but *Azkaban* gives Harry a cut that is styled similarly to Antoine's (although Harry wears it longer). In Cuarón's adaptation the classrooms at Hogwarts, with their old-fashioned desks, have been slightly rearranged when compared to *Chamber*, desktops cleared of the clutter that we see in the earlier film, the rows neater and broken into a pattern of three rows of desks with two students sharing a desk, thereby more suggestive of the classroom in *The 400 Blows*. However, in contrast to the educational system depicted in *The 400 Blows*, *Azkaban* emphasizes teaching moments that take place outside that traditional classroom. Only Snape, as a substitute for Lupin, teaches Defense Against the Dark Arts in a traditional classroom setting. Lupin's lesson plan for defending against the boggart is hands-on (or wands out), loose, and improvisational, involving neither lectures nor books. The mentoring relationship that Lupin develops with Harry also takes place outside the traditional space of the classroom—with one exception. When Lupin confiscates the Marauder's Map from Harry, thus playing a traditional authoritative role, he does so in the Defense Against the Dark Arts classroom.

There are also moments in *Azkaban* when Daniel Radcliffe's performance recalls that of Jean-Pierre Leaud. After Antoine's lie—that his absence was caused by his mother's death—is (quickly) found out, he runs away and eventually has to spend the night on the Paris streets. He steals a bottle of milk, and hides in an alley to drink it. Leaud's facial expressions in this sequence, which convey desperation and a fear of being caught, provide a template for Radcliffe's portrayal of Harry at a similar moment, when he has angrily left the Dursleys, fearing that his use of magic will result in his expulsion from Hogwarts, and not knowing which way to turn next. For Antoine, however, there is no Knight Bus to rescue him.

As both films involve the theme of developing identity, it is not surprising that both feature mirrors and mirror images. We see Antoine looking into a foggy bathroom mirror, which he wipes clean with one hand, remembering as he does so a comment from his teacher (which we hear in voiceover as Antoine looks pensively into the mirror). The composition of this frame is remarkably similar to the moment when we observe Harry looking at his image in the rain-streaked train window, and when, like Antoine, he is momentarily lost in memory, his face pensive, uncertain. Later in the film, we see Harry standing behind the face of Hogwarts's tower clock, isolated and confined visually by the metalwork of the clock, his face momentarily barred as the clock hand sweeps slowly past it, a shot that in both composition and emotional content recalls images of Antoine in various prison cells.

Although the way we experience time is also a theme of *The 400 Blows*, the emphasis, in keeping with the film's central dialectic of confinement and freedom, alternates between the way timekeeping is used to regulate individual behavior and individual resistance to regulated time. "In the theory of relativity," Stephen Hawking writes, "there is no unique absolute time, but instead each individual has his own personal measure of time that depends on where he is and how he is moving."[26] If the theory of relativity forces us to acknowledge that we each carry our own personal measure of time, the collective imposition of a single clock seeks to hold back the chaos of relativity. In Antoine's world, timekeeping functions as a disciplinary apparatus. Time is regulated in the wizarding world as well, but the sheer multiplicity of timekeeping devices suggests a greater fluidity in the way individuals experience time. Although authority figures insist on keeping time exactly—recall the punctual enactment of Buckbeak's punishment—an individual literally carrying her own personal measure of time (Hermione and her Time-Turner) can thwart the efforts of official timekeepers.

In *The 400 Blows*, Antoine's friend, Rene, sets a clock forward to make his father think he is late for his club meeting—a less magical means of time manipulation than Hermione's Time-Turner but effective nonetheless. Even without magic, children in *The 400 Blows* find multiple ways of "stealing" time, of experiencing time differently than by the timekeeper's clock. They lose themselves and their sense of time at the movies, on a carnival ride, at a puppet show; they wander freely the streets of Paris, moving spontaneously from one place to another. In one of the film's most famous scenes, a gym instructor leads a line of students as they jog through the streets. Viewed from above, we watch as one student after another breaks away from the uniformity of a double row of single-file lines, each running off in his own individual direction, each choosing to spend his time in his own way, as the line dwindles to one inattentive instructor and a handful of dutiful students following behind him.[27]

Both *The 400 Blows* and *Azkaban* end with their protagonists taking "flight," and, significantly, both films end with a still image, in each case a close-up of the protagonist's face. To reflect in film form Antoine's escape from this regulated world, Truffaut breaks from convention in terms of the representation of cinematic time, filming part of the escape in a long (eighty-one seconds) single take of Antoine running. The sequence ends with Antoine reaching the ocean, where he wades briefly out into the water and turns back to the shore, at which point the film freezes his image as the camera moves slowly toward a close-up of his face. The film thus ends in another radical departure from conventional form, with this now famous freeze-frame.

Cuarón's decision to end *Azkaban* with a freeze-frame seems a deliberate homage to the earlier film (as well as being another example of the way cinema manipulates the experience of time). If the freeze-frame conclusion suggests an association between the two films, the content of each still image exemplifies the difference between the two—Antoine tentatively looks back at the camera, his expression ambiguous, his "flight" to the ocean's edge at an end, his future uncertain; Harry triumphantly and ecstatically takes flight on his new broom, having not yet reached the edge of his future possibilities but still zooming upward toward them.

Linda Hutcheon suggests that adaptation is not only a product (a particular type of film) and a process (of transcoding a novel into a film) but also a mode of reception. Adaptations are adaptations because we recognize them as such. Hutcheon observes, "To deal with adaptations *as adaptations* is to think of them as . . . inherently 'palimpsestuous' works, haunted at all times by their adapted texts. If we know that prior text, we always feel its presence shadowing the one we are experiencing directly."[28] In comparing *Azkaban* and *The 400 Blows*, I am suggesting that we regard *Azkaban* as an adaptation not only of Rowling's novel but also of Truffaut's film. To do so, we need to take up a position as a "knowing" reader of the text, one who is aware of, or who is in the process of recognizing, the relationship between not just two but three texts (and, potentially more, as any text can be the site of multiple "hauntings").[29]

As a prior text, Rowling's novel has a much more direct relationship to the *Azkaban* film than does *The 400 Blows*. It is perhaps more accurate to describe the relationship of Truffaut's film to *Azkaban* as a "haunting," and the relationship of the novel to the film as something more embodied—a doubling, or a transfiguration, as I suggested earlier. Our knowledge of the connection to *The 400 Blows* is evoked only in indirect ways, but by leaving "clues" alluding to the ghostly presence of the other text, the film encourages us as readers to complete the materialization of that ghost. By so doing, director Cuarón not only brings "something new" to the story, but he also suggests an understated critique of that story. *The 400 Blows* is a work of realism that shows how the social system responds to imaginative misfits such as Harry and Antoine in a world where there is no Hogwarts, where magical experience is fleeting, and where reform school and prisons are the likely destinations of unwanted, neglected, adolescent boys who are "up to no good." Harry's final flight embodies the dream of escape that cannot be fully realized in Antoine's world. If we position ourselves as "knowing" readers, then considering Harry as Antoine's dream double adds a troubling note to Harry's triumphant flight, which is haunted by our knowledge of his double's uncertain fate. As Hutcheon observes, becoming a "knowing" reader or viewer involves "understanding the interplay between works" and involves a process "of opening up a text's possible meanings to intertextual echoing."[30] Like the time traveler, the knowing reader has a more complicated understanding of such seemingly distinct categories as original and adaptation, past, present, and future. As I hope I have demonstrated here, an expanded notion of what constitutes an adaptation enables us to move beyond expectations of fidelity and toward other more productive and interesting ways of talking about the relationships between books and films.

## NOTES

1. Robert Stam, Introduction, *Literature and Film: A Guide to the Theory and Practice of Film Adaptation*, Robert Stam, ed. (Malden, MA: Blackwell, 2005), 1–45, 14.

2. Glen Whipp, "Director Remains Faithful to Harry," *Toronto Star* (21 September 2002), H4, quoted in Linda Hutcheon, *A Theory of Adaptation* (New York: Routledge, 2006), 123.

3. As Robert Stam writes, "The conventional language of adaptation criticism has often been profoundly moralistic, rich in terms that imply that the cinema has somehow done a disservice to literature. Terms like 'infidelity,' 'betrayal,' 'deformation,'

'violation,' 'bastardization,' 'vulgarization,' and 'desecration' proliferate in adaptation discourse, each word carrying its specific charge of opprobrium." Stam, Introduction, 3.

4. J.K. Rowling, *Harry Potter and the Prisoner of Azkaban* (New York: Scholastic Inc., 1999).

5. Kamilla Elliott, *Rethinking the Novel/Film Debate* (Cambridge: Cambridge UP, 2003). Linda Hutcheon, *A Theory of Adaptation* (New York: Routledge, 2006).

6. Hutcheon, 20.

7. Ibid.

8. *Azkaban*, 29.

9. *Harry Potter and the Prisoner of Azkaban*. Dir. Alfonso Cuarón. Screenplay by Steve Kloves. Perf. Daniel Radcliffe, Rupert Grint, Emma Watson, Robbie Coltrane, Michael Gambon, Richard Griffiths, Gary Oldman, Alan Rickman, Fiona Shaw, Maggie Smith, Timothy Spall, David Thewlis, Emma Thompson, Julie Waters. DVD, Warner Home Video, 2004.

10. Film is a collaborative art form, and I recognize that it is potentially problematic to assign to a film's director a role similar to that of the author of a novel. However, as *auteur* theory came out of the film criticism that preceded the French New Wave, and as my essay discusses that cinematic movement as an influence on the style of *The Prisoner of Azkaban* film, it seems appropriate to claim Alfonso Cuarón as an *auteur*, and, despite the flaws in *auteur* theory, present practice in film criticism continues to use the director's name as a kind of shorthand for all the creative artists involved in making a film.

11. Karen Manners Smith, "Harry Potter's Schooldays: J.K. Rowling and the British Boarding School Novel," in *Reading Harry Potter: Critical Essays*, ed. Giselle Liza Anatol (Westport, CT: Praeger, 2003), 69–87, 70.

12. Hutcheon, 20.

13. Rowling, *Azkaban*, 176.

14. Ibid., 195, 211.

15. Ibid., 220.

16. Hutcheon, 10.

17. According to Naomi Greene, techniques such as the long take and depth of focus were particularly important to the philosophy of New Wave filmmakers, who favored them over a reliance on montage/editing, which "fragment[ed] reality" rather than allowing us [as Andre Bazin puts it] "to experience the continuity and ambiguity of reality much as we do in real life." Naomi Greene, *The French New Wave* (New York: Wallflower, 2007), 20.

18. Ibid., 13.

19. The poster consists of a moving mug shot, with actor Gary Oldman moving his head to show left profile, front, right profile, and then back in the other direction, a sequence that we see continually repeated. Additionally, the actor's motions, the exaggerated side-to-side movement of his head, his open-mouthed laugh when facing the camera, suggest (as did Uncle Vernon's similar movements in the opening scene) the motions of a clock's "cuckoo." That Sirius seems to be continually chiming the hour suggests as well the way the manipulation of time is part of the punishment in Azkaban.

20. Housed in a cabinet, the Kinetoscope was designed for an individual viewer and used a continuous loop of film that could play and then replay the filmed scene. The cabinet could accommodate no more than fifty feet of film, most often less, and depending on the rate of frames-per-second at which the scene was filmed and projected, the clips lasted anywhere from ten seconds to a maximum of thirty seconds.

21. *The 400 Blows (Les quatre cents coups)*, Dir. François Truffaut. Perf. Jean-Pierre Leaud, Claire Maurier, Albert Remy, and Patrick Auffay. 1959. DVD, The Criterion Collection, 2006. I would also like to acknowledge the influence of Professor Brian Stonehill's audio commentary track on my own understanding of the film. The commentary is useful not only in terms of Professor Stonehill's insights but also in his summaries of critical thought regarding *The 400 Blows*.

22. The source of this observation is Brian Stonehill's audio commentary track to *The 400 Blows*.

23. Greene, 4. Rowling, *Azkaban*, 192.

24. Greene, 75.

25. Jeff Jensen, "Inside 'Harry 3': The Scary New World of 'Azkaban,'" *Entertainment Weekly*, No. 789 (11 June 2004), *Entertainment Weekly* Archive, http://www. ew.com/ew/article/0,644599_5,00.html (accessed 26 May 2008).

26. Stephen J. Hawking, *A Brief History of Time* (New York: Bantam, 1996), 34.

27. Playing hooky is in itself stealing time, but the punishment for such transgressive behavior for Antoine is reform school, where time is regulated even more strictly than in the outside world—as indicated by an establishing shot of a ringing bell that signals the time for beginning and ending activities. At lunch, Antoine bites into a piece of bread while the other boys stand at attention. For starting too early, Antoine is punished by sharp slap to the face, administered after the guard removes his wristwatch, and the scene ends with Antoine staring at the watch, as if it, rather than the guard's hand, is the cause of his pain and punishment.

28. Hutcheon, 6.

29. I draw the term "knowing" from Linda Hutcheon: "If we know the adapted text, I prefer to call us 'knowing,' rather than the more common descriptors of learned or competent.... The term 'knowing' suggests being savvy and street-smart.... If we do not know that what we are experiencing actually *is* an adaptation or if we are not familiar with the particular work that it adapts, we simply experience the adaptation as we would any other work. To experience it *as an adaptation*, however ... we need to recognize it as such and to know its adapted text, thus allowing the latter to oscillate in our memories with what we are experiencing." Hutcheon, 120–21.

30. Ibid., 117.

# Selected Bibliography

American Library Association website. "Challenged and Banned Books http://www
.ala.org/ala/oif/bannedbooksweek/challengedbanned/challengedbanned.cfm
(accessed 28 August 2008).

Anatol, Giselle Liza, ed. *Reading Harry Potter: Critical Essays.* Westport, CT: Praeger,
2003.

Anelli, Melissa, John Noe, and Sue Upton. "PotterCast Interviews J.K. Rowling,
part one." *PotterCast #130.* http://www.accio-quote.org/articles/2007/1217-
pottercast-anelli.html (accessed August 2008).

Arden, Heather and Kathryn Lorenz. "The Ambiguity of the Outsider in the Harry
Potter Stories and Beyond." In *The Image of the Outsider in Literature, Media,
and Society,* edited by Will Wright and Steven Kaplan. Pueblo, CO: Society for
the Interdisciplinary Study of Social Imagery, 2002, 430–34.

Baggett, David and Shawn E. Klein, eds. *Harry Potter and Philosophy: If Aristotle Ran
Hogwarts.* Chicago: Open Court, 2004.

Barrow, Simon. "Reading Harry Potter too religiously." *Ekklesia,* 30 July 2007. http://
www.ekklesia.co.uk/node/5504. (accessed June 2008).

Beam, Lindy. "What Shall We Do With Harry?" *Plugged In (Focus on the Family)*
http://www.family.org/pplace/pi/genl/A0008833.html (accessed 5 May 2001).

Blake, Andrew. *The Irresistible Rise of Harry Potter.* London: Verso, 2002.

Boucher, Geoff. "Final 'Harry Potter' book will be split into two movies." *Los Angeles
Times,* 13 March 2008. http://www.latimes.com/entertainment/news. (accessed
June 2008).

Cani, Isabelle. "Lily et James Potter, ou les visages morcelés de l'unité perdue,"
*Belphégor: Littérature Populaire et Culture Médiatique,* 6.1 (2006): n.p. http://
etc.dal.ca/belphegor/vol6_no1/fr/main_fr.html (accessed 15 June 2008).

Cherland, Meredith Rogers. *Private Practices: Girls Reading Fiction and Constructing
Identity.* London: Taylor and Francis, 1994.

Cockrell, Amanda. "Harry Potter and the Witch Hunters." *The Journal of American Culture* 29.1 (2006): 24–30. http://www.ebschost.com (accessed 9 June 2008).

Deavel, Catherine Jack and David Paul Deavel. "Character, Choice, and Harry Potter." *Logos* 5.4 (2002): 49–64.

DeMitchell, Todd A. and John J. Carney. "Harry Potter and the Public School Library." *Phi Delta Kappan* 87 (2005): 159–65. 163. http://www.ebschost.com (accessed 9 June 2008).

Diamond, Laura. "Hearing draws Potter Foes, Fans." *The Atlanta Journal-Constitution*, 21 April 2006: J1. http://www.proquest.com/proquest (accessed 9 June 2008).

Diffendal, Lee Ann. "Questioning Witchcraft and Wizardry as Obscenity: Harry Potter's Potion for Regulation." *Topic: The Washington & Jefferson College Review* 54 (2004): 55–62.

Eden Communications. "Is 'Harry Potter' Harmless." *ChristianAnswers.Net*. http://christiananswers.net/q-eden/harrypotter.html (accessed 11 June 2008).

Elliott, Kamilla. *Rethinking the Novel / Film Debate*. Cambridge: Cambridge UP, 2003.

Ford, James Ishmael. "Dumbledore is gay. Ain't it loverly?" "Breaking News," *Monkey Mind* (21 October 2007). http://monkeymindonline.blogspot.com (accessed 24 January 2009).

Frazier, Sir James George. *The Golden Bough: A Study in Magic and Religion*. New York: Macmillan, 1951.

Freud, Anna. "Adolescence." *The Psychoanalytic Study of the Child* 13 (1958): 255–78.

Gibbs, Nancy. "J.K. Rowling." *Time* 130, no. 27, 31 December 2007. http://www.time.com/time/specials/2007/personoftheyear (accessed June 2008).

Gilbert, Sandra M. and Susan Gubar. *The Madwoman in the Attic: The Woman Writer and the Nineteenth-Century Literary Imagination*. 2nd ed., 1979. New Haven, CT: Yale UP, 2000.

Goldstein, Dana. "Harry Potter and the Complicated Identity Politics." *The American Prospect*, 24 July 2007), web only. http://www.prospect.org/cs/articles?article=harry_potter_and_the_complicated_identity_politics (accessed 19 September 2008).

Griesinger, Emily. "Harry Potter and the 'Deeper Magic': Narrating Hope in Children's Literature." *Christianity and Literature*, 51.3 (2002): 455–80.

Grossman, Lev. "The Doubting Harry." *Time*, 23 July 2007, 15. http://www.ebschost.com (accessed 9 June 2008).

Hallet, Cynthia Whitney. *Scholarly Studies in Harry Potter: Applying Academic Methods to a Popular Text*. Studies in British Literature, Vol. 99. Lewiston, NY: Edwin Mellin Press, 2005.

*Harry Potter and the Chamber of Secrets*. Dir. Christopher Columbus. Perf. Daniel Radcliffe, Rupert Grint, and Emma Watson. Warner Bros., 2002.

*Harry Potter and the Order of the Phoenix*. Dir. David Yates. Perf. Daniel Radcliffe, Rupert Grint, and Emma Watson. Warner Bros., 2007.

*Harry Potter and the Philosopher's Stone*. Dir. Christopher Columbus. Perf. Daniel Radcliffe, Rupert Grint, and Emma Watson. Warner Bros., 2001.

*Harry Potter and the Prisoner of Azkaban*. Dir. Alfonso Cuarón. Perf. Daniel Radcliffe, Rupert Grint, and Emma Watson. Warner Home Video, 2004.

"Harry Potter: A Sorcerers Tale." *Let Us Reason Ministries* website. http://www.letusreason.org/current16.htm (accessed 24 January 2009).

"Harry Potter Foe Loses Challenge." *American Libraries* (1 August 2007): 21. http://www.ebschost.com (accessed 10 June 2008).

Harvey, Linda. "Harry Potter and Anti-Christian Bigotry." *WorldNetDaily*. http://www.worldnetdaily.com/news/article.asp?ARTICLE_ID=56715 (accessed 9 June 2008).

Heilman, Elizabeth E., ed. *Critical Perspectives on Harry Potter*. New York: Routledge, 2009.

———, ed. *Harry Potter's World: Multidisciplinary Critical Perspectives*. New York: Routledge, 2003.

Hemmens, Daniel. "Harry Potter and the Doctrine of the Calvinists." *FerretBrain*. 17 August 2007. http://www.ferretbrain.com/articles/article-161.html (accessed June 2008).

Hjelm, Titus. "Between Satan and Harry Potter: Legitimating Wicca in Finland." *Journal of Contemporary Religion* 21.1 (2006): 33–48. http://www.ebschost.com (accessed 10 June 2008).

*J.K. Rowling* official webite. http://www.jkrowling.com (accessed June 2008).

Jensen, Jeff. "Inside 'Harry 3': The Scary New World of 'Azkaban.'" *Entertainment Weekly*, No. 789, 11 June 2004, *Entertainment Weekly* Archive, http://www.ew.com/ew/article/0,,644599_5,00.html (accessed 26 May 2008).

Karolides, Nicholas J., Margaret Bald and Dawn B. Sova. *120 Banned Books*. New York: Checkmark Books, 2005.

Keller, Lindy. Review of *Harry Potter and the Deathly Hallows. Plugged In Online*. http://www.pluggedinonline.com/articles/a0003326.cf (accessed 9 June 2008).

Kenn, Edmund M. *The Wisdom of Harry Potter: What Our Favorite Hero Teaches Us About Moral Choices*. New York: Prometheus Books, 2008.

Kennedy, Matt. "Christian themes in Potter books make good evangelism tools, some say." *Associated Baptist Press*, 31 July 2007. http://www.abpnews.com/www/2682.article.print (accessed June 2008).

King, Stephen. "Potter Gold," *EW.com: From Entertainment Weekly*, 11 July 2003, http://www.ew.com/ew/article/0,,462861,00.html (accessed 3 May 2008).

Kjos, Berit and Andy. "Harry Potter Articles." *Kjos Ministries* http://www.crossroad.to/articles2/007/harry-links.htm (accessed 9 June 2008).

Knutsen, Torbjørn L. "Dumbledore's Pedagogy: Knowledge and Virtue and Hogwarts." In *Harry Potter and International Relations*. Ed. Daniel H. Nexon and Iver B. Neumann. Lanham, MD: Rowman & Littlefield Publishers, Inc., 2006. 197–212.

Kopel, Dave. "Deconstructing Rowling." *National Review Online*, 9 June 2003. http://www.nationalreview.com/kopel/kopel062003.asp (accessed June 2008).

Lackey, Mercedes, with Leah Wilson, eds. *Mapping the World of Harry Potter*. Dallas: BenBella Books, 2005.

Lee, Patrick. "Pottermania lives on in college classrooms." *CNNU*, 25 March 2008. http://www.cnn.com/2008/SHOWBIZ/books/03/25/cnnu.potter/index.html (accessed June 2008).

Lewis, James R. *Legitimating New Religions*. New Brunswick, NJ: Rutgers University Press, 2003.

Lux, Mike. "Ministers and Their Sermons." *Huffington Post*, 28 April 2008. http://www.huffingtonpost.com (accessed June 2008).

Maughan, Shannon. "Rowling's Rare Book to Hit Shelves in December." *Publishers Weekly*, 31 July 2008. http://www.publishersweekly.com/article/CA6583159 .html?nid=2788 (accessed 9 September 2008).

McCarron, Bill. "Power vs. Authority in *Harry Potter and the Order of the Phoenix*." *Notes on Contemporary Literature* 34.5 (2004): 8–10.

McVeigh, Dan. "Is Harry Potter Christian?" *Renascence* 54.3 (2002): 197–214.

Mudhar, Raju. "More Than Robes in Wizard's Closet." *Toronto Star*, 23 Oct. 2007. http://www.proquest.com/proquest (accessed 7 November 2007).

Neal, Connie. "A Christian Defense of Albus Dumbledore" (21 October 2007). *Dallas Morning News* religion blog, 1 May 2008. http://religionblog.dallasnews.com (accessed June 2008).

Nel, Philip. *J.K. Rowling's Harry Potter Novels: A Reader's Guide*. New York: Continuum, 2001.

Nodelman, Perry. *The Hidden Adult: Defining Children's Literature*. Baltimore: The Johns Hopkins University Press, 2008.

O'Brien, Michael. "Harry Potter and the 'Death of God.'" *LifeSiteNews.com* http://www.lifesitenews.com/ldn/2007/aug/07082003.html (accessed 9 June 2008).

Olsen, Ted. "(A Bit Less) Positive about Potter." *Christianity Today Magazine Online*, 26 July 2007. http://www.christianitytoday.com/ct/2007/julyweb-only/130–43 .0.html?start=2 (accessed June 2008).

Patel, N., M. L. Crismon, K. Hoagwood, M. Johnsrud, K. Rascati, J. Wilson, et al. "Trends in the Use of Typical and Atypical Antipsychotics in Children and Adolescents." *Journal of the American Academy of Child and Adolescent Psychiatry* 44.6 (2005): 548–56.

Pennington, John. "From Elfland to Hogwarts, or the Aesthetic Trouble with Harry Potter." *Lion and the Unicorn* 26.1 (2002): 78–97.

Pitts, Leonard. "So Dumbledore Is Gay: (Yawn), It's All in the Details." *Sunday Gazette-Mail* (Charleston, WV), 28 October 2007, 3C. http://www.proquest .com/proquest (accessed 9 June 2008).

Prewitt, Janice C. "Heroic Matriculation: The Academies of Spenser, Lewis, and Rowling." *Philological Papers* 53 (2006): 25–34.

Rankin, Bill and Sherry. "Bringing Harry Potter to Church." Workshop at *The Upside Down Kingdom: Living the Sermon on the Mount*. 65th Annual Bible Lectures at Pepperdine University, Malibu, CA. 1–2 May 2008.

Rivadeneira, Caryn. "Bringing Harry Potter to Church." *Gifted for Leadership: A Community of Christian Women*, 23 July 2007. http://blog.christianitytoday.com/ giftedforleadership (accessed June 2008).

Rowling, J.K. *Harry Potter and the Chamber of Secrets*. New York: Arthur A. Levine–Scholastic, 1999.

———. *Harry Potter and the Deathly Hallows*. New York: Arthur A. Levine–Scholastic, 2007.

———. *Harry Potter and the Goblet of Fire*. New York: Scholastic, 2000.

———. *Harry Potter and the Half-Blood Prince*. New York: Arthur A. Levine–Scholastic, 2005.

———. *Harry Potter and the Order of the Phoenix*. New York: Arthur A. Levine–Scholastic, 2003.

———. *Harry Potter and the Prisoner of Azkaban*. New York: Arthur A. Levine–Scholastic, 1999.

———. *Harry Potter and the Sorcerer's Stone.* New York: Arthur A. Levine–Scholastic, 1997.

———. "J.K. Rowling Interview." Transcript from *CBCNewsworld: Hot Type.* CBC Toronto. July 13 2000. CBCNewsworld. 14 April 2006. http://www.cbc.ca/programs/sites/hottype_rowlingcomplete.html (accessed May 2008).

———. "World Exclusive Interview with J.K. Rowling," *South West News Service,* 8 July 2000.

———. "Straight Talk on Harry Potter." *With One Accord Ministries.* http://www.withoneaccord.org/store/potter.html (accessed June 2008).

Seiler, Casey. "Opinion: Tolerance Thrives in Fantasyland." *Times Union,* 28 Oct. 2007. http://www.proquest.com/proquest (accessed 7 November 2007).

Sink, Mindy. "The Split Verdict on Harry Potter." *The New York Times,* 8 March 2003, B6. http://www.proquest.com/proquest (accessed 5 June 2008).

SLJ Staff, "Paperback Edition of 'Deathly Hallows' Slated for July 2009." *School Library Journal* (29 September 2008). http://www.schoollibraryjournal.com/article/CA6599861.html (accessed November 2008).

Smith, Kathy A. "Who Is Harry Potter?" *Fill the Void Ministries.* http://www.fillthevoid.org/children/HarryPotter2.html (accessed 9 June 2008).

Stam, Robert. "Introduction." In *Literature and Film: A Guide to the Theory and Practice of Film Adaptation,* edited by Robert Stam. Malden, MA: Blackwell, 2005, 1–45.

Taylor, Betsy. "'Potter Event Led to Rights Violations,' ACLU Says." *St. Louis Post-Dispatch* B7, 28 May 2008. http://www.proquest.com/proquest (accessed 9 June 2008).

Trites, Roberta Seelinger. *Waking Sleeping Beauty: Feminist Voices in Children's Novels.* Iowa City: U of Iowa P, 1997.

Vann, Allison Bergman. "Why I Love Harry Potter." Preached at Temple Beth-El, San Antonio, TX, 3 August 2007. http://www.beth-elsa.org/abv080307.htm (accessed June 2008).

"Vatican Questions New Age, Supports Harry Potter." *America,* 17 February 2003, 4–5. http://hwwilsonweb.com (accessed 1 June 2008).

Vineyard, Jennifer. "Kreacher Comfort: MTV Solves A 'Harry Potter' Mystery." *MTV Movie Blog,* posted 25 June 2007. http://moviesblog.mtv.com/2007/06/25/kreacher-comforts-mtv-solves-a-harry-potter-mystery (accessed 21 May 2008).

Waetjen, Jarrod and Timothy A. Gibson. "Harry Potter and the Commodity Fetish: Activating Corporate Readings in the Journey from Text to Commercial Intertext." *Communication and Critical/Cultural Studies* 4.1 (2007): 3–26.

Ward, Michael. *Planet Narnia.* Oxford: Oxford University Press, 2008.

Watkins, Jon. "Harry Potter: A New Twist on Witchcraft." *Exposing Satanism and the New World Order.* http://www.exposingsatanism.org/harrypotter.htm (accessed 11 June 2008).

"Webchat with J.K. Rowling, 30 July 2007." http://www.bloomsbury.com/jkrevent (accessed 15 May 2008).

Whipp, Glen. "Director Remains Faithful to Harry," *Toronto Star,* 21 September 2002, H4, quoted in Linda Hutcheon, *A Theory of Adaptation,* New York: Routledge, 2006.

Whited, Lana A., ed. *The Ivory Tower and Harry Potter: Perspectives on a Literary Phenomenon.* Columbia: University of Missouri Press, 2004.

Wilson, Heather. "Hermione Clinton." *New York Times Op-Ed Section*, 8 June 2008. http://www.nytimes.com/2008/06/08/opinion/08wilson.html?_r=1 (accessed 15 November 2008).

"Wotcher Harry! or, Accio Friday Five!" *Magdalene's Musings*, 13 July 2007. http://magdalenesmusings.blogspot.com (accessed June 2008).

Zeitlin, Matt. "Harry Potter and the Jewish Goblins," *Matt Zeitlin: Impetuous Young Whippersnapper*, 24 July 2007. http://whippersnapper.wordpress.com/2007/07/24/harry-potter-and-the-jewish-goblins/ (accessed 15 November 2008).

Zipes, Jack. *Sticks and Stones: The Troublesome Success of Children's Literature from Slovenly Peter to Harry Potter*. New York: Routledge, 2001.

# Index

to totalitarianism, 133, 177–80; sadism, 77, 94–95, 111
*Uncle Tom's Cabin* (Stowe), 167–68

Virtue Theory. *See* Aristotle
Voldemort, 84, 110; as anti-Muggle, 18–19, 144–46; as aristocrat, 133; childhood of, 49, 132; and education, 149–50; as a killer, 67, 81–82, 144; as politician, 175–76; relationship to Harry, 7, 47, 49–50, 183–84; relationship with mother, 97–99, 136; response to prophecy, 51–52, 54–55, 197; as Tom Riddle, xiii, 78, 111, 149, 152

*A Voyage Round the World in the Years 1740–4* (Anson), 119

Weasley family, 78, 104, 139; Arthur (Mr.), 121, 139; Bill, 92, 112, 120; Ginny, 1, 139; Molly (Mrs.), 70, 97, 103; Percy, 139; Ron, 19, 67, 91, 121, 128, 137, 139–40, 162–63, 168–69, 187, 195; twins Fred and George, 141–42 n.34, 156 n.30, 182–83, 189 n.37
*The Weirdstone of Brisingamen* (Garner), 68
Wicca, 15–17, 24, 25
Wu, Frank, 120, 121, 126 n.88

# About the Editor and Contributors

GISELLE LIZA ANATOL is also the editor of *Reading Harry Potter: Critical Essays* (Praeger 2003). An associate professor of English at the University of Kansas, she specializes in children's literature, Caribbean women's writing, and literature of the African-Americas. In addition to *Reading Harry Potter Again,* she is working on a book-length manuscript that explores the cultural implications of vampires in African diasporic folk traditions and contemporary literature.

TRACY L. BEALER is a visiting assistant professor at the University of South Carolina. Her research interests include the twentieth-century American novel and pop culture. She has published essays on William Faulkner, Zora Neale Hurston, and Quentin Tarantino.

BRYCCHAN CAREY is a Reader in English Literature at Kingston University, London. He contributed a chapter to Anatol's *Reading Harry Potter: Critical Essays* (2003) and is the author of *British Abolitionism and the Rhetoric of Sensibility: Writing, Sentiment, and Slavery, 1760–1807* (Palgrave 2005). He is currently completing a book on the origins and development of Quaker antislavery rhetoric in the seventeenth and eighteenth centuries.

LISA DAMOUR, also a contributor to Anatol's *Reading Harry Potter: Critical Essays* (2003), is a clinical psychologist who treats children, adolescents, and adults in her private practice. She is an adjunct faculty member in the Department of Psychology at John Carroll University and a Clinical Instructor at Case Western Reserve University.

PATRICIA DONAHER is an associate professor of English and Graduate Faculty at Missouri Western State University in Saint Joseph, Missouri. Her scholarship centers on language attitudes and popular linguistics and popular literature studies. She is the national area chair for language attitudes and popular linguistics for the Popular Culture Association.

PEGGY LIN DUTHIE is an independent scholar working out of Nashville, Tennessee. A graduate of the University of Chicago and the University of Michigan, she has contributed to the *Oxford Encyclopedia of Children's Literature* (2006), *Books and Beyond: The Greenwood Encyclopedia of New American Reading* (2008), and other reference works.

LESLEE FRIEDMAN holds a B.A. from Oberlin College and an M.A. in English from the University of Kansas, where she wrote her master's thesis on the politics of women's reading and writing in selected Young Adult literature. She works full-time at the Harvard Graduate School of Education and will begin her study of copyright law in August 2009.

XIMENA GALLARDO C. and C. JASON SMITH, who contributed the chapter on gender in Anatol's *Reading Harry Potter: Critical Essays* (2003), are the authors of *Alien Woman: The Making of Lt. Ellen Ripley* (Continuum, 2004), which was awarded the 2005 Popular Culture Association Ray and Pat Browne Book Award for excellence in research in popular culture. Gallardo and Smith both teach English for the City University of New York-LaGuardia.

LISA HOPKINS is Professor of English at Sheffield Hallam University and co-editor of *Shakespeare*, the journal of the British Shakespeare Association. Her previous publications include "Harry Potter and the Acquisition of Knowledge" in Anatol's *Reading Harry Potter: Critical Essays* (2003).

MICHAEL K. JOHNSON teaches at the University of Maine-Farmington. He is author of *Black Masculinity and the Frontier Myth in American Literature* and has published in *African American Review, Literature/Film Quarterly*, and *Quarterly Review of Film and Video*.

CHANTEL M. LAVOIE received her B.A. and M.A. at the University of Ottawa and her Ph.D. at the University of Toronto. She has published on early women writers, poetic collections, Canadian verse, and children's literature (with thoughts now on *Gregor the Overlander*). She contributed a chapter on the sorting ritual to Anatol's *Reading Harry Potter: Critical Essays* (2003). She lives and teaches in Toronto with her two sons.

MARGARET J. OAKES is an associate professor of English at Furman University in Greenville, South Carolina, specializing in English Renaissance literature, including Shakespeare, Herbert, and Cavendish. Her chapter in Anatol's *Reading Harry Potter: Critical Essays* (2003) focused on technology in the wizarding world.

JAMES M. OKAPAL received his Ph.D. in Philosophy from the University of Tennessee. He currently teaches Ethics and Social and Political Philosophy at Missouri Western State University.

SHAMA RANGWALA lives in Montreal and received her master's degree in English Literature from McGill University. Her M.A. thesis examined the influence of cinema on Elizabeth Bowen's novels. She has published previously on *Harold and Kumar Go to White Castle*.

REBECCA L. STEPHENS is a professor of English at the University of Wisconsin-Stevens Point. Her teaching and research interests include young adult literature, nationalism, censorship, and performance. She contributed "Harry and Hierarchy" to Anatol's *Reading Harry Potter: Critical Essays* (2003).

CPSIA information can be obtained
at www.ICGtesting.com
Printed in the USA
BVOW06*0430060118
504491BV00002B/13/P